D1187774

**Iran's Natural Gas Industry
in the Post-Revolutionary Period**

# Iran's Natural Gas Industry in the Post-Revolutionary Period

## Optimism, Scepticism, and Potential

ELHAM HASSANZADEH

Published by the Oxford University Press
for the Oxford Institute for Energy Studies
2014

# OXFORD

UNIVERSITY PRESS

Great Clarendon Street, Oxford OX2 6DP

Oxford University Press is a department of the University of Oxford.
It furthers the University's objective of excellence in research, scholarship
and education by publishing worldwide in

Oxford New York

Auckland Cape Town Dar es Salaam Hong Kong Karachi
Kuala Lumpur Madrid Melbourne Mexico City Nairobi
New Delhi Shanghai Taipei Toronto

with offices in

Argentina Austria Brazil Chile Czech Republic France Greece
Guatemala Hungary Italy Japan Poland Portugal Singapore
South Korea Switzerland Thailand Turkey Ukraine Vietnam

Oxford is a registered trade mark of Oxford University Press
in the UK and in certain other countries

Published in the United States
by Oxford University Press Inc., New York

British Library Cataloguing in Publication Data

Data available

Library of Congress Cataloguing in Publication Data

Data available

Cover designed by Cox Design Limited
Typeset by Philip Armstrong, Brighton
Printed by Berforts Information Press Ltd, Witney

ISBN 978-0-19-872821-4

The contents of this book are the sole responsibility of the authors.
They do not necessarily represent the views of the
Oxford Institute for Energy Studies or any of its members.

1 3 5 7 9 10 8 6 4 2

*To my parents Javad and Fatemeh and
my siblings Arash, Arezoo, Azadeh, and Arsalan
whose presence in my life has been the greatest
source of love, support, and determination.*

# CONTENTS

# LIST OF MAPS

# LIST OF FIGURES

## LIST OF TABLES

# PREFACE

For much of the past 30 years, the Iranian gas industry has been a subject on which researchers – other than noting the country's huge reserves, production, and export potential – have had little to say. The reasons for this are well known: the post-Revolution Islamic regime was anathema to many western governments and companies which found their ability to conduct political discourse with, and commercial activities in, the country much reduced; problems which were compounded by the Iran–Iraq war. A period of reduced tensions followed, but since the mid 2000s, the increasingly problematic relationships between Iran and the international community on a range of issues, but particularly the country's nuclear power programme, resulted in the imposition of progressively onerous sanctions, the withdrawal of international companies from the country, and international political and commercial isolation. With the arrival of President Rouhani's government in 2013, the resumption of international negotiations and renewed determination to resolve the nuclear question holds out the promise of bringing Iran back into the international community, and renewed prospects for gas development and exports. This is therefore a very good time to publish a book reviewing the history and future potential of the Iranian gas industry.

The origins of this book date back to 2009 when I first met Elham Hassanzadeh and agreed to supervise her doctoral thesis at the University of Dundee. The work proceeded a little more slowly than we had anticipated, but by the time it was completed in 2013 it clearly contained research which would make a considerable contribution to natural gas literature and Elham was invited to spend a year at the Oxford Institute for Energy Studies turning the thesis into a book. Even given Elham's enormous personal energy, enthusiasm, knowledge, and ability, this has been a big task to complete on a demanding schedule and I am really grateful to her for producing this excellent and timely study.

Jonathan Stern, Oxford, May 2014

## ACKNOWLEDGMENT

I would like to acknowledge with much gratitude the support given to this book by colleagues from the Oxford Institute for Energy Studies (OIES) and by many people from organizations inside and outside Iran. First and foremost, completion of this book would not have been possible without the generous help provided by Jonathan Stern, to whom I am greatly indebted for both invaluable research advice and endless support. This book owes its existence to, and has benefited immensely from, his aid both in terms of content and language. I also owe a debt of gratitude to Howard Rogers for giving me the opportunity to turn my PhD dissertation into this book and for his valuable technical insights. I am grateful to my other colleagues from the Institute, especially Bassam Fattouh, Patrick Heather, Simon Pirani, Anouk Honoré, Katja Yafimava, and Anupama Sen for their kind intellectual support. I am also thankful for the administrative and organizational support of Kate Teasdale, Susan Millar, and Jo Ilott at OIES.

My special thanks also go to those from the Iranian Oil Ministry and its affiliated companies who provided me with important data and information, all of which helped to depict a clearer picture of the Iranian natural gas industry. I would also like to thank Hassan Sedigh from Azad Tehran University for all his help and advice which encouraged me to choose an academic and professional path in the oil and gas industry. I am also thankful to those who made great intellectual contributions to this work but who would prefer that neither their names nor their organizations are named.

# UNITS

| | |
|---|---|
| bbl | barrel |
| bcm | billion cubic metres |
| cm | cubic metre |
| Mbbl | million barrels |
| mcf | million cubic feet |
| MMBtu | million British thermal units |
| mmcm | million cubic metres |
| mt | million tonnes |
| tcm | trillion cubic metres |

# GLOSSARY

| | |
|---|---|
| AIPC | Anglo-Iranian Petroleum Company |
| APOC | Anglo-Persian Oil Company |
| BG | British Gas |
| BIT | Bilateral Investment Treaty |
| BOT | build, operate, and transfer |
| Capex | capital cost |
| CISADA | Comprehensive Iran Sanctions Accountability and Divestment Act |
| CNOOC | China National Offshore Oil Cooperation |
| CNPC | China National Petroleum Corporation |
| CPC | Crescent Petroleum Company |
| EER | Energy–Environment Review |
| EIA | US Energy Information Administration |
| EOR | Enhanced oil recovery |
| EPC | Engineering, Procurement, and Construction contracts |
| FIPPA | Foreign Investment Promotion and Protection Act |
| FTZ | Free Trade Zones |
| GGFR | Global Gas Flaring Reduction Partnership |
| GTL | Gas-to-liquids |
| IAEA | International Atomic Energy Agency |
| ICOFC | Iranian Central Oil Fields Company |
| ICSID | International Centre for the Settlement of Investment Disputes |
| IEG | Independent Evaluation Group of the World Bank |
| ILNG | Iran LNG Ltd. |
| ILSA | Iran–Libya Sanctions Act |
| IOOC | Iranian Offshore Oil Company |
| IPC | Iran Petroleum Contract |
| IRGC | Islamic Revolutionary Guard Corps |
| ISA | Iran Sanctions Act |
| JCC | Japan Customs-cleared Crude (also known as Japan Crude Cocktail) |
| JMC | Joint Management Committee |
| LAPFI | Law for Attraction and Protection of Foreign Investment |
| LIBOR | the London Interbank Offered Rate |

| | |
|---|---|
| LICA | The Law on International Commercial Arbitration |
| LPG | liquefied petroleum gas |
| LRAIC | long-run average incremental cost |
| MDP | Master Development Plan |
| MoU | Memorandum of Understanding |
| NICO | Naftiran Intertrade Company |
| NIGC | National Iranian Gas Company |
| NIGEC | National Iranian Gas Export Company |
| NIOC | National Iranian Oil Company |
| NIPC | National Iranian Petrochemical Company |
| NISOC | National Iranian South Oil Company |
| NITC | National Iranian Tanker Company |
| Non-Capex | non-capital cost |
| OFAC | US Treasury's Office of Foreign Assets Control |
| OIETAI | Organization for Investment and Economic and Technical Assistance of Iran |
| Opex | operation cost |
| PEMEX | Petroleos Mexicanos |
| POGC | Pars Oil and Gas Company |
| PSEEZ | Pars Special Economic Energy Zone |
| SLH | Synthetic Liquid Hydrocarbons |
| SNSC | Supreme National Security Council |
| TAP | Trans-Adriatic Pipeline |
| TAPI | Turkmenistan–Afghanistan–Pakistan–India pipeline |
| TPAO | Turkish Petroleum Corporation |
| TSC | Technical Service Contracts |
| UNCITRAL | United Nations Commission on International Trade Law |
| UNSC | UN Security Council |
| USSR | Soviet Union |
| WTO | World Trade Organization |

# INTRODUCTION

The Iranian natural gas industry has faced tremendous upheavals since the beginning of its development in the mid 1960s. It has gone through numerous historical and political events which, despite its massive growth potential, have seriously undermined its world-class development. Owning the world's largest proven natural gas reserves,[1] the country could potentially become a major player in the global gas trade; stringent US and international sanctions, however, coupled with the domestic politicization of the petroleum industry, an unfavourable legal and contractual investment regime, and rapidly growing domestic demand have all made the country unable to capitalize on its huge potential in both domestic and international markets.

This academic book is the first of its kind in any language which is entirely devoted to the Iranian natural gas industry, focusing on both its domestic and export development since the Islamic Revolution in 1979. Despite abundant gas reserves with the potential to evolve as a major regional and international gas player, Iran's natural gas industry is little discussed in academic literature. This can to a large extent be attributed to the lack of accurate and detailed information and data on the subject matter on the one hand, and to international sanctions on the other. The aim of sanctions has been to isolate Iran and exclude its energy resources from global markets, thus creating a discouraging atmosphere for the country's petroleum sector. With the election of the moderate government of Rouhani in 2013, however, there are brighter prospects, following the new government's more conciliatory foreign policy towards the international community over the nuclear programme. Sanctions might be eased or removed, reviving opportunities for the participation of Iran as a player in the international oil and gas industry, and hence justifying the importance of this book.

The significance of this book is, first of all, derived from the increasing importance of global gas markets and the role that Iranian natural gas resources could play in them. The expansion of natural gas in global energy balances, which is predominantly a result of global demand for a cleaner source of energy to tackle environmental problems, highlights the importance of securing access to reliable sources of supply. Uneven global distribution of natural gas resources and the importance of diversification of sources of supply, require increasing trade across borders. Iran, given its huge natural gas resources, geographical proximity, ease of access to regional and international markets, as well as the relatively low cost of its resource development and developed infrastructure, could be in a unique position from which to contribute to growing demand in global markets. Due to numerous political, legal, and economic obstacles over the past 30 years, however, the country has displayed a completely different picture.

Secondly, for academic discussions as well as corporate strategies, a comprehensive literature on the state of Iranian natural gas is required for a better understanding of the sector, the barriers to its development, and the political and commercial implications of such development at domestic and international levels. Issues related to natural gas production and exports are increasingly important for a country which is itself heavily reliant on these resources. In this context, an objective and comprehensive assessment of gas supply potential can provide greater knowledge both for domestic and international consumers.

Thirdly, this book offers a new perspective on discussions about the Iranian petroleum sector. The political structure is analysed within the context of major historical and political events, which have inevitably affected the decision-making process in the oil and gas industry. This gap in the literature has resulted in uncertainties in many aspects of the gas sector's development, including the direction of government policy and the question of whether an alternative approach can be adopted.

Finally, the book provides a unique methodological approach, presenting a multidisciplinary study of various historical, political, legal, and economic variables affecting the development of the gas industry. This is not an approach which has been taken before in any language, publication or academic work on this subject. One of the direct benefits of such an approach is to permit readers to comprehend the current state and future development of the gas industry, giving access to it by means of a single comprehensive analytical study in English, rather than from scattered, less detailed, and translated resources, available mostly in Persian. The study will also benefit Iranian readers, by providing a hybrid, analytical overview of the flaws within the current political, legal, and fiscal frameworks and, therefore, highlight the need for reform of certain aspects of government policies in the petroleum sector.

This book therefore aims to address the primary issue of the major obstacles to further substantial development of the Iranian natural gas industry. It also tries to illuminate the prospects for changes in the current status of the industry and to examine the potential that any future development can offer to domestic, as well as regional and international, gas markets. Along these lines, it also reassesses the possibility that Iran could or should become the 'next Qatar', and that the country has lost the game of extensive development of its export capacity to competitors. In answering these questions, the book aims to present a realistic picture of the industry and its potential, using the lenses of optimistic and pessimistic future scenarios, in particular to assess its relations with the international community.

Prior to embarking on the analysis of the natural gas industry in the forthcoming chapters, it is important to briefly review the political–economic backdrop of post-Revolutionary Iran, together with key issues relating to the country's power structure and decision making. This will be the foundation of the political discussions throughout this book which have direct implications for different aspects of gas sector development.

## The post-Revolutionary political structure

The political structure after the Revolution in 1979 developed into an opaque system, often hard to understand. Perhaps it is the first system of its kind where an overlapping mixture of formal and informal political, religious, military, and business authorities, all directly and indirectly, influence the decision-making process in critical matters such as security and foreign policy.

The 'formal' political structure is clearly articulated in the Constitution through which each centre of power, including the Executive, the Judiciary, and the Legislature, is explicitly defined and assigned particular autonomies and responsibilities. However, behind the facade of a constitutionally clear power structure, there is a complicated, informal political system which influences the country's domestic and foreign politics. These competitive and 'loosely-connected' power centres are established as religious–political associations, revolutionary foundations, and paramilitary organizations which are heavily supported by differing factions of the powerful clerical leadership.[2] In parallel with the formal centres of power, these powerful and decentralized informal institutions compete politically and economically with the central government to enforce their factional ideologies.

Each of these divided, competing factions has different and, in most cases, opposing ideologies relating to the country's objectives and how these should be achieved. Contrary to widespread perceptions, this highlights the fact that domestic and foreign policy are 'neither a blank slate nor set in concrete'; meaning that there are always choices to make, and they are made by these divided factions through indirect influence on formal decision-making processes.[3] Since the Revolution, the different approaches taken towards regional and international matters by different governments show that political rivalries and ideological conflicts have been playing an important role in the formation of Iranian foreign policy. Since the death of Ayatollah Khomeini in 1989, the support of and intervention by different factions and political institutions have given rise to periods of pragmatism and moderation in foreign policy, supporting moderate policy and promoting the easing of tension between Iran and the international community (as they did for example during the Rafsanjani and Khatami governments). Conversely, there have been periods of confrontation and defiance when hardline, fundamentalist groups saw Iran as a revolutionary state which should adopt an assertive foreign policy in defence of Islamic interests and confrontation with imperial powers (as for example they did during the Ahmadinejad era).[4]

Therefore, although the political system has formal institutions whose roles and responsibilities are clearly articulated in the Constitution, these institutions are a playing field for informal centres of power, individuals, networks, and factions which are predominantly overseen, and at times engaged, by the Supreme Leader.[5] In other words, while the pendulum of decision-making may swing towards conservatism or pragmatism depending on the prevailing political faction in power, its range of action is limited to what is set by the Supreme Leader. In major foreign and security issues, the Supreme Leader has the ultimate authority to approve or reject policy initiatives.[6] He is the most important official in the country, the commander-in-chief with the constitutional power to declare war and mobilize troops. The Supreme Leader is not often involved in day-to-day affairs but guides the overall direction of domestic and foreign policy.

Even though in the 'formal' political power structure the President, through the foreign ministry, and the Supreme National Security Council (SNSC), plays important roles in foreign policy-making, it is the Supreme Leader who holds the highest authority over the overall direction of policy that should be followed by the regime. While the President is responsible for the day-to-day administration of the country and participates in decision-making on domestic and foreign matters, his authority to a large extent depends on the degree of freedom that the Supreme Leader decides to grant him.[7] In the SNSC also, decisions on defence and national security matters should be made within the framework of general policies determined by the Supreme Leader.

But while it is true to maintain that the Supreme Leader holds the most power, as Thaler and et.al (2010) argue, he is not 'omnipotent'.[8] There is a misconception that the Supreme Leader is all-powerful – that he can dictate policies and take decisions based on his own preferences.[9] While describing the Supreme Leader as the single most powerful individual in a highly factionalized, autocratic regime, Sadjadpour (2008) argues that the Supreme Leader does not make national decisions on his own, although no major decision can be taken without his consent.[10] The Supreme Leader frequently consults with influential religious, military, and business factions and has representatives in almost all key political institutions. This also has strategic importance since he can oversee and engage with these factions and institutions to maintain his position. In other words 'he must balance a multitude of competing interests to ensure that no single faction or group becomes so dominant that it threatens his power'.[11] For example, the presence of representatives from various institutions, including the President and the Islamic Revolutionary Guard Corps (IRGC) commanders, at the SNSC and their collective decision making in its deliberations, particularly during times of crisis, ensures that if anything goes wrong, all parties take responsibility.[12]

Therefore, decision making on critical issues, such as foreign and security policy, is a process which cannot be mapped or predicted in advance. It is 'a highly dynamic and periodic' process that does not follow any certain, pre-defined pattern. The multiplicity of bodies of power, each having competing interests and ideologies, means that such a pattern has never been established in the post-Revolutionary political system.[13]

## Economic and foreign policy of post-Revolutionary governments

Since the 1979 Islamic Revolution, Iran has undergone major changes in its economic and foreign policy. The Revolution radically transformed the economy from a Western-oriented, free-enterprise system to a state-controlled theocratic oligarchy.[14] The new economic strategy promoted by the Islamic ideology of social justice – openly hostile to capitalism and multinational institutions – involved extensive state intervention in the economy.[15] The inward-oriented economy which resulted from the revolutionary ideology of self-sufficiency and independence strengthened the dominance of state-owned companies, as well as the unregulated and opaque para-governmental organizations.[16] The expulsion of international oil companies from Iran and cancellation of all oil and gas development contracts were consequences of such policies.

The Islamic Republic's overall economic policy has always been to reduce its dependence on oil revenues. Yet factors such as costs of war, deteriorating economic conditions, and a population boom eventually led to an increase of such dependence. The ailing economic situation, which had been further exacerbated by the start of the Iran–Iraq war, helped the revolutionary regime to expand state ownership and operation and encourage distribution of the oil wealth among people in forms of energy and commodity subsidies to gain support.[17] It was during the war period that the revolutionary goal of encouraging high population growth was promoted, leading to a sharp increase in population to which much of Iran's economic hardships, including unemployment and low national productivity, have been attributed.

Post-Revolutionary foreign policy was, to a large extent, influenced by the historical experiences of foreign political and economic intervention in Iran; this led to the formulation of the principle of 'equilibrium', which in effect meant establishing political and diplomatic relations based on equality.[18] The US embassy hostage crisis, however, led to strong anti-imperialism sentiments, manifested in a confrontational foreign policy with the West and the controversial policy of exporting Revolution, which referred to an ideal Islamic world order to legitimize its policies. The legacy of the hostage crisis has been a detrimental impact on Iran–USA relations which, throughout the post-Revolutionary era, has manifested itself in the form of sanctions, political and economic isolation, threat of military attack, and support of opposition groups.

The changes of economic and foreign policy in the aftermath of the Iran–Iraq war are illustrated during the three crucial periods of the Rafsanjani, Khatami, and Ahmadinejad presidencies.

## Rafsanjani and the construction era (1989–1997)

Akbar Hashemi Rafsanjani took power in Iran in 1989 after the Iran–Iraq war had left large parts of the country destroyed and with deteriorating economic conditions. The fall of oil prices around the end of the war, rising unemployment, and mounting foreign debt forced Rafsanjani to adopt construction and economic development through economic liberalization and the promotion of foreign investment as his principal policies.[19] To speed up reconstruction and economic recovery, the government was forced to change its overall foreign policy, ending the revolutionary ideology of antagonism with the West, in order to open doors to foreign investment and engage in more constructive relations with the outside world. His pragmatic approach – although seriously opposed by fundamentalist and conservative factions supported by Supreme Leader Khamenei following the power struggle after Khomeini's death – made significant contributions to the post-war economic recovery and revitalization of the oil and gas sector.[20]

In the petroleum sector, Rafsanjani adopted contrasting policies: reducing the country's dependence on oil by encouraging industrialization, while increasing the production and export of oil to boost the hard currency revenues vitally needed for his reconstruction plans. As a result, he directed funds towards development of the country's gas industry and the domestic consumption of gas – policies which had already been started in the mid-1980s by Prime Minister Mir Hossein Mousavi. The post-war reconstruction and industrialization process substantially increased oil and gas consumption in domestic markets, highlighting the need for increased production and vast investment. The policy of increasing the share of natural gas in the country's primary energy mix was envisaged in both the First (1991–1995) and Second (1996–2000) Economic Development Plans, encouraging domestic market expansion, and conversion of power generation from oil to gas. The idea of gas export to neighbouring countries was also first discussed by the Rafsanjani government, but as production was insufficient to meet additional supply commitments, it was abandoned. Although this administration made the unprecedented move of welcoming foreign investors to develop oil and gas, US sanctions and domestic sources of opposition placed serious constraints on the success of this policy.

## The reformist government of Khatami (1997–2005)

President Mohammad Khatami's election followed the unfavourable economic conditions – resulting from low oil prices, inflation, growing dominance of Bonyads,[21] and corruption – which emerged during Rafsanjani's second term. These conditions encouraged certain societal groups, particularly youths, women, and elites, to seek political change and economic reform. In response, Khatami adopted a policy of gradual transition to democracy through establishing the rule of law, promoting civil society, economic and civil liberalization, and a move towards more integrated relations with the international community through expansion of trade ties and diplomatic dialogue.[22] His economic agenda primarily focused on the control of inflation and unemployment, and the promotion of foreign investment to develop major industries such as oil and gas.

During the Khatami presidency, a major breakthrough occurred in the development of both the oil and, particularly, the gas sector as a result of the participation of major oil companies. Improved political and diplomatic relations with the EU helped his administration to attract foreign investment while benefiting from the EU–USA confrontation over US economic sanctions against Iran. One of Khatami's major successes in the attraction of foreign companies was the introduction of the 2002 Foreign Investment Promotion and Protection Act (FIPPA), which offered the guarantees and protections needed by foreign investors. Opening up Iran's petroleum sector to foreign investment, albeit under the unattractive framework of buyback contracts, provided international oil companies with their first opportunities to return to Iran's oil and gas sector since they had left or were expelled following the Revolution.

The Khatami administration essentially continued Rafsanjani's pragmatic development policy of the petroleum sector, though at a faster pace in the natural gas sector. The exception was gas export policy which, thanks to the fast development of South Pars Phases, was extensively pursued via the conclusion of many pipeline and LNG export contracts to regional and international markets. In line with the Third Development Plan (2001–2005), top priority was given to expansion of the domestic market and natural gas substitution in power generation, to release more oil for export.

## The fundamentalist government of Ahmadinejad (2005–2013)

A radical shift in domestic and foreign policy was the most important consequence of Mahmoud Ahmadinejad's election as Iran's sixth president. To the surprise of many, his victory in the election was a result of the strong support he received from conservative factions, and of his success in presenting the image of a simple and humble servant, something which seemed to appeal to the urban poor.[23]

The revolutionary ideology of independence and resistance further intensified during his tenure, and in the view of some scholars this turned into ideological paranoia.[24] Ahmadinejad's foreign policy was formed by finding external threats around which to mobilize support, thereby increasing the dependency of society on the state; this had the effect of diverting attention from domestic economic problems and political deficiencies. The political tension between Iran and the West increased following Ahmadinejad's strong support for Iran's nuclear programme and radical rhetoric, mobilizing not only the USA and the EU, but also China and Russia, his close allies, against the country. On the domestic front, Iran also witnessed an unprecedented rise in the political and economic power of the military and security services (such as the IRGC) during his term, together with the growing participation of informal centres of power in economic affairs.

Ahmadinejad's economic policy focused more on independence and the exploitation of national capabilities, including national companies, investments, and technologies. This resulted in a more unfavourable stance toward foreign investors, and their replacement by powerful military and economic institutions such as the IRGC. His hardline conservative foreign policy also facilitated a transition away from a market economy (which had been advocated by Rafsanjani and Khatami) towards a nationalistic, state-controlled economy; this ultimately resulted in the intensification of international sanctions.

The departure of international oil companies, as a result of intensifying international sanctions, helped Ahmadinejad to take a tighter grip on the rentier system of the oil and gas sector by offering more active roles to institutions such as IRGC and its subsidiaries. The advancement of such institutions in Iran's political and economic system was a product of the Ahmadinejad administration's need to make trade-offs with them to sustain its power. In the light of growing international pressures, the dominance of domestic and Asian companies in the oil and gas sector – lacking experience, technology, and adequate investment – led many development projects to be cancelled, suspended, or substantially delayed. By the time Ahmadinejad left office in the summer of 2013, the economy had been devastated, mostly as a result of international sanctions and badly implemented economic reforms.

## The moderate government of Rouhani and the prospect for change

Almost one year has passed since the election of Hassan Rouhani in June 2013, and available evidence suggests that Iran is on a different domestic and foreign policy path from that of the previous administration. The victory of Rouhani, a moderate cleric who promised the establishment of a prudent and moderate government, has revived hope in the West for a more friendly and less confrontational approach from Iran's foreign policy makers.

President Rouhani has pledged to engage in 'constructive interaction' internationally, highlighting his approach to solving domestic and international challenges by 'addressing their underlying causes' in order to secure 'win–win solutions'.[25] Rouhani's foreign policy has enjoyed the unprecedented support of the Supreme Leader, who has ultimate authority over the country's national security and foreign affairs (see above). Such a change of approach by Ayatollah Khamenei, described as an event of 'heroic flexibility',[26] is interpreted as permission for a compromise over the nuclear dispute, and as a signal to the West that President Rouhani has his blessing to negotiate on this basis. International sanctions, worsening economic conditions, and public demands for a change in domestic and international affairs (which had led to the election of Rouhani) are some of the reasons behind such a change of policy. Therefore, this foreign policy shift from confrontation with the West to conciliation and 'heroic flexibility' could potentially signal a breakthrough in the nuclear dispute and consequent easing or removal of international sanctions. Such a potential is further amplified by President Rouhani's assertion that he has 'full authority' in negotiations with the international community over Iran's nuclear programme, a level of authority which has rarely been seen in former governments.[27]

On the domestic front, the return of Bijan Namdar Zanganeh as petroleum minister has been welcomed by industry players and experts alike after eight years of mismanagement under Ahmadinejad.[28] His previous term in that post (1997–2005) was the most glorious era for the Iranian petroleum sector since the Revolution. His notable achievements in office included: the attraction of foreign investors, a substantial expansion of the gas sector, an increase in the share of gas in the primary energy mix (with consequent freeing up of oil for export), development of the country's petrochemical sector and of local companies as private contractors to the National Iranian Oil Company (NIOC), as well as the development of many gas export projects and a strengthening of the country's energy diplomacy in the region and beyond. In his new term as petroleum minister, he has moved rapidly to break the taboo on buyback contracts being the only and unchangeable contractual framework for the development of the Iranian petroleum sector, and has ordered the modification of oil contracts in a bid to make them more attractive to potential investors.

## Structure of the book

This introductory chapter, while introducing the objectives of this book, has presented readers with the intellectual foundation of Iran's political structures and decision-making mechanisms; these play an important role in the development of the country's natural gas industry.

It is important to stress from the outset that some of the knowledge relating to issues and challenges highlighted in this chapter may remain limited, due to the limited scope of the data and information in the public domain, as well as to the lack of openness of governmental organizations or international companies. This is particularly challenging for studies of the Iranian energy sector, where official data and statistics are either not available or are considered confidential.

The book has six chapters. Chapter 1 provides a descriptive background to Iran's natural gas industry and reviews its development before and after the Islamic Revolution. Chapter 2 identifies domestic political challenges which have slowed the progress of the industry, particularly export projects. It analyses the roots and ramifications of the politicization of the country's petroleum sector and establishes linkages between the various historical and political events which have contributed to the sensitivity of the sector. The background to US and international sanctions, along with their impact on the development of Iran's oil and gas sector, is addressed in Chapter 3, which also considers the likelihood of Iran reaching a final agreement with the international community on the timing and scale of sanctions removal, together with the overall impact that such a development could have on the natural gas industry. Chapter 4 examines the investment regime in the oil and gas sector and presents an analytical review of the Iranian petroleum contractual regime and the new reforms made to the investment framework under the Rouhani government. It also tries to answer the question of whether legal and contractual reform would be sufficient to ensure long-term participation of foreign investors in the development of the gas sector. Chapter 5 focuses on the issue of energy subsidies and their impact on the development of the natural gas industry. It also reviews the 2010 subsidies reform programme and evaluates its overall success in controlling domestic consumption and freeing up revenues for the development of natural gas projects. Chapter 6 examines the prolonged political debate over optimal allocation of natural gas resources. This highlights the importance of the secure and adequate supply of gas to domestic markets on social equity grounds; it also presents a qualitative economic analysis of allocating gas to different options, and reassesses the justification for support of gas exports as a component of foreign diplomacy. The final chapter summarizes the conclusions on each of the different themes in the previous chapters and offers some forecasts of how the industry may develop up to and beyond 2020.

# CHAPTER 1

# IRAN'S NATURAL GAS INDUSTRY: AN OVERVIEW

## Introduction

Iran's natural gas industry cannot be understood without examining the country's past and present policies and how they have affected its development. While priority was given to the policy of gas export before the Revolution, a drastic policy shift from export to domestic consumption led to an 'aggressive expansion' of the domestic market after it. The post-Revolutionary era also witnessed a recommencement and expansion of export projects – thanks to the discovery of mammoth natural gas reserves, as a result of which the country announced substantial pipeline and LNG export projects in the late 1990s. Due, however, to numerous political, legal, fiscal, and economic challenges (to be examined in forthcoming chapters), most of these projects were cancelled, suspended, or not allowed to fully materialize.

This chapter provides a detailed background to Iran's natural gas industry, including: the history, government policies, infrastructure, organization, production and consumption trends, and natural gas export–import projects in order to set the stage for forthcoming analytical discussions on challenges facing the development of the industry.

## The history of natural gas in Iran

The history of natural gas in Iran dates back to the ancient era when natural gas reserves were found, surprisingly, near the wreckage of fire temples, such as 'Eternal Fire' near Kirkuk, also known as 'Nebuchadnezzar'.[1] Evidence also proves the consumption of natural gas in ancient Zoroastrian temples in the vicinity of Masjed Soleyman, where oil was first discovered in 1908. The first historical evidence showing the commercial consumption of natural gas goes back to the Qajar dynasty when Naser-al-Din Shah, during his first visit to London in 1873, saw that streets were lit by gas lamps. After returning to Iran, he ordered the construction of the first gas lamp factory in Tehran, which started production in 1881.[2]

Limited consumption of natural gas continued until 1908 when, following the discovery of the first oil field in Masjed Soleyman, the gas industry entered a new stage of substantial flaring of gas produced in association with oil production.[3] In 1916, Iran signed its first 70-year natural gas field development contract with a Russian subject, Mousier Mededivitch Khoshtaria, for exploration and exploitation of oil and gas resources in some northern provinces, which included Gilan, Mazandaran, and Estarabad. This agreement, however, was never approved by the Parliament.[4]

It was only after the 'White Revolution' of Mohammad Reza Shah Pahlavi in 1963, and his revolutionary vision for rapid economic development of the country, that utilization of natural gas became part of a strategic goal to maximize economic revenues and prevent the waste of natural resources. In a famous rhetorical speech, he emphasized that 'the flames that are burning the nation's wealth must be extinguished at once and forever',[5] underlining the immense economic potential of the natural gas industry, both in the development of domestic markets and exports. As a result, the National Iranian Gas Company (NIGC) was established to manage and control gas development projects, including exports.

The Shah's new gas policy encouraged the consumption of gas as a fuel for electricity generation with commercial and residential uses, particularly in regions rich in natural gas resources, such as Masjed Soleyman, Agha Jari, Haft Gol, and Abadan. Natural gas was first used as a feedstock in the Shiraz' Fertilizer Manufacturing Complex in 1964, for which a 10 inch, 215km pipeline was constructed by NIOC from Gachsaran to Shiraz.[6] A few years later, the same pipeline supplied gas to Shiraz's Namazi Hospital – the first time the country's gas was consumed for non-industrial purposes.

Substantial development of the natural gas industry took place in the mid-1960s following the implementation of the Third and Fourth Economic Development Plans. These strongly emphasized industrialization and tried to attract foreign investment for the development of gas resources. As a result, the country started negotiations for gas exports to the then Soviet Union (USSR) which led to the conclusion of a Fifteen-Year Economic and Technical Co-operation Agreement in January 1966. This committed Iran to the export of 10 bcm/year of natural gas to the USSR, in return for credit finance of 260 million Soviet Roubles and the construction of various mega projects which included a steel plant, the first Trunkline pipeline (IGAT 1), and an automotive factory in Arak.[7] The two countries agreed to review the contract in 1980 with the possibility of extension for another 10 years.

The construction of the 40 and 42-inch IGAT 1 pipeline started immediately and gas exports to the USSR commenced in 1970 after a 10-year sale and purchase agreement was reached between the two countries. Natural gas exports to the USSR started at less than 1 bcm/year, and reached a record of 9.4 bcm in 1977. In the sale and purchase agreement, the price of gas was set at 6 Roubles/thousand cubic metres of gas, or $0.185/MMBtu.[8] The government's annual revenue from gas exports was estimated at around $41 million in 1970, which amounts to an aggregate income of $950 million throughout the life of the contract.[9]

Besides gas exports to the USSR, Iranian officials also planned to transmit and distribute 6.5 bcm of gas a year in domestic markets via future extensions from the IGAT 1 pipeline.[10] Therefore, IGAT 1 was not only an export-designated pipeline, but was also another mega project made up of various smaller projects to supply gas to domestic markets (see Map 1.2).

As of the mid-1970s, Iran was estimated to hold around 17 per cent of the world's natural gas resources.[11] As a result, it initiated further negotiations with other countries, including those in Europe, in order to expand its gas exports ties with global markets. Before this, gas destined for export had been mostly associated with oil production from fields such as Maroon, Agha Jari, Koranj, Fars, Pazanan, Bibi Hakimeh, Gachsaran, and Rageh Sefid. Only later, after the discovery of non-associated gas in Shiraz boosted production capacity in the mid-1970s, was the Iranian government encouraged to start negotiations for new swap contracts with the USSR to export gas to West Germany and Europe. Prior to the Europe gas agreement, talks to promote the export of Kangan LNG to the Japanese and US markets were underway, but the unexpected conclusion of the Europe gas agreement (between Iran, USSR, Germany, France, and Austria) cast major doubts over the finalization of the former deal. These doubts were later proved to have been wrong as the Kangan LNG project continued until it was cancelled as a result of the Islamic Revolution (rather than the Europe gas agreement).[12] The Europe gas agreement was a trilateral swap contract between Iran and the USSR on the one hand, and the USSR and European countries on the other. Iran's growing economic ties with the USSR during the cold war period triggered much concern among US and British officials about losing influence over Iran to the USSR. There were even rumours that the 1977 explosion of the IGAT 1 pipeline was planned by the US and British intelligence services in retaliation for close Iran–USSR cooperation and for the Shah's ultimatum to western countries that he would review the oil contract of the 1953 Consortium (see Chapter 2).[13]

Based on the Europe gas agreement, Iran committed to export an additional volume of 15 bcm/year of gas to the USSR once the construction of the second export pipeline was completed, while the latter committed to export the same volume to Germany.[14] Of this 15 bcm of gas, 50 per cent had been allocated to West Germany, 33.33 per cent to France, and 16.67 per cent to Austria.[15] The duration of the contract was 20 years and the price was fixed, based on the prices of alternative fuels in West Germany's market, and was estimated to generate a total revenue of DM20 million for Iran.[16] In addition to the Europe gas agreement, another export contract was also concluded with Czechoslovakia; this, however, never went beyond the planning stage and was cancelled following the Revolution.

Iran had also planned to diversify its gas export options and, along with pipeline projects, it embarked on the development of LNG capacity. The first LNG project goes back to the early 1970s when the country made an agreement with a consortium of Japanese, Norwegian, and US companies to construct facilities and to produce and export 4.8–7.2 mt/year of LNG from the North Pars field.[17] As a result, a consortium named Kangan Liquefied Natural Gas, also known as Kalingas, was established to design and conduct feasibility studies for three potential export projects: the first, known as MRW, was for the export of LNG to the US market, and it was cancelled in the late 1970s; the second project, relating to exports of LNG to West Europe, was also abandoned at the negotiation stage; the most promising project was the third one, also known as JKC, for exports of 2.8 mt/year of LNG to Japan.[18] In the JKC project, the gas price was set at $0.36/MMBtu, which was expected to gradually increase to $0.46/MMBtu by 1979.[19] The Kalingas project was also cancelled in 1979 as a result of the Islamic Revolution.

The Islamic Revolution dramatically transformed Iran's natural gas development prospects. The 1970s had been a decade of prosperity for the natural gas industry, particularly on the export front; one major export project was already successfully implemented and plans for further expansion of production and export capacities were underway. The positive trend of the industry's development had assumed that once all planned projects had materialized, Iran would become a leading gas exporter to international markets.[20] But the Revolution diverted the process by implementing policies stemming from the revolutionary theories of independence, self-reliance, and prohibition of foreign influence. (see introductory chapter)

Eleven months after the Revolution, in 1980, a special commission encompassing revolutionary figures was established to reassess all oil and gas contracts. According to its single-article mandate, contracts whose terms were considered inconsistent with the provisions of the 1950 Petroleum Act had to be declared null and void.[21] This resulted in the cancellation of almost all petroleum contracts to which foreign companies were party. The gas export project to the USSR was also suspended after the two countries failed to reach an agreement on the terms of the contract's extension and pricing beyond 1980. In addition, one effect of the war with Iraq (1980–1988) had been to support the policy of domestic consumption of gas as it would release more oil for export, yielding more revenue for use by the government to tackle the financial difficulties resulting from the war. Moreover, the infrastructure damage, along with the expulsion or withdrawal of oil companies, left the country with major challenges in sustaining the production capacity required to meet export commitments, which forced the country to suspend its export contract with the USSR.

Despite the abandonment and cancellation of many post-Revolutionary projects in the period between the 1980s and early 1990s, those activities relating to gas export continued, with small-scale feasibility studies for potential LNG projects. In 1987, for example, British Gas (BG) examined the feasibility of exports of 6 mt/year of LNG from Iran to western European markets in a comparative study with exports of the same volume from Nigeria, Qatar, and Trinidad and Tobago.[22] Another study was conducted by a Japanese company in 1988 on the construction of a liquefaction plant with a capacity of 24 mmcm/day of gas from the South Pars field.[23] This study showed that export of LNG from Iran could be economically viable if the prices were set at $5.3/MMBtu c.i.f Japan delivery.[24]

As the post-war economic situation was improving progressively, gas exports to the USSR resumed in 1990, recording a rate of 2.2 and 2.7 bcm of gas in 1990 and 1991 respectively.[25] But, following the collapse of the USSR and the continuation of domestic market expansion, exports were reduced to 487 mmcm in 1992 and suspended thereafter. In 1992, Tehran and Baku signed a 10-year contract for exports of 250 mmcm of Iranian gas to Azerbaijan in return for the import of gasoline.[26] Supplies were suspended in 1993 and cancelled in 1995 due to Baku's failure to pay for the exported gas.[27] During the two-year suspension period NIGC attempted to use this pipeline for storage of gas destined for consumption in the north-western part of the country, but this was not successful.[28]

## Iran's natural gas policy

Since the beginning of natural gas commercialization in the 1960s, different governments adopted various and, in most cases, contradictory policies with regard to the development of the industry. In the pre-Revolution era, Iran's gas policy was dominated by export objectives designed to maximize the net income from international sales, while securing access to international markets through direct participation in refining, marketing, distribution, and sales and purchase activities in major energy consuming countries. In the 1970s, in addition to its focus on export markets, the government decided to develop domestic market infrastructure in order to expand and encourage domestic consumption. After the Revolution, however, the gas export policy was changed in favour of domestic market expansion policies, resulting in the cancellation of almost all export contracts and projects. The industry was severely affected by the Iran–Iraq war, which was followed by an urgent need for reconstruction, which led to hasty development planning and mismanagement.

Perhaps for the first time since the Revolution, a transparent set of policies was introduced by the Khatami administration (1997–2005); this led to the promotion and improvement of both domestic and export markets, to the pursuit of increased development of the sector, and flourishing international relations (see introductory chapter). Based on the Third Five-Year Development Plan (2000–4), exports of natural gas were the government's second priority, after fulfilling the needs of the domestic market. The country's key policy instrument, namely the 20-Year Economic Perspective (2005–25),[29] was also designed and introduced during the Khatami administration; this required substantial development of the gas sector, and was referred to as the country's 'pillar of development'.[30] The Perspective envisaged that, as the development of the country's huge natural gas resources required massive financial and technological investment, it could be used as a strategic tool to strengthen economic and political relations with the outside world.[31] The Perspective defined the country's overall policy in the petroleum industry as the maintenance of its position as the second-largest oil producer in OPEC,[32] with the intention of improving its position to the third-largest gas producer in the world, and the aim of becoming the largest producer of oil and gas combined in the region.[33]

During the Ahmadinejad administration (2005–13), there was a further change of policy in which the focus was primarily on domestic market expansion; new export projects were effectively abandoned and existing ones, particularly gas exports to Turkey, faced serious difficulties. In practice, his government put an end to the Khatami government's long-term strategic planning for development of the gas industry. Ahmadinejad's radical stand against the international community, together with the controversies over the country's nuclear programme, also led to the termination of almost all investment and development activities by foreign companies, leaving the country seriously challenged in the development of its oil and gas industry (see Chapter 3). Despite increasing deterioration in the industry, the Fifth Five-Year Development Plan (2011–15) remained fairly optimistic and articulated yet another 'ambitious' plan for the development of the gas industry. It urged the attraction of investment worth \$140 billion in the oil and gas upstream sector, and the export of around 75 bcm/year of gas by the end of the Plan.[34] To this end, the Plan required the government to:

- increase natural gas production to 450 bcm/year,
- increase the share of natural gas in the country's energy balance (to 75 per cent, compared with its share of 55 per cent in 2011) by substituting oil products with natural gas as well as accelerating the completion of reinjection projects,
- developing natural gas exports through both pipeline and LNG, and
- developing natural gas-based industries such as petrochemicals and GTL.[35]

None of these objectives has materialized and they are highly likely to remain unachievable in the near future.

The Plan addressed the notorious problem of the lack of coherent, long-term strategic planning in the energy sector. Its Article 125 requires the government to prepare and present to Parliament the 'National Bill for Energy Strategies' to govern all energy activities in the country for a 25-year period. The Bill is designed to determine the country's overall energy strategies, such as those relating to oil and gas production capacity, energy balance, resource exploration and development, and export projects. The Bill was supposed to have been prepared by the Petroleum Ministry and ratified by the Parliament within one year from the coming into force of the Fifth Development Plan, but its final ratification has been reportedly delayed by Parliament and is unlikely to be approved before the end of the Plan implementation period.[36]

The election of the Rouhani government in June 2013 has raised hopes that in addition to improving relations with the international community and strengthening prospects for the return of international companies, the industry would again witness consistent and coherent decision making and policies. The available evidence since its election shows that the new administration has adopted policies in line with those implemented by the Khatami administration, meaning parallel development of domestic markets and export capacity. In order to implement these policies, however, the administration has to tackle the daunting task of substantially increasing the country's production capacity, which previous administrations failed to achieve due to international sanctions and unfavourable legal and fiscal terms.

## Organization of Iran's natural gas industry

Three major companies control and manage Iran's gas industry: the National Iranian Oil Company (NIOC), the National Iranian Gas Company (NIGC), and the National Iranian Gas Export Company (NIGEC). Depending on upstream and downstream segments of the industry, one of these companies manages the relevant development activities. NIOC handles upstream activities, including exploration, development, and production of gas. It controls these activities through several other subsidiaries such as the National Iranian South Oil Company (NISOC), the Iranian Central Oil Fields Company (ICOFC), the Iranian Offshore Oil Company (IOOC), and the Pars Oil and Gas Company (POGC).

NIGC, established in 1965, is one of four principal companies affiliated to the Ministry of Petroleum. It is responsible for downstream activities, including gas transmission and distribution, downstream project engineering and construction, and underground storage. NIGC itself has more than 40 subsidiaries; these include eight gas processing companies,[37] 30 provincial gas companies,[38] and four administrative companies.[39]

To manage natural gas marketing and sales in regional and international markets, NIGEC was established in 2003 as a subsidiary of NIOC. It manages all international-related investments and projects on behalf of NIOC. Its key responsibilities include: marketing of natural gas and related products; establishing joint ventures with potential buyers/investors; negotiating and finalizing natural gas and LNG sales and purchase agreements; and managing and carrying out GTL projects and developing markets for GTL products. In July 2012, following an unexpected decision by NIOC, NIGEC was dissolved and its responsibilities were assigned to the international division of NIOC. This was said to have been a pre-emptive attempt by NIOC to block the Petroleum Ministry's decision to incorporate NIGEC with NIGC in order to broaden the latter's responsibilities in forthcoming natural gas projects.[40] NIGEC was revived a few months later, but its future remains unclear as there are still disagreements among officials about whether to keep its affiliation with NIOC, to assign it to NIGC, or to dissolve it.[41]

As a result of this unintegrated system, the management of the gas industry is scattered among various state-owned companies with overlapping responsibilities. The resulting mismanagement, in the absence of a long-term strategic vision for development of the industry, has created serious institutional complications. It has also caused confusion among stakeholders, particularly those involved in export projects, in identifying which body is responsible for the different elements of project development – when exploration and production is controlled by NIOC, transmission by NIGC, and export planning by NIGEC. The situation becomes even more complicated when political disagreements break out among officials (as was the case in the dissolution of NIGEC), causing a deliberate disconnection between these organs.

**Natural gas reserves and production**

As of 2012, Iran had proven natural gas reserves of around 34 tcm.[42] The country has 18 per cent of global gas reserves, and is the largest gas resource holder in the world (followed by Russia).[43] Nearly two-thirds of Iranian reserves are located in non-associated fields which remain to be developed. The increase in the country's proven gas reserves in 2012 (compared with the 2010 figure), can be attributed to NIOC's new discoveries of Shoorijeh, upper and lower Mozdooran, Toosan Rood, Forooz and Sefid, Neiriz of Azadegan, and Dehrom fields which increased the country's proven reserves by more than 1 tcm.[44]

According to Iran's Energy Balance, as of 2012 there were 28 major natural gas fields in Iran which include onshore, offshore associated and non-associated reserves, the most important of which are South Pars, Golshan, Ferdowsi, Kish, North Pars, Hengam, Tabnak, Aghar, Dalan, Naar, Kangan, Sarkhoon, Sooroo, Assaluyeh, and Varavi.

Among the fields, South Pars is strategically very important as it is shared with neighbouring Qatar which has substantially developed its production capacity (see Map 1.1). The giant South Pars gas field constitutes over 47 per cent of Iran's gas reserves and accounts for 40 per cent of its gas production. Discovered 100 km offshore in the Persian Gulf in 1988, the South Pars field has a 24-phase development scheme to produce around 270 bcm/year (or 750 mmcm/day) gas.[45] Each phase has a combination of natural gas, condensates, and/or natural gas liquids production (see Table 1.1).

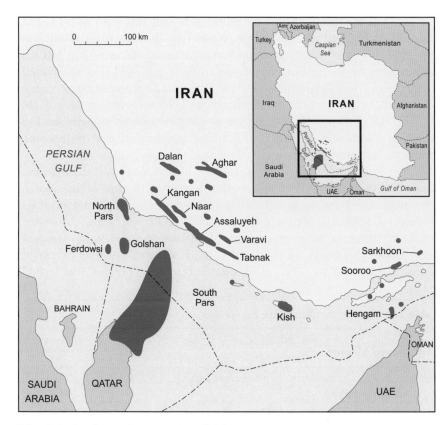

**Map 1.1:** Iranian major natural gas fields

Source: NIOC (2009).

As of 2014, 11 phases of South Pars (phases 1–10 and 12) were operational, while the remaining phases are under development with completion dates varying between 2014 and 2018 (see Table 1.1).[46] Natural gas produced from the South Pars field is mainly allocated for the domestic market, especially for oil field reinjection, with a few phases being designated for export and GTL projects.[47] Since 2007, more than $30 billion has been invested in the development of the South Pars phases, and a further estimated additional investment of $40 billion is required for developing other phases within the next five years.[48]

In addition to the South Pars field, Iran owns other major gas fields with substantial gas reserves such as North Pars, Kish, Golshan, and Ferdowsi. Located in the east of Lavan Island, Kish gas field is estimated to have 1.8 tcm of proven gas[49] and is known as the 'country's second gas pole'. It is estimated that its production will reach 30 to 50 bcm/ year ultimately, and when its three phases become fully operational it is expected to supply domestic and export markets.[50] According to NIOC, 70 per cent of the drilling operation in Kish gas field was completed in 2012 and initial production from three wells is expected to come on stream by the end of 2014.[51] Kish gas field and phases 12, 15, 16, 17, and 18 of South Pars have been assigned urgent priority by Oil Minister Zanganeh, in order to increase production and reduce the country's gas deficit.[52]

North Pars is another major gas field which is located 120 km to the south-east of Bushehr. The four-phase development plan of the North Pars field has been assigned to the Chinese oil company CNOOC through a buyback contract for production of 36 bcm/year when the field becomes fully operational. Golshan and Ferdowsi are two other major gas fields, with an estimated reserve of 1.4 tcm of gas in place.[53] In December 2007, a 66-month buyback contract was signed

---

**Table 1.1:** Production from South Pars phases

### Completed phases

| Phase | Capacity (Natural Gas & Condensate) | Participating Companies | Operation year |
|---|---|---|---|
| 1 | 25 mmcm/day 40,000 bbl/day | Petropars | 2004 |
| 2 | 50 mmcm/day 80,000 bbl/day | Total; Gazprom; Petronas | 2003 |
| 3 | | | |
| 4 | 50 mmcm/day 80,000 bbl/day | Eni; Petropars; NIOC | 2005 |
| 5 | | | |
| 6 | 104 mmcm/day 158,000 bbl/day | Statoil; Petropars | 2009 |
| 7 | | | |
| 8 | | | |
| 9 | 50 mmcm/day 80,000 bbl/day | South Korean GS Construction and Engineering Company; National Iranian Oil Engineering and Construction Company; Iranian Offshore Engineering and Construction Company | 2009 |
| 10 | | | |
| 12 | 78 mmcm/day 110,000 bbl/day | Petropars; Sonangol; PDVSA | 2014 |

**Table 1.1:** *continued*

**Phases under development**

| Phase | Capacity (Natural Gas & Condensate | Participating Companies | Operation year |
|-------|-----------------------------------|------------------------|----------------|
| 11 | 50 mmcm/day 80,000 bbl/day | NIOC; Chinese CNPC | 2017–18 |
| 13 | 50 mmcm/day 80,000 bbl/day | MAPNA; SADRA; Petro Paydar | 2016–17 |
| 14 | 50 mmcm/day 77,000 bbl/day | Iranian Offshore Engineering and Construction Company; Iran Shipbuilding & Offshore Industries Complex Co; Organization of Industrial Development and Renovation; MAPNA; Payandan Co; Mashin Sazi Arak Engineering & Construction Co; Iran Industrial Plans Management Co; | 2015–16 |
| 15 16 | 50 mmcm/day 80.000 bbl/day | Khatam-al-Anbia Contraction Headquarter; Iranian Offshore Engineering and Construction Company; SAAF; Iran Shipbuilding & Offshore Industries Complex Co. | 2014–15 |
| 17 18 | 50 mmcm/day 80.000 bbl/day | Organization of Industrial Development and Renovation; National Iranian Oil Engineering and Construction Company; Iranian Offshore Engineering and Construction Company | 2015–16 |
| 19 | 50 mmcm/day 77.000 bbl/day | Petropars; Iranian Offshore Engineering and Construction Company | 2017–18 |
| 20 21 | 50 mmcm/day 75.000 bbl/day | National Iranian Oil Engineering and Construction Company | 2016–17 |
| 22 23 24 | 50 mmcm/day 77.000 bbl/day | Petro Sina Aria; SADRA | 2017–18 |

Source: Pars Oil & Gas Company (2014) and author's data collection.

between NIOC and the Malaysian SKS Company for development and production of 20 and 5 bcm/year from Golshan and Ferdowsi fields, respectively.[54] The contract, however, was cancelled in 2012 and no new contract has been awarded since then. As the development of South Pars has been of strategic importance for the government, few resources have been allocated for the development of these other three fields. It is not surprising, therefore, to see long delays in their development.

Despite exposure to numerous challenges in developing its natural gas resources, the country has a remarkable record in natural gas production (see Figure 1.1). In 2012, with production around 161 bcm, the country was the third largest gas producer in the world after the USA and Russia.[55]

It is important to mention that the production in Figure 1.1 shows only the volume of processed gas and does not include the aggregate volume of rich gas produced. This is substantially higher and includes associated, gas cap,[56] and non-associated gas. (see Table 1.2)

Rich gas, unless processed and dehydrated, cannot be commercially utilized. Processing removes water, together with hydrocarbons which can cause blockage and corrosion of valves and pipelines. In 2012, from the total volume of rich gas produced, 79 per cent (around 176 bcm) was transferred to processing and dehydration plants. (see Table 1.3)

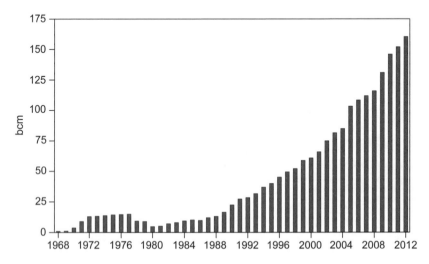

**Figure 1.1:** Iran's natural gas production, 1968–2012 (bcm)

Source: Iran Energy Balance (1968–2012), BP Statistics (2013).

**Table 1.2:** Rich gas production, 2005–2012 (bcm/year)

| Year | Associated | Gas cap | Non-associated | Total |
|------|------------|---------|----------------|-------|
| 2005 | 34.0 | 12.7 | 110.1 | 156.8 |
| 2006 | 35.1 | 12.2 | 119.8 | 167.2 |
| 2007 | 36.0 | 14.1 | 131.7 | 182.0 |
| 2008 | 36.3 | 12.9 | 149.4 | 198.6 |
| 2009 | 36.1 | 10.3 | 163.2 | 209.7 |
| 2010 | 37.1 | 12.8 | 172.2 | 222.2 |
| 2011 | 37.4 | 10.7 | 179.0 | 227.1 |
| 2012 | 27.7 | 11.4 | 184.7 | 223.9 |

Source: Iran Energy Balance (2012).

**Table 1.3:** Rich gas consumption in different sectors, 2005–2012 (bcm/year)

| Year | Gas and liquid gas factories | Refinery plants and dehydration units | Reinjection* | Others | Total |
|------|------------------------------|----------------------------------------|--------------|--------|-------|
| 2005 | 27.6 | 108.5 | 1.4 | 19.3 | 156.8 |
| 2006 | 28.9 | 118.2 | 1.5 | 18.6 | 167.2 |
| 2007 | 32.4 | 120.6 | 10.3 | 18.7 | 182.0 |
| 2008 | 33.6 | 134.9 | 9.6 | 20.5 | 198.6 |
| 2009 | 30.9 | 149.0 | 9.5 | 27.3 | 209.7 |
| 2010 | 31.4 | 163.3 | 9.2 | 18.3 | 222.2 |
| 2011 | 28.1 | 168.9 | 11.3 | 18.8 | 227.1 |
| 2012 | 26.6 | 176.9 | 6.5 | 13.9 | 223.9 |

\* The reinjection figures include gas reinjection to Haft Gol, Bibi Hakimeh, Gachsaran, Doroud, and Darkhovin oil fields.

Source: Iran Energy Balance (2012).

## Natural gas processing capacity

After the Revolution, Iran made significant progress in developing relatively reliable gas processing capacity. In 2013, there were 12 refining and dehydration units spread across the country in Bushehr, Khoozestan, Hormozgan, Khorasan Razavi, Fars, Ilam, and Qom, where the gas comes from fields such as Nar and Kangan, Aghar, Agha Jari, and South Pars. Processing capacity in 2012 reached 546.9 mmcm/day, which is 6.1 per cent higher than the 2010 level.[57] The figure for dehydration units stood at 28.3 mmcm/day in 2012, indicating an annual growth rate of 5.5 per cent since 2005.

As the country has been facing growing domestic consumption, in parallel with developing production capacity, the government has serious plans for expansion of processing capacity. In the period 2005–12, several large processing plants were brought into production including: Masjed Soleyman, Ilam, and South Pars phases 9 and 10. There are also plans to build additional plants such as Parsian to upgrade and increase the processing capacity of some other plants such as Sarkhoon and Qeshm.

**Table 1.4:** Nominal capacity of processing and dehydration units, 2005–2012 (bcm/year)

| Processing units | 2005 | 2007 | 2009 | 2011 | 2012 |
|---|---|---|---|---|---|
| Fajr (Kangan) | 39.6 | 39.6 | 39.6 | 45.0 | 45.0 |
| Khangiran (Hasheminejad) | 16.0 | 16.0 | 16.0 | 18.3 | 18.3 |
| Bid Boland 1 | 8.1 | 8.1 | 8.1 | 9.7 | 9.7 |
| Masjed Soleyman | - | 0.3 | 0.3 | 0.3 | 0.3 |
| Sarkhoon and Qeshm | 5.0 | 5.1 | 5.1 | 5.2 | 5.2 |
| Dalan | 7.2 | 7.2 | 7.2 | 7.2 | 7.2 |
| South Pars (phases 1–5 and 9 and 10) | 50.4 | 50.4 | 68.4 | 75.6 | 75.6 |
| Parsian | 9.0 | 29.1 | 29.1 | 29.7 | 29.7 |
| Ilam | - | 2.4 | 2.4 | 2.4 | 2.4 |
| Goorzin | 0.6 | 0.7 | 0.7 | 0.7 | 0.7 |
| Gonbadli and Shoorijeh D and B dehydration unit | 1.6 | 1.6 | 1.6 | 1.6 | 1.7 |
| Sarajeh dehydration unit | 0.2 | 0.2 | 0.2 | 0.2 | 0.2 |
| Total | 137.8 | 161.1 | 179.1 | 196.8 | 196.9 |

Source: Iran Energy Balance (2012).

## Natural gas transmission system

After the Revolution, the shift of policy to domestic market development led to extensive expansion of trunklines, import–export pipelines, and distribution networks. The 'backbone' of the country's domestic pipeline system is provided by the gas trunklines (IGAT pipelines), which transport gas from processing plants to end users in both domestic and export markets. These pipelines are fed by the gas produced from the operational phases of the South Pars and onshore associated gas. Construction of IGAT 3 to IGAT 8 started when the development of the South Pars phases began.[58] Except for IGAT 1, 2, 5, and the North and North East pipeline, the remaining IGATs are either under construction or are only partially operational.

In 2012, Iran had around 35,000 km of high-pressure transmission pipelines which were capable of transferring 700 mmcm/day gas across the country (see Table 1.5).[59] The 20-Year Economic Perspective (2005–25) envisaged that the aggregate length of the transmission network should reach 65,000 km by 2025 which would substantially increase the country's transmission capacity.[60]

**Table 1.5:** Transmission pipelines, 2005–2012 (km/year)

| Year | 2005 | 2006 | 2007 | 2008 | 2009 | 2010 | 2011 | 2012 |
|------|------|------|------|------|------|------|------|------|
| Construction every year | 2,249 | 2,911 | 2,821 | 2,416 | 1,902 | 1,042 | 1,056 | 624 |
| Total length | 22,005 | 24,916 | 27,737 | 30,153 | 32,055 | 33,097 | 34,153 | 34,778 |

Source: Iran Energy Balance (2012).

## IGAT 1

IGAT 1, 42-inch in diameter, was the first nationwide transmission pipeline, constructed before the Revolution between the Bid Boland gas processing plant and Astara to export gas to the USSR.[61] The 1101 km pipeline has the capacity to deliver 32 to 46 mmcm/day of gas from Bid Boland, Aghar and Dalan, Naar and Kangan, and phase 19 of South Pars.[62] The pipeline has 10 compressor stations and is divided into two parts: the first runs from the Bid Boland plant to the fourth compressor station close to Isfahan, and the second from there to the measurement station in Astara.[63] Gas is exported to Turkey and Armenia through this pipeline.

## IGAT 2

IGAT 2 is a 1037 km 56 inch pipeline with a transmission capacity of 90 mmcm/day.[64] The pipeline was constructed to supply gas from Naar and Kangan fields to the northern cities of Semnan, Golestan, Mazandaran, and Southern Khorasan. According to NIGC, this pipeline has been planned to improve gas transmission infrastructure in the northern and north-eastern regions in order to reduce their dependence on imports from Turkmenistan.[65]

## IGAT 3

IGAT 3 is a 1079 km, 56 inch pipeline constructed to supply gas from South Pars Phases 1–5 to Kangan, Saveh, and Rasht.[66] Its transmission capacity is 100 mmcm/year and it has nine compressor stations.[67] IGAT 3 also has a 273 km extension between Saveh and Rash which became operational in 2013.[68] IGAT 3 will be connected to IGAT 1 through a 36-inch, 700-metre loop pipeline in Dehagh in Isfahan in 2014, and there are also plans for it to loop with IGAT 2, for which the technical studies are still underway.[69]

### IGAT 4

IGAT 4 transports 110 mmcm/day of gas from the South Pars and Parsian processing plants to central and northern provinces of Iran.[70] It is a 1145 km, 56 inch pipeline with 10 compressor stations[71] and is divided into two parts: the main part (which came on stream in 2004) is a 351 km pipeline to Fars province connecting the processing plants in Assaluyeh to Pol-Kaleh compressor station in Isfahan; the second part, which is partially operational, includes various pipelines supplying gas to Kerman province (42-inch), Fars petrochemical plant (24-inch), Yazd (40-inch), and Isfahan Mobarakeh (40-inch).[72]

### IGAT 5

The 56-inch IGAT 5 can supply 90 mmcm/day of sour gas to the Agha Jari oil field for reinjection from South Pars phases 6, 7, and 8.[73] The 503 km pipeline has five compressor stations – two stations in Assaluyeh and three in the cities of Khormoj, Ab Pakhsh, and Sar Dasht.[74] Construction finished in 2008 and the pipeline became operational a year later.

### IGAT 6

IGAT 6, mainly in parallel with IGAT 5, has a 110 mmcm/day capacity and supplies gas to nearly 30 cities in Bushehr and Khoozestan provinces, while also serving reinjection purposes.[75] It will deliver gas from South Pars phases 9 and 10 to the Bid Boland processing plant, is 493 km long and 56 inches in diameter, and has four compressor stations en route.[76] Its construction has been delayed for many years and it is unlikely to become operational before 2016.

### IGAT 7

The 907 km, 56 inch IGAT 7 delivers 110 mmcm/day gas from the South Pars and Kish gas fields to 48 southern towns and cities including

17 cities in Kerman and Hormozgan provinces, and 31 cities in Sistan and Baluchistan province, with export potential to the UAE, Pakistan, and India.[77] The pipeline extends to Gavbandi, Rudan, and Kahnooj and terminates in Iranshahr. There are two compressor stations and this figure can increase to 11 in case of exports.[78] The first phase of the pipeline from Assaluyeh to Iranshahr was inaugurated in 2010, but its 400 km second phase from Iranshahr to the Pakistani border has been suspended due to uncertainties about gas exports to Pakistan and financing problems.[79]

### IGAT 8

IGAT 8, a 983 km 56 inch pipeline with nine compressor stations supplies 110 mmcm/day of natural gas from Assaluyeh to the Parsian gas processing plant in Fars province and from there to Isfahan and Tehran provinces.[80] The first and second phases of the project (from the Parsian processing plant to Abarkooh and from there to Tehran) became operational in 2008 and 2009, respectively.[81] Technical studies are underway to connect IGAT 8 to IGAT 5 in Tehran.

### IGAT 9

The 56-inch IGAT 9 is another gas export pipeline designed to connect South Pars field to European markets.[82] The 1863 km pipeline has 17 compressor stations and aims to transfer gas from Assaluyeh to the border city of Bazargan. According to reports, 23 per cent of the pipeline construction will be handled by Iran and the remaining 77 per cent by the Turkish partners.[83] A memorandum of understanding (MoU) was signed by the two countries in 2008; this contains plans for cooperation and calls for the participation of the Turkish state petroleum company TPAO in the development of phases 22, 23, and 24 of South Pars, along with the construction of the IGAT 9 gas trunkline from Assaluyeh to Bazargan.[84] Although the construction of the project has been suspended due to international sanctions, once completed, it could export 35 bcm/year gas to European markets via Turkey.

### IGAT 10 (Loop line)

IGAT 10 has two tranches and transports gas from Assaluyeh to Fajr treatment plant in Pataveh and from there to Pol Kalleh in Isfahan. The pipeline is 422 km long and has a transmission capacity of 90 mmcm/day.[85] It is designed to compensate for the gas deficit in IGAT

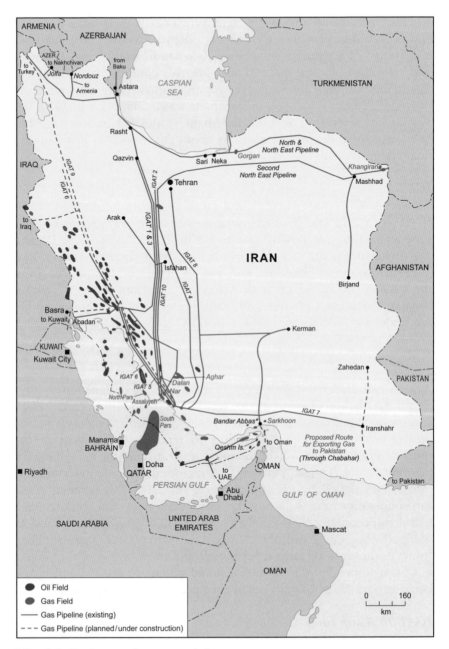

**Map 1.2:** Iran's natural gas transmission system

Source: Author's data collection.

2 and to free up some capacity in IGAT 7 for domestic consumption by supplying additional gas volume for potential export to Pakistan and India.[86] A hundred kilometres of the pipeline between Assaluyeh and the Pataveh processing plant is operational,[87] but further work on the construction of the remaining phases of the project has been suspended due to lack of investment sources.

### North and North-East Pipeline

This pipeline, which started operation in 2010, is 1024 km long and has diameters of both 42 and 48 inches. It has six compressor stations and consists of two phases: phase one, operational since 2009, extends 418 km between Parchin and Miami, and 106 km between Miami and Dasht.[88] The second phase is a 500 km, 48 inch pipeline between Miami and Sang Bast which transfers 58 mmcm/day of gas from the second import pipeline from Turkmenistan to the Shahid Hasheminejad gas processing plant.[89]

### Natural gas distribution system

As a result of domestic market expansion, Iran has also extensively developed its distribution network. In 2012, the aggregate urban and rural distribution network was 236,600 km, supplying gas to more than 16.3 million customers, including households, commercial, and industrial units in 920 cities, 12,504 villages, and 69 power plants.[90]

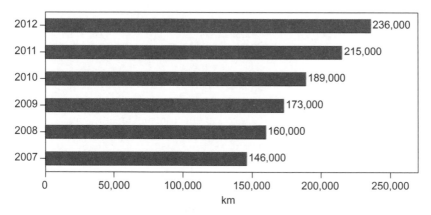

**Figure 1.2:** Iran's natural gas distribution network, 2007–2012 (km)

Source: Iran Energy Balance (2012).

Tehran, Isfahan, Khorasan Razavi, and Fars have the most developed natural gas grids in the country.[91] In the period 2007–12, more than 90,000 km of pipeline were added to the national distribution network, an average construction rate of 15,000 km/year.[92] (Figure 1.2)

## Natural gas domestic consumption in Iran

Natural gas consumption has accelerated rapidly during the last 25 years, reaching 151 bcm in 2012.[93] In 2012, Iran was ranked the third largest gas consumer in the world after the USA and Russia.[94] Aside from the government's domestic market expansion policy (the low prices charged nationwide are due to energy subsidies), major causes of rapid growth of the domestic market are gas reinjection into old oilfields to enhance the rate of recovery and population growth, with the consequent increase in household and industrial consumption.

**Table 1.6:** Natural gas domestic consumption in different sectors 2005–2012 (bcm)

| Sector | 2005 | 2007 | 2009 | 2010 | 2011 | 2012 |
|---|---|---|---|---|---|---|
| **Non-Energy Sector** | | | | | | |
| Residential | 31.49 | 40.44 | 41.39 | 40.86 | 44.05 | 40.13 |
| Public & Commercial | 4.29 | 5.41 | 5.67 | 5.92 | 6.43 | 5.90 |
| Transportation | 0.3 | 1.04 | 3.43 | 5.54 | 6.24 | 6.91 |
| Agricultural | - | 0.17 | 0.4 | 0.47 | 0.61 | 0.76 |
| Industrial | 11.33 | 14.84 | 17.52 | 19.87 | 24.01 | 25.70 |
| Petrochemical | 7.18 | 12.81 | 14.30 | 16.17 | 22.12 | 20.60 |
| **Energy Sector** | | | | | | |
| Oil refinery | 4.43 | 3.80 | 5.62 | 4.42 | 4.47 | 4.72 |
| Gas processing plant fuel | 3.21 | 3.72 | 4.34 | 5.47 | 5.21 | 5.49 |
| Power generation | 35.05 | 36.97 | 43.40 | 44.89 | 38.90 | 40.60 |
| Turbines and compressors fuel | 0.50 | 0.41 | 0.39 | 0.48 | 0.44 | 0.44 |
| Others | 0.22 | 0.24 | 0.21 | 0.24 | 0.18 | 0.35 |
| Total | 98.00 | 119.90 | 136.50 | 144.40 | 152.70 | 151.60 |

Source: Iran Energy Balance (2012).

In 2012, natural gas constituted 54 per cent of the country's energy demand of which the residential, commercial, and public sectors consumed around 30 per cent, power generation 28 per cent, industry 17 per cent, the petrochemical sector 14 per cent, oil refineries 6 per cent, and transportation and agriculture 5 per cent.[95]

## Residential and commercial sector

Households are the largest sector in the natural gas domestic market, consuming around 40 bcm in 2012.[96] The consumption per capita in the household sector has fallen since 2011 (when consumption was above 44 bcm), most likely due to the price rise resulting from the 2010 subsidies reform (see Chapter 5). More than 96 per cent and 54 per cent of the urban and rural population (around 55 million people) have access to gas.[97] The heavy dependence of the residential sector has caused major challenges for the supply to other sectors, particularly during cold winters when supply to the power and industrial sectors are either cut or limited. In the public and commercial sector, consumption experienced an increase of 8.6 per cent in 2011 and stood at slightly less than 6.5 bcm.[98] In 2012, however, consumption fell to 5.8 bcm, which again can be attributed to a large extent to the price rise of 2010.

## Power generation and petrochemical sectors

Power generation accounts for the second-largest share of natural gas consumption. In the period between 2010 and 2012, consumption in power generation fluctuated, consuming 44 bcm, 38 bcm, and 41 bcm in 2010, 2011, and 2012 respectively. The 11 per cent fall in 2011 is an indication that the price rise of 2010 had an impact on affordability and the level of consumption in power generation. However, as the government rigorously pursues the policy of using gas as a substitute for fuel oil in power generation, it is not surprising that consumption began to rise again in 2012. It is also important to mention that most power generation plants in Iran have reached the end of their design lives and need to be replaced or upgraded. As a result, the low energy efficiency rate can, to a large extent, be attributed to the age of the capital stock in this sector.

The petrochemical industry is also a major natural gas consuming sector. Iran has 10 major petrochemical plants where natural gas is consumed both as feedstock and fuel. In 2012, the total volume of gas consumed in the petrochemical sector was about 20 bcm, of which 10 bcm was used as feedstock.

## Industrial, transportation, and agricultural sectors

Around 75 per cent of the energy consumed in the industrial sector is supplied by natural gas. In 2012, the industrial sector consumed around 26 bcm of gas, an increase of 30 per cent compared with 2010.

This was mostly due to the increase in oil product prices which forced industries to consume more natural gas.

Consumption in the transportation sector has also increased substantially as a result of the government's policy of expanding a natural gas vehicle fleet which is ranked first in the world. In 2012, the number of vehicles using gas was 2.8 million (or around 25 per cent of the country's total vehicle fleet) consuming around 7 bcm of gas, a 15 per cent increase compared with 2012.[99] In the agricultural sector consumption increased by around 81 per cent, from 0.4 bcm in 2010 to 0.7 bcm in 2012.[100]

## Gas reinjection into oil fields

Gas reinjection is a technique applied in ageing oil fields to prevent the reservoir pressure from dropping, in order to facilitate the recovery of a greater percentage of crude oil. Natural gas reinjection technology was first introduced by NIOC in 1971. In the period 1971–4, a comprehensive study conducted by a group of reservoir engineers urged natural gas reinjection to Haft Gol, Gachsaran, Lab Sefid, Maroon, Agha Jari, Parsi, and Bibi Hakimeh oilfields. Gas was first reinjected into Haft Gol and Gachsaran oil fields in 1976–7.[101] In 2002, and during the 25-year period since the start of reinjection, the aggregate injected gas to these oilfields was estimated at 22.51 bcm and 219.99 bcm respectively, adding 154 and 2500 million barrels of oil to the production output.[102]

In 2012, the Petroleum Ministry had 34 reinjection projects in oil-producing regions, 18 of which were located in the southern part of the country. South Pars phases 6, 7, and 8 are designated to supply gas for reinjection purposes. In 2009, construction of the 56 inch, 503 km IGAT 5 pipeline from South Pars to the Agha Jari oilfield was completed, facilitating the delivery of up to 40.3 mmcm/year of gas for reinjection to oil fields located in the south and south-west of the country (20.8 mmcm/year for Agha Jari and 19.5 mmcm/year for other oil fields). Gas reinjection in Agha Jari has been operational since 2010, although the injection capacity has been significantly lower than planned.[103] In 2012, the aggregate volume of gas reinjection fell by around 10.6 per cent to 77.7 mmcm/day (see Table 1.7).[104] This is mainly due to shortage of gas in domestic markets. For technical reasons, gas reinjection is usually used in onshore gas fields, whereas for offshore and continental shelf fields, water and a mixture of water and gas can also be used. In 2012, the injection of water into offshore

**Table 1.7:** Natural gas and water injection into Iran's oilfields (2000–12)

| Year | 2000 | 2001 | 2002 | 2003 | 2004 | 2005 | 2006 |
|---|---|---|---|---|---|---|---|
| NG (mmcm/day) | 71 | 75 | 72 | 77 | 80 | 77 | 73 |
| Water (Mbbl/year) | - | 106 | 92 | 99 | 75 | 98 | 130 |

| Year | 2007 | 2008 | 2009 | 2010 | 2011 | 2012 | |
|---|---|---|---|---|---|---|---|
| NG (mmcm/day) | 87 | 77 | 79 | 88 | 86 | 77.7 | |
| Water (Mbbl/year) | 132 | 420 | 152 | 152 | 403 | 130.6 | |

Source: Iran Energy Balance (2012).

oil fields witnessed a dramatic decline, falling to 130.6 Mbbl. (see Table 1.7)

Gas reinjection has never been implemented as planned – either due to lack of gas caused by growing domestic demand, or to the high cost of reinjection, or to a combination of both. The failure can also be attributed to reconstruction problems in the aftermath of the Iran–Iraq war and challenges resulting from the lack of coordination between the gas producing company NIOC, and the distribution company NIGC, which has led to the extensive expansion of the domestic market with no regard to the country's production capability to meet such growth.

In 2014, there is an urgent requirement for gas reinjection, due both to declining oil production rates and to high oil prices, which promise higher revenues for the government (see Chapter 6). Oil production capacity has been decreasing at a rate of around 300–600 thousand bbl/year.[105] In the Fourth Development Plan (2005–9), the required volume for natural gas reinjection was envisaged to reach around 53 bcm by the end of the plan, but the actual reinjection was only 31 bcm. The Fifth Development Plan (2011–15) has also required gas reinjection of 93 bcm by 2015.[106] However, as the total gas reinjection in 2012 was only 28.3 bcm, it is highly unlikely that this objective will be met.

### Natural gas flaring

Estimates show that 30 per cent of onshore associated gas, mainly in Khoozestan, Ilam, Bushehr, Lorestan, and Kermanshah provinces, and 80 per cent of offshore associated gas in Kharg and Bahregansar, is flared. According to the World Bank-led Global Gas Flaring Reduction Partnership (GGFR), Iran's flared gas production is only exceeded by Russia and Nigeria. Iran's flaring rate was around 11.4 bcm in 2011, the last year for which official data is available (Table 1.8); this is about a quarter of gas demand in South Korea, which is the second largest LNG buyer in the world.[107]

**Table 1.8:** Estimated flared gas volumes, 2005–2011 (bcm)

| Volumes | 2005 | 2007 | 2009 | 2011 |
|---------|------|------|------|------|
| Russia | 55.2 | 52.3 | 46.6 | 37.4 |
| Nigeria | 21.3 | 16.3 | 14.9 | 14.6 |
| Iran | 11.3 | 10.7 | 10.9 | 11.4 |
| Iraq | 7.1 | 6.1 | 8.1 | 9.4 |
| USA | 2.0 | 2.2 | 3.3 | 7.1 |

Source: World Bank (2012).

Gas is flared due to a lack of the infrastructure required to process and transport gas to the market. Relatively low domestic gas prices also reduce incentives to develop new, or to improve existing, infrastructure to reduce flaring. In countries like Iran, where prices are fixed by the government to cover the average costs of gas production from abundant non-associated fields, investing in the required infrastructure to gather and process the gas associated with oil seems uneconomic; thus it is less costly if the associated gas is flared instead of being gathered, processed, and transported to markets. In the case of Iran, under stringent international sanctions, restricted access to the necessary equipment and finance has diminished the chance of any success in the reduction of flaring.

### Natural gas storage capacity

NIGC has two natural gas storage areas, located near Qom and Sara-khs. The primary reason to retain gas in (mainly underground) storages is to ensure it is available during periods of high demand, particularly during cold winters. Storage is also important in order to respond to accidents or natural disasters which can affect consumption or supply.

Sarajeh storage, located 40 km from Qom, has an aggregate capacity of 3.3 bcm/year of gas and is the only operational gas storage in Iran. Seven months of injection is required to fill the storage capacity. The stored gas can be withdrawn at a rate of 9.8 mmcm/day during a four month period.[108]

Shoorijeh is another gas storage area, which is located in the vicinity of Shahid Hasheminejad refinery, 165 km from Mashhad. Its maximum storage capacity is 2.4 bcm/year which should be injected during an eight month period. The stored gas can be withdrawn at the rate of 20 mmcm/day during a four month period.[109] Shoorijeh storage is planned to start operation in 2015.[110]

Gas storage capacity is not yet in line with the growing rate of gas consumption where, during cold weather for example, supply to major sectors such as industry and power generation has to be cut off or reduced. Future development of storage capacity is also unlikely to solve these problems as limited production capacity leaves insufficient gas for reinjection into storage facilities.

## Export projects

Following the Revolution, Iran's first rigorous attempts to develop new gas export projects date back to the Khatami administration (1997–2005). Export plans were in line with the development of the South Pars field and Iran's policy to improve its trade ties with its neighbouring countries and with Europe. In other words, the plans were consistent with the Khatami government's overall policy of reducing tensions between Iran and the international community and promoting the country's presence in international economic and trade transactions. It was during this era that many gas industry development plans, including export to Turkey, conclusion of contracts for construction of LNG plants, and development of the South Pars gas field were implemented. In the mid-2000s, however, following the coming to power of Ahmadinejad and the seventh Parliament, opposition to gas exports intensified; this, combined with increasing international sanctions, eliminated prospects for further development.

Despite its massive reserves, Iran is a relatively small and strictly regional exporter to neighbouring countries: Turkey, Armenia, and Azerbaijan. It supplies less than 1 per cent of global natural gas exports and has no capability to export gas to global markets via LNG.

### Pipeline exports

#### The Turkish contract
In August 1996, NIGC signed a 25-year contract with Turkey's BOTAŞ for export of 10 bcm/year of gas to Turkey via pipeline (a total export of 228 bcm). The pipeline (40 inch diameter, 253 km in length) delivers gas through the border city of Bazargan in Iran to Dogubeyazit in Turkey.[111] The agreement provided for the initial export of 4 bcm of

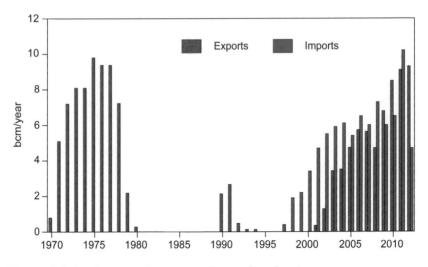

**Figure 1.3:** Iranian natural gas export–import (bcm/year)

Source: Iran Energy Balance (2012) and BP Statistics (2013).

gas in 2002 and its gradual increase to 10 bcm in 2007. When exports started in December 2001, the actual volume was only 0.35 bcm, much lower than was initially agreed upon by the parties.[112] During the first few years, gas trade never came close to contractual volumes. Only since 2010 has Iran managed to export above 8 bcm, as a result of the new South Pars phases coming on stream[113] (see Figure 1.3).

Gas exports to Turkey have been interrupted several times, particularly during times of spiking domestic demand in cold winters or by attacks on the pipeline by regional terrorist groups. Iran has also been demanding comparatively high prices, while gas quality and quantity often allegedly fall below the agreed levels.[114] The resulting dispute over a 'take or pay' clause regarding the price and gas volume agreed upon between the two countries caused Turkey to take the issue to international arbitration twice, in 2005 and 2012.[115] The dispute actually began in 2002 when Turkey halted imports due (according to the Turkish side), to unsatisfactory technical specification of the gas. The dispute later intensified following delivery shortfalls by Iran in 2004. Turkey first took the matter to arbitration where, in 2009, it was awarded $800 million in compensation.[116] In the second arbitration, still pending, in addition to seeking compensation for gas cuts in December 2011 and January 2012, the Turkish side has also requested a 30 per cent reduction in the price, claiming that the latter is substantially higher than that of gas imported from Russia and Azerbaijan.[117] According to unofficial reports, Turkey pays $490 mcm for Iranian gas while it pays $335 and $425 mcm for Azeri and Russian gas, respectively.[118] The Iranian government has suggested that it might agree on a price reduction if Turkey doubles its gas import volume. This is believed by some to be a tactic by the Iranian authorities to indirectly start exporting gas to European markets through Turkey.[119]

As is evident, gas trade and relations between Iran and Turkey have encountered many problems, are lacking in trust, and have failed to demonstrate long-term reliability on the part of either gas importer and exporter. Moreover, Iran's unsatisfactory export record to Turkey has, to a large extent, affected the country's reputation as a potentially reliable supplier to European markets.

*The Armenia contract*
In 2004, Iran signed a gas export contract with Armenia in exchange for electricity. The contract provides for the supply of 1.1 to 2.3 bcm/year of gas for a 20-year period.[120] The Iran–Armenia gas pipeline is 113 km long and 30 inches in diameter, connecting Tabriz to the Armenian border. Export to Armenia started in 2009 after a two-year delay, and supplied around 0.4 bcm of gas in 2012 – significantly lower than the volume envisaged in the contract. In exchange for every cubic metre of gas, Armenia exports 3kwh of electricity to Iran. In March 2012, there were further negotiations for a six-fold increase in exports. Although no progress has been made, this could have translated into an increase of total export capacity of 2.3 bcm/year.[121]

*The Azerbaijan swap contract*
Based on a 25-year swap contract with Azerbaijan, Iran started exporting an average of 300–350 mmcm/year of gas to Azerbaijan in 2005 through a 16-inch pipeline connecting Jolfa (on the Iranian border) to Nakhchivan.[122] In exchange, Azerbaijan supplies an equal volume of gas to Iran's northern city of Astara. The Iran–Azerbaijan gas swap deal had resulted from a prolonged territorial dispute between Azerbaijan and Armenia, preventing the former's domestic pipeline system from reaching Nakhchivan.

*The Iran–Pakistan–India 'Peace Pipeline'*
The Iran–Pakistan–India pipeline, also known as the 'Peace Pipeline', is another controversial export line planned to export Iranian gas from South Pars to the Asian subcontinent. With a proposed length of 2,800 km and around 40 bcm/year of export capacity, pipeline construction stalled in both Pakistan and India due to various problems including

prolonged political tension between the two countries, pricing disputes, and the US government's opposition to the project.[123] Consequently, in 2007, India decided to suspend negotiations and has become more interested in the US-backed pipeline from Turkmenistan to Afghanistan and Pakistan (TAPI).[124] The USA also intensified political pressure on Pakistan; this came particularly from the Obama administration, which has described Pakistan's interest in the Peace Pipeline as 'inexplicable'.[125]

On Iranian territory, the construction of 900km of pipeline (an extension of IGAT 7, to the Iran–Pakistan border) is complete, avoiding the need for construction of a new parallel pipeline.[126] The pipeline in Pakistan is planned to start from southern Baluchistan and proceed to Nawabshah in Sindh province. The section on Pakistani territory is expected to be around 750 km. Pakistan has so far been unable to secure funding for the project. It approached foreign companies including OAO Gazprom, International Petroleum Investment Co., and China National Petroleum Corporation with no success.[127] In 2012, Iran offered funding of $500 million, which was only one third of the total cost of construction.[128] The offer, however, was cancelled by the Rouhani government, which warned the Pakistani side that if it fails to complete construction of the pipeline by the end of the contract (2014) – realistically improbable – the country will be exposed to the risk of substantial financial payments to Iran under the 'take or pay' clause in the contract.[129]

In 2009, Iran and Pakistan, in the absence of India, finalized the gas sales and purchase agreements. The initial pricing formula was based on 47 per cent linkage to Japan Crude Cocktail (JCC).[130] The new formula is 79 per cent linked to the JCC price which, at an average oil price of around $100/barrel, means that Pakistan should pay around $14.5/MMBtu. Adding transportation and transit fees, the final gas price jumps to around $16/MMBtu, which is highly unlikely to be affordable by Pakistan. There are also other problems which make completion of the project unlikely in the near future. As the project is planned to continue without India, some experts believe that the pipeline is no longer economic as there is virtually no chance for further expansion of the pipeline beyond the Pakistani border.[131] Also, the availability of other alternatives, including LNG and the construction of the US-backed Turkmenistan–Afghanistan–Pakistan pipeline, has cast doubt on the future of the project.[132] Equally important is the issue of security: the planned pipeline route is exposed to terrorist attacks in the troubled border province of Baluchistan, while political disputes and occasional military conflict between India and Pakistan have also created security risks.

*Other export pipelines*

**Nabucco** was, perhaps, the most promising pipeline project for the export of gas to Europe.[133] In January 2004, Iran signed a Memorandum of Understanding (MoU) with the Nabucco project leader OMV of Austria and its 50 per cent-owned Austrian gas marketing arm EconGas to assess the flow of the Iranian gas in the project, as well as upstream development cooperation with Iran. However, a few years later, as a result of international sanctions, it was announced that the Nabucco project would proceed without Iranian gas.[134] The Nabucco pipeline was formally abandoned in June 2013 after the Shah Deniz Consortium chose the Trans-Adriatic Pipeline (TAP) as the preferred route to deliver Azeri gas to Europe.[135]

The 520km **TAP** was also another pipeline with the potential to link gas from the Caspian region, including Iran, to Greece, Albania, and Italy via Turkey. Gas exports to the Swiss market were also expected to be made using the same pipeline. A 20-year gas purchase contract between the Swiss-based EGL Company and NIGEC was signed in 2008 for export of 5.5 bcm/year of gas to the Swiss market using existing infrastructure via Turkey.[136] US government pressure on Switzerland, together with the EU ban on gas imports from Iran, meant that the partners were forced to use other sources.

There are also proposed pipelines for exports to Europe via Armenia and Ukraine. But as there are doubts over the long-term profitability of such projects, due to the lack of strong markets and economic infrastructure in these transit countries, and given Russia's relatively strong influence over the region's transit pipelines, the chances of developing additional export pipelines to Europe through Armenia and Ukraine are very slim.[137]

Another potential export project is the **Iran–Iraq–Syria–Mediterranean Pipeline** for which an MoU was signed between Iran and Syria in 2011 for exports through Iraq, Syria, and the south of Lebanon to Mediterranean Europe. The decision to build the pipeline, also known as the 'Islamic pipeline', was taken when Iran was excluded from the Nabucco pipeline. The project is increasingly unlikely to make significant progress for the foreseeable future, due to the civil war and possible collapse of the Syrian Assad regime, which has had strong political and trade ties with Iran. But exports to two Iraqi major cities – Baghdad and Basra – are expected by NIGC officials to proceed as planned.[138] In July 2013, an agreement was reached between Iran and Iraq for export of 9 bcm/year of gas in the first phase of the agreement, which is planned to increase to 14 bcm/year in the second phase when fully completed in 2015.[139]

The 10-year gas export project to Iraq is expected to come on stream by the end of 2014, with a minimum export volume of 7 mmcm/day using the existing infrastructure in Iran to transfer gas to the Basra power plant close to the Iranian border. Phases 12 and 15–18 of South Pars (to be completed in 2014–16) are expected to supply the Iraqi market through IGAT 6 and two extension pipelines (227 and 142 kilometres respectively) to Baghdad and Basra. Contracts for pipeline construction have been awarded to Iranian contractors and, as of March 2014, 75 per cent of the pipeline is reportedly completed.[140] The price of gas sold to Iraq is unknown and remains contentious.[141]

*Export to GCC Countries*

Since the early 2000s, there have been ongoing negotiations for potential gas exports to some GCC countries including Kuwait, Oman, and individual Emirates of the UAE. In 2004, during the OPEC Ministerial Conference, Iran and Kuwait signed an agreement worth $7 billion for the export of gas to Kuwait for 25 years.[142] The 260 km offshore pipeline was planned to export 2.5 bcm/year of gas to Kuwait, but did not make any significant progress beyond the negotiation stage.

The joint natural gas field of Hengam between Iran and Oman brought the parties to the negotiation table in 2000 and this eventually led to the conclusion of a contract for joint development of the field, and the export of 10 bcm/year of gas to Oman.[143] In September 2013, the Rouhani government resumed negotiations with Omani counterparts and an agreement was reached to accelerate the construction of the project to export an estimated $60 billion worth of gas through an offshore pipeline during a 25-year contract.[144] In late 2013, the Iranian authorities held talks with their Omani counterparts about the possibility of using the Omani LNG facilities to liquefy a percentage of the exported gas and market it as Iranian LNG.

In 2001, NIOC and Crescent Petroleum Company (CPC) signed a 25-year contract for the export of 5.2 bcm/year of sour gas from the Salman field to the Emirate of Sharjah.[145] Although the initial completion date of the project was December 2005, there have been substantial delays due to a price dispute between the two companies and the failure of the contractor (Petro Iran) to develop the field and the export pipeline to the Mubarak oil platform. Some Iranian officials and members of the Parliament opposed the price formula used in the UAE gas export deal (set at around $1/MMBtu) which they considered very low, accusing the negotiating team of corruption and misconduct.[146] In July 2009, Crescent Petroleum took the dispute to an arbitration tribunal, seeking compensation from NIOC for the four year delay in supplying gas. The arbitration award is still pending.

Following the dispute with Crescent Petroleum, the Iranian government decided to divert the gas from the Salman field to the domestic market. Construction of a 287 km pipeline connecting Sirri to Assaluyeh started in 2008, but its completion has been delayed for many years. Production from the Salman field started briefly in 2010, but was suspended due to technical problems occurring in the pipeline to Sirri. No gas has yet been produced from Salman field.

## Liquefied Natural Gas (LNG)

Post-Revolution initiatives designed to develop LNG production resumed in the late 1990s when the country started negotiations with European and Asian companies to construct several LNG projects, which included Iran LNG, Pars LNG, and Persian LNG. It was planned that LNG would be produced from South Pars phases 11–14 through partnerships between NIOC or its subsidiaries (such as NIGEC) with foreign companies. As will be seen below, none of these projects has materialized due, most significantly, to the imposition of international sanctions on the export of such technologies to Iran.

### Iran LNG

The Iran LNG project consists of two 5.5 mt/year trains and is located in the port of Bandar Tombak, 50 km from Assaluyeh.[147] It was planned that the gas for the project would be supplied from phase 12 of South Pars. The project is owned by NIGEC (49 per cent), the NIOC Pension Fund Co (50 per cent), and the NIOC Pension Investment Fund Co. (1 per cent).[148] The feasibility study for Iran LNG was first conducted in 1996 by Linde, GES, and OIEC. In 1997, the study was completed by Daewoo and JGC and was eventually reviewed and finalized in 2000 by the Iranian Oil Engineering and Construction Company.[149] Iran LNG is the most advanced LNG project in Iran (around 50 per cent physically completed) and is managed by NIOC's subsidiary, Iran LNG Ltd. (ILNG).[150] The project was expected to come on stream in late 2014; however, the construction of the liquefaction plant (the most important part of an LNG project), has not made any progress, as a result of restricted access to the required technologies and the inability of Iranian and Chinese contractors to provide such technologies.[151] Moreover, ILNG was never successful in marketing potential production. Some contracts which had been signed a few years ago – such as exports to India – were reviewed and cancelled by the Iranian side due to low gas prices. Other preliminary development and sales and purchase contracts with Austria's OMV, China's Sinopec, and India's ONGC companies are also highly unlikely to materialize.[152]

*Pars LNG*
Pars LNG is located in Tombak Port in Assaluyeh and its feed gas was planned to come from phase 11 of South Pars. The shareholders of the project were NIOC (50 per cent), Total (40 per cent), and Petronas (10 per cent).[153] The project included two liquefaction plants with a capacity of around 5 mt/year each. Pars LNG exports were expected to reach markets in Japan, South Korea, the UK, and France. The withdrawal of Total and Petronas from the project in 2008, as a result of mounting international sanctions, caused the Iranian government to cancel the project in 2010.[154]

*Persian LNG*
Persian LNG is also located in Tombak Port and consists of two liquefaction plants with a total production capacity of 16.2 mt/year. NIGEC, Shell, and Repsol held shares of 50 per cent, 25 per cent, and 25 per cent in the project, respectively. The plants' feed gas was planned to come from South Pars phases 13 and 14. The project consisted of two phases: the first phase included two units for sweetening and condensate extraction together with one unit for LNG production. The second phase, in addition to sweetening and condensation units, included another LNG train.[155] Shell and Repsol marketed the LNG to India and Europe. Prices were expected to be linked to a crude oil basket, including JCC and Brent, but not at a fixed price. Industry sources reported that NIOC had offered gas to Shell from South Pars at a wellhead price of $0.7/MMBtu.[156] The project, however, was cancelled due to international sanctions and the withdrawal of foreign partners from the project in 2007.[157]

*Other LNG projects*
In addition to the major LNG projects reviewed above, agreements were reached with some Asian companies for construction of other LNG plants. For most of these potential projects, no progress towards physical completion has been reported, and all signed MoUs have already expired.[158] The **North Pars** project is an example where NIOC signed an MoU with the China National Offshore Oil Cooperation (CNOOC) for development of the field and export of 20 mt/year of LNG. Despite the conclusion of a buyback contract in 2008, the project never got off the ground because of political pressures and the Chinese company's

lack of technical expertise. **Qeshm LNG** is a project for which NIOC signed an agreement with the Australian LNG Ltd. Company in 2006, for production of 3–3.5 mt/year of LNG in Qeshm Island. However, as the Australian counterpart had no experience in construction and development of such projects, it was suspended. **Golshan LNG** is another project for which NIOC signed a contract, this time with the Malaysian company SKS Venture for production of 10 mt/year of LNG from Golshan and Ferdowsi gas fields. The development of the fields was assigned to the same Malaysian company based on a seven year buyback contract. According to the contract, NIOC is responsible for the marketing of 5 mt/year of LNG, while sale of the remaining capacity is tentatively assigned to SKS.[159] Another potential LNG project was **Lavan LNG**, for which the Iranian Offshore Oil Company (IOOC), one of NIOC's subsidiaries, had negotiated a deal with a Polish company, PGNiG, for the development of Lavan gas field with the prospect of LNG export. Liquefaction capacity was estimated at around 2–3 mt/year. But, due to the slow pace of negotiations and sanctions, the project never materialized.

## Imports from Turkmenistan

Poor transmission facilities in the north-east of Iran, and the country's inability to produce adequate volumes of gas to meet growing domestic consumption, forced Iran to import gas from Turkmenistan. The 25-year contract, signed in 1995, provided for imports of 8 bcm/year. Turkmen imports started in 1997 through a 200 km , 40-inch diameter pipeline which stretches from Korpedzhe in Turkmenistan to Kurd Kui in Iran (see Map 1.2).[160] Import volumes were initially 0.4 bcm and reached around 6.5 bcm in 2010 following the inauguration of the second import pipeline from Turkmenistan. The second pipeline is 35 km long and 48 inches in diameter, was constructed between Dauletabad in Turkmenistan and the Shahid Hasheminejad gas processing plant, and is connected to the North and North East pipeline in the Sang Bast region in Khorasan Razavi.[161] Although the new pipeline increased gas import capacity to 14 bcm/year,[162] imports from Turkmenistan surprisingly fell to 4.7 bcm in 2012 – this was 5.5 bcm less than in 2011 (Figure 1.3).[163] According to Iran Energy Balance 2012, the fall in gas imports had several causes, including enhanced efficiency in domestic gas consumption, inauguration of two compressor stations in Semnan and Parchin, increased efficiency in the dispatching system, and completion and operation of IGAT 3, making the north less dependent on gas imports from Turkmenistan.[164] Some speculate that the decline in imports was mainly due to a gas price dispute between Iran and Turkmenistan. Such disputes over pricing have caused interruptions to exports on several occasions, most recently in November 2012.[165] It is difficult to ascertain the exact price Iran pays for its natural gas imports from Turkmenistan; analysis published by PFC Energy, however, shows that Iran paid $9–10/MMBtu in the first half of 2009.[166] Although the pricing terms were changed in the second half of 2009, and Iran now pays an oil-linked price for its imports, the Turkmenistan government is still dissatisfied. Hence, future interruptions remain likely, particularly during periods of cold weather.

## Conclusion

The factual review of the Iranian natural gas industry in this chapter has shown that the country possesses giant gas resources to which new discoveries are added annually. It also showed that the country is the third-largest gas producer and consumer in the world, but that the rate of growth of the latter surpassed that of the former, leaving the country with no option but to import gas to meet the resulting gas deficit. To the surprise of many, the Iranian natural gas industry has a paradoxical dimension, meaning that despite having the largest gas reserves in the world, the country has mostly remained a net gas importer since the mid-2000s.

This review of in-place or planned domestic infrastructure showed how a strong policy to expand the role of natural gas in the domestic market resulted in very rapid growth of household, commercial, in-dustrial, and power generation consumption after the Revolution. In the period 1997–2005, when the reformist government of Khatami was in office, extensive attempts were made to restart gas exports to regional and international markets for which a handful of pipeline and LNG contracts were signed. The natural gas industry in previous and subsequent administrations followed inconsistent policies which eventually led to the disproportionate development of the domestic markets, without giving due consideration to whether the country's production could meet such growth.

This chapter has shown that despite a relatively rapid increase in production, the enormous growth of the domestic market has made the country struggle to fulfil its domestic and export commitments. This has resulted in frequent interruptions of gas supply to sectors with less strategic importance during cold winters, cancellation of export projects, and increasing imports. Reasons attributed to the country's failure to substantially develop its natural gas industry, ranging from political to legal, fiscal, and economic, are the subject of detailed analyses in the following chapters.

# CHAPTER 2

# POLITICIZATION OF THE PETROLEUM INDUSTRY

## Introduction

The Iranian petroleum industry has suffered chronically from domestic politicization. A historical account of the political events affecting the industry since the discovery of oil in the early 1900s shows that the fear of foreign control of petroleum resources has pushed the country towards domestic political interventions and a culture of mistrust and xenophobia in the oil and gas sector. Iran's petroleum industry history is based on a handful of concession contracts in which exclusive privileges were granted to foreign participants, resulting in their securing cheap and easy access to the country's petroleum resources. In the post-Revolutionary era, the fear of victimization, foreign exploitation, and betrayal combined with the Revolutionary political system of parallel centres of power, further exacerbated the politicization of the industry. This has been largely responsible for mismanagement, lack of transparency in the decision-making process, and, more importantly, systematic corruption.

This chapter reviews the historical events that played a major role in the politicization of the petroleum industry and examines the impacts of this political intervention on the long-term development of the gas industry.

## A historical overview of the petroleum sector's political sensitivity

Iran, once a country with a long and rich history as a great empire and ruling power, has gone through long periods of hardship during which it has experienced western powers interfering in its internal affairs, ignoring its sovereignty, and humiliating it by means of military intervention, political manipulation, and lucrative economic privileges. The beginning of the twentieth century, and the discovery of oil in particular, left unpleasant memories and deep resentment towards foreign countries which, under the guise of developing Iran's natural resources, orchestrated events which merely served their own political and economic interests, at a price which cost Iranians dearly. This period planted the seeds of great political sensitivity in dealings with a sector which became not only the most vital source of economic revenue on which the very essence of Iranians' livelihood has been dependent, but also a symbol of sovereignty and national self-determination. In the following sections, some of the most influential events in this period will be reviewed to demonstrate how the historical intervention of foreign powers in the petroleum sector led to its political sensitivity, and ultimately to its politicization.

## *The 1901 D'Arcy concession*

In the history of the Iranian petroleum industry, an important milestone was the first Middle East oil concession granted for exploration and development of petroleum resources. It dates back to 1901, when Mozaffar-al-Din Shah of Qajar granted a 60-year oil exploration and production concession to a British speculator, William Knox D'Arcy, covering the entire country apart from the five northern provinces bordering Russia.[1] The concession was widely and rightly perceived to favour foreign interests in return for payment of the costs of the Qajaris' extravagance, including their luxurious trips to Europe. The scope of the exploration and production area was striking considering the fact that the right was exclusive and effective for 60 years. Also, the number of exploitable commodities and resources was unprecedented in comparison to current oil and gas field development contracts.[2] Interestingly, and contrary to the common practice in concession agreements, the D'Arcy concession had a tax-free clause stipulating that all lands granted by this arrangement to the concessionaire (or that may be acquired by him), and also all products exported, should be free of all custom duties and taxes during the term of the concession. It also provided that all material and apparatuses necessary for the exploration, operation, and development of the deposits, and for the construction and development of pipelines, should enter the country free of all taxes and duties.[3] The tax-free status given to the concession's operations deprived the country of revenues which could have been obtained and injected into the economy from a technologically massive operation such as the exploitation of oil fields. At that time, there was an argument that, as the government was to inherit all the equipment and structures built during the course of the operations, the tax-free clause was defensible; but given the 60-year length of the concession, the depreciated equipment would hardly be useable after the termination of the concession.[4]

Only one month after the original concession, in June 1901, the Shah issued a royal decree to be added to the original concession; this was perceived by many as a sign of foreign pressure on Iran to give away its natural resources free. The decree provided that:

> Pursuant to the concession granted to Mr. William Knox D'Arcy, as a result of the particularly friendly relation which united powerful Great Britain and Persia, it is accorded and guaranteed to the Engineer William D'Arcy, and to all of his heirs and assigns and friends, full power and unlimited liberty for a period of 60 years, to probe, pierce and drill at their will the depths of Persian soil; in consequence of which, all the subsoil products wrought of him without exception will remain the property of D'Arcy. We declare that all the officials of this blessed Kingdom and our heirs and successors will do their best to help and assist the honourable D'Arcy, who enjoys the favour of our splendid court.[5]

To some scholars, the flattering and ornate language used in this appendix highlights the extent of British influence on the process of decision making in Iran, particularly with regard to the oil concessions.[6]

The Anglo-Persian Oil Company (APOC)[7] was established for the development of oil resources after the initial discoveries in 1908. It was a foreign company in which the British government held 51 per cent of the shares.[8] The British government had a strong influence over the company and made substantial tax revenues from its operation, to the extent that it was believed that Britain earned more money from Persian oil than Iran ever did.[9] The British government also had a strong grip on the company's management since it had the right to appoint two directors to the managing board who would have the power of veto on any issue relating to British national interests.[10] The British government's strong involvement in the D'Arcy concession was predominantly due to the fact that the development of oilfields in Iran coincided with the decision of the British Admiralty to substitute coal with oil, as the means of fuelling their warships.

### The 1933 concession

Less than two decades later, in the 1920s, the exploitive approach of the British government, and unfair clauses of the concession, caused serious political confrontation between Reza Shah, who deposed the Qajari Shah in 1925, and the British government. Resentment against British influence had also been exacerbated by the 1919 Anglo-Iranian Agreement, concluded in order to bring stability to the country and prepare the ground for modernization within the framework of a constitutional monarchy. But Iranians perceived this as a British attempt to turn Iran into a protectorate, and hence strongly opposed its implementation. Furthermore, Reza Shah, as a part of his modernization programme, needed a substantial source of funding for which the small revenues earned from APOC as a part of the oil concession were not sufficient. From an Iranian perspective, APOC represented 'the epitome of foreign intervention' as it controlled and exploited Iran's greatest natural asset while giving it 'a miserable pittance in return for the millions it took away'.[11] Therefore, on assuming power, Reza Shah made it clear that Iran was no longer willing to give away its natural resources practically free. To curtail the expansion of foreign influence and secure more profits for Iran, he called for renegotiation of the terms of the concession and announced in a public speech that:

> Iran can no longer tolerate watching huge oil revenues go into the pockets of foreigners while it is deprived of them.[12]

Many years of negotiations attempting modification of the concession's terms were of no avail. In 1932 Reza Shah ultimately decided in fury, and to the surprise of the British government, to declare the D'Arcy concession null and void. The decision was taken after the company had declared that Iran's revenue would be reduced to a quarter of that received the previous year, which was perceived by the Shah as a personal affront as much as a great loss of finance and foreign exchange.[13] In response to the Shah's decision, Britain took the matter to the League of Nations and, in a frightening and humiliating move, mobilized the British Navy to the Persian Gulf threatening a possible attack on Iran. The parties to the dispute were called by the Security Council to seek a solution through negotiation, which resulted in the 1933 Concession.

The new concession granted the company:

> ... the exclusive right, within the territory encompassed by the Concession, to look for and extract petroleum as well as to refine or treat in any other way and render suitable for commerce the petroleum obtained through this process.[14]

It also permitted the company:

> ... to conduct various logistical operations without special license, for all imports necessary for the exclusive needs of its employees, subject to the payment of the custom duties and other duties and taxes in force at the time of importation.[15]

In effect, the new agreement provided for a new business framework in which annual royalty, minimum annual payment to the government, and payments of 20 per cent dividends earned from distribution were integrated. The agreement also granted Iran the right to conduct investigations into oil company finances in a new effort to ensure that the previous challenges to fair distribution of profits would not occur again.

Notwithstanding the fact that the terms of the new concession appeared more favourable to the Iranian side, there were serious criticisms that the conditions were by no means fair to domestic interests. First and foremost, the term on the extension of the agreement for another 30 years triggered great public resentment towards the company. Second, the company had the right to terminate the concession, but similar rights had not been granted to the Iranian government. Third, the government remained uncompensated for the decreasing value of the pound sterling, attributable to the use of official, rather than market, gold prices used in calculations of currency rates by the company. Fourth, payments to the government were made after British income tax had been deducted. And last but not least, the British government had unfairly limited the Iranian share of distributed profits.[16] The sale of oil at low prices to the British Navy and British Air Forces was also seen by many as another factor which lowered the company's distributable profits. Further, the company often avoided customs duties and charges. For example, tax was not levied on the allied forces, resulting in losses of up to $18 million to the Iranian government.[17] Moreover, the conditions of employment of Iranian workers were poor, and unions were banned. For all these reasons, despite some improvements in the contractual terms, Iranians still held a substantial grudge against the concession, and the company.[18]

### The invasion of Iran by Allied forces

An equally important historical event which added to petroleum sector sensitivity was the country's occupation by Allied forces during World War II.[19] Although Iran formally declared its neutrality during the war, the pro-German rhetoric of some Iranian rulers aroused serious Allied concern about the German army taking control of Iran's oil resources and putting at risk their secure access to oil supply from Iran. This led to the Allied forces' occupation of Iran in 1941, with the Allied air forces operating in the Far East, Europe, and Middle East being highly dependent on fuel from the Abadan refinery.

During the Allied occupation, Iranians endured huge suffering. In some regions, famine broke out, resulting in food rationing and loss of life.[20] It was mainly because of the country's petroleum resources that, for the first time in its contemporary history, Iran experienced invasion by foreign forces, leaving deep scars on the nation's sense of property and territorial integrity. During the invasion, foreign intervention in the country's internal affairs continued, indirectly resulting in the abdication of Reza Shah (who was believed to have connections to the Axis powers) and the succession of his son Mohammad Reza Shah to pursue pro-Allied policies.

### The 1951 oil nationalization

After World War II, the mounting political competition between global powers to acquire a larger share of Iranian oil resources, together with resentment among Iranians caused by the occupation of their homeland and by the terms of the concession, culminated in the nationalization of the oil industry in March 1951.[21] Added to this was the disappointing experience of trying to renegotiate contracts perceived by both the people and the authorities to be unbalanced, only to find themselves contractually bound by foreign pressure to submit to even more unfair terms.[22] As a result, a radical transformation occurred in the 1950s, changing the landscape of the Iranian oil industry.

The nationalization of the oil industry was strongly supported by Dr Mohammad Mosaddeq, the popular Iranian prime minister, who had proclaimed that 'nationalization of oil would abolish poverty in Iran at one stroke'.[23] His government's initiative in nationalizing the oil industry also received strong support from Parliament, which passed a proposal to take over all the installations of AIOC without immediate compensation. The single-article bill enacted by the Parliament in 1951 stipulates:

> For the happiness and prosperity of the Iranian nation and for the purpose of securing world peace, it is hereby resolved that the oil industry through all part of the country, without exception, be nationalized, that is to say, all operation of exploration, extraction and exploitation shall be carried out by the government.[24]

The 1951 nationalization did not occur in a historical vacuum, but was instead a logical progression to the series of events which started when outside forces intervened in Iran's political and economic development.[25]

The first immediate consequence of nationalization was a worldwide embargo on the purchase of Iranian oil, the freezing of Iran's sterling assets, and a ban on export of goods to the country.[26] As a result, Iran's principal source of public revenue and foreign exchange was cut off, while it had to pay the labour and maintenance costs of a virtually idle industry. In the 18 months from the beginning of 1952, the National

Iranian Oil Company only sold 118,000 tonnes of oil, compared with Anglo-Iranian Oil Company's exports of 31 million tonnes in 1950.[27] Iran started offering its oil at discounts as high as 50 per cent in the hope that a significantly cheaper price for oil would break the British blockade. To fully paralyse the Mosaddeq government, the British directed the Bank of England to make it practically impossible for the Iranian government to exchange its sterling balances.

In order to overcome these economic hurdles, Mosaddeq introduced and implemented a policy of perseverance and austerity based on 'an oil-less economy'.[28] In reality, however, Iran was heavily dependent on oil revenue for budgetary and trade purposes. Direct revenues from oil dropped from £16 million in 1950 to £8.3 million in 1951, and to practically nil in 1952.[29]

From the start of the dispute, the British Conservative government rejected direct negotiations with Iran, continued its campaign against Mosaddeq, and looked for a suitable successor. The British demanded that Iran should either give another concession with more favourable terms for Iran (something that was later granted in the post-coup consortium agreement), or it should compensate the company for all the oil that the company would have exported up to 1990, had the Iranians not nationalized the industry. The company and the British government were of the opinion that nationalization of the oil industry was unlawful, and appealed to the International Court of Justice, declaring that it would protect British property and assets in Iran.[30] The Court issued an order for interim measures to be taken for the protection of both parties' rights.[31] Mosaddeq represented Iran himself at the Court, arguing that nationalization of the oil industry was a purely domestic matter and therefore outside the jurisdiction of the Court, or of any foreign state. The eventual ruling was that, as the Court's jurisdiction was limited to treaties and conventions only, and the 1933 Agreement was a concessionary contract to which the British government was not a party, the Court had no jurisdiction to adjudicate on the matter referred to it by the British government.

### The 1953 coup d'état

As mentioned above, the oil embargo, together with deficits accumulated in previous years and the loss of foreign exchange and oil revenues, led to an economic crisis in Iran. The deteriorating economic conditions triggered a move against the reform-minded Mosaddeq government which was pursuing initiatives to abolish the Parliament and depose the Shah. At the same time, the British were seeking to undermine the Mosaddeq government and replace it with one that would be more receptive to their interests.[32] As a result, the British MI6, backed by the US CIA (Operation Boot), planned and executed the so-called 1953 *coup d'état* which led to the fall of the Mosaddeq government. The opposition group aiming to bring down the government also received major support by the US and British governments through their diplomatic and intelligence staff and agents in Iran.[33] Hence, the coup was a product of the close collaboration between both Mosaddeq's domestic and foreign opponents, although the role of foreign governments (especially that of the USA) in organizing and financing it was crucial.

According to Katouzian (2010), the fall of Mosaddeq's government was not inevitable. It would have had a good chance of survival if Mosaddeq had settled the oil dispute, highlighting the extent to which the petroleum industry had turned into a central element in the political battle between nationalistic movements and foreign intervention.[34] The nationalization of the oil industry led to a situation in which sovereignty was gravely undermined. The overthrow of the country's first democratically elected government had a serious impact, and significantly changed the way Iranians viewed the western world. From this, much can be understood about the origins of the current suspicions toward foreign participation in the petroleum industry.

### Post-nationalization and the 1954 Consortium Agreement

After the coup, the British were well aware of the fact that the AIOC could not return to Iran under any form or guise due to the immense degree of resentment towards it. It was therefore advisable to participate in an international consortium led by US oil companies to continue exploiting Iranian oil.

During the course of negotiations for a new petroleum contract, Iranians strongly resisted management of the oil industry by the consortium and the figure of 50 per cent for Iran's profit share. But, unsurprisingly, the new government installed by the Anglo-American coup, was in a weak and vulnerable position, negotiating with companies supported by the coup makers. Famously, whenever the Iranian negotiators requested better terms, the US oil companies' chief representative, Howard Page, would respond by saying that:

> The US Government has asked us to find markets for your oil; if you don't like our terms we will go back home.[35]

Iran's share of the 1954 agreement was nominal ownership of the Iranian oil industry's assets along with 50 per cent of the net profits, under a complicated formula which disguised Iran's unfair share of profit. Profits payments to Iran were designated to be in the form of taxes that the operating companies were to pay to the Iranian government, so that they could obtain tax exemption from their respective governments against these payments. More significantly, and despite the objectives of the oil nationalization movement, NIOC did not have any role in the management and control of the industry, this was the prerogative of the two operating companies formed to explore, produce, and refine oil on behalf of NIOC. Based on this agreement, these powers could not be revoked or modified by any general or special legislative and administrative measures, or any act whatsoever emanating from Iran. To save Iran's face and NIOC's usefulness, the latter was given the task of 'non-basic' operations such as housing, health, and education of staff.[36] The agreement period was 25 years and was renewable at the consortium's option, for up to three five-year terms; meaning that the agreement was valid up until 1994, more or less as lengthy a period as that covered by the AIOC's concessionary agreement of 1933 which had been nullified by the nationalization of the oil industry.

There was also a confidential agreement between the parties that the operating companies would control the amount of oil to be produced, in an attempt to tie this to the production levels of consortium members in other countries where they were operating. This would allow companies to control a large share of global oil production, and hence oil prices. Therefore, there was little difference between the 1933 concession and the 1954 Consortium Agreement, as Iran still had no say in the management of its own oil industry. The agreement was clearly against the interests of the country, nationalization, and the long-held aspiration for independence. As Elm (1994) laments 'Iran paid heavily for going after shadow nationalization under the consortium agreement.'[37] In fact he argues that the only things that were nationalized and transferred to Iran were the country's internal distribution facilities, the Natfi-Shah oil fields, and the Kermanshah refinery, whose products were not exported; the total worth of this was at most £10 million. Yet in return for these assets Iran paid £25 million and was forced to waive over £100 million of indisputable claims.[38] Therefore, it is not surprising that many scholars described the Consortium Agreement as unfair, exploitative, and a catastrophic defeat for Iran.[39]

In the 1960s, Iran and the consortium planned to substantially develop the petroleum sector and to increase oil production to 8 million bbl/day by the late 1970s; the construction of the required infrastructure enabling such a target to be reached was well under way by that time. In the early 1970s, Iran began to accumulate capital from oil rents at an accelerated pace and developed an awareness of its own economic potential.[40] The most important single factor in determining the pattern and the speed of economic change and industrialization was oil revenue. In this period revenues began to rise steeply as a result of a continuous growth in exports. From the early 1970s, the increase in revenue was explosive both because of export levels and, more especially, because of the significant increase in real oil prices.[41] In 1973, being aware of the shortcomings of the 1954 Agreement, in which Iran's long-term interests were not preserved, the Shah gave an ultimatum to the oil consortium that unless a new arrangement was agreed, Iran would not extend the existing Agreement beyond 1979, and that the consortium members would then be treated simply as buyers of Iranian oil.

### *1979 Islamic Revolution*

The Islamic Revolution did not happen in a political vacuum. On the contrary, the historical events preceding the oil nationalization, including the 1953 coup and the Consortium Agreement, played a key role in uniting contentious political groups and mobilizing nationwide protests. The anti-imperialist and anti-western theories of the revolutionary leader, Ayatollah Khomeini, also stemmed from the political and economic implications of the same course of events which had helped him to attract millions of supporters. Against the background of a legacy of perceived foreign economic and political domination, the Shah's decades of alliance with western powers, particularly the USA, were considered the apex of the prolonged monarchical betrayal of the national interest, causing mounting hatred and ultimately the fall of his regime.[42]

Oil was more than the fuel that maintained the Revolution. The development of the oil industry, independent of foreign involvement, had become a national aspiration and a driving force for toppling the Shah, who was perceived to have surrendered the industry to foreigners. Oil also became the most important means of power in the hands of the revolutionary forces. As the Revolution gathered strength, the forces of opposition resorted to oil strikes to cut revenues, facilitating the Shah's collapse.

As promised, the revolutionary leaders annulled all petroleum contracts with foreign companies which had been concluded before the Revolution, promoting the theoretical ideas of independence and self sufficiency as well as the preservation of natural resources for future generations. In order to avoid interruption in the flow of oil, Iranian technicians took over the fields, in the belief that they were sufficiently experienced to conduct such operations. The government's notorious decision to cancel oil and gas development contracts, combined with the US embassy hostage crisis which further accelerated the departure of major oil companies from the oil sector, subjected Iran to costly and prolonged litigation in US domestic courts and international arbitration tribunals, condemning the country to payments of hundreds of millions of dollars in damages.

### *Iran–Iraq war*

The post-Revolution initiative for independent development of Iran's petroleum resources was hard hit by the start of the Iran–Iraq war in September 1980, as it inflicted serious damage on the sector's infrastructure, making it extremely difficult to maintain the flow of oil production and exports. Throughout the war, the entire Iranian economy was highly dependent on the export of crude oil. Aware of this Achilles heel, Iraqi forces targeted oil and gas production, processing, refining, transportation, import/export, and distribution networks throughout the war.[43] The destruction of the Abadan refinery in 1980 (which produced an average of 628,000 bbl/day of refined oil products), along with the bombing of refineries and shuttle tankers, and the embargo on purchases of Iranian oil by Japan, the USA, and major European countries, seriously exacerbated Iran's economic crisis.

The Iraqi initiative of interrupting Iran's oil export supply first took place in February 1984, when Iraq attacked tankers shuttling between Khark and Sirri islands. Within a short period, Iranian production dropped from an average 4 million bbl/day to less than 1.5 million bbl/day in 1982.[44] Although oil production slightly increased in the following years as a result of rapid reconstruction of the infrastructure, subsequent heavy damage, inflicted as a result of tanker wars, reduced oil exports to 1 million bbl/day in 1986, having been estimated at 1.9 million bbl/day a year earlier.[45] As the economy was largely geared to the war effort, shortages of consumer goods became inevitable and a system of rationing was introduced. Evidence showed a sustained decline in the average standard of living, and in 1988 alone (the last year of the war), GDP shrank by almost 8 per cent. There was a sharp rise in inflation and civilian unemployment, and a continuing decline in the rate of exchange of the national currency. The cost of the war, both in local currency and foreign exchange, had left hardly any room for productive investment, while both war and revolutionary struggles resulted in the flight of large amounts of capital and human resources.

The war with Iraq did not take place independently of support from the Western powers. Since discovery of huge petroleum resources in the Persian Gulf, the region has long been considered a strategic location by colonial powers – they tend to claim it as part of their sphere of influence and assert their right to intervene whenever they feel their interests are threatened.[46] Iran, a revolutionary state, has always rejected this hegemonic attitude and opposed such interference. The country's foreign policy following the Islamic Revolution has been based on rejection of all forms of foreign domination, and preservation of the independence of the country from foreign intervention.[47] Hence, as a means of combatting Iran's anti-western policy, the USA, along with other western powers, indirectly supported the Iraqi government's war against Iran which, as mentioned above, targeted Iran's most vital sector, petroleum.

### US and international sanctions

Following the war, Iran was left in a state of serious and multifaceted crisis which was characterized by negative economic growth, high unemployment, low productivity, and underutilization of capacity; the country also faced shortages of investment capital and high import dependency.[48] In the absence of foreign investment and other immediately available and accessible resources, Iran's economic difficulties reinforced the country's dependence on oil and the need to attract foreign investment, technology, and expertise.[49] During the post-war reconstruction period, President Rafsanjani (1989–1997) implemented a moderate foreign policy and encouraged foreign investment and stronger economic relations with the West (see the introductory chapter).

The Clinton Administration's economic sanctions, however, targeted any foreign participation which encouraged the development of Iran's oil and gas sector. Being aware of Iran's extensive dependence on oil and gas revenues, the USA and (later in the mid 2000s and 2012) the UN and the EU tightened their economic pressure on Iran by imposing sanctions on sales of Iranian oil and gas and on any investment activities intended for the development of its petroleum sector (see Chapter 3). Taking advantage of Iran's dependence on its hydrocarbon sector, and imposing sanctions with the aim of weakening the country's economy to create political pressure, has been interpreted as an 'indirect' intervention of western states in the country's internal affairs. This has reaffirmed the fact that in its political confrontation with the West to protect national interests, the petroleum sector has been Iran's Achilles heel, through which foreign powers can put pressure on its economy, emphasizing the political sensitivity of the industry.

## The impact of foreign intervention on the political mindset in the oil and gas sector

In dealing with Iran, the country's history cannot just be interpreted in the context of the timing and detail of events but also, more importantly, on the impacts they have left on Iran as a nation. The awareness of history and its influence on Iranians as a whole, and on its decision makers in particular, leads us into the puzzling world of Iranian politics, and allows us to make it seem less complex and challenging. As it has been put by Limbert (2009), the US senior diplomat who was taken hostage during the US embassy hostage crisis, such a consciousness of history will protect foreigners from being confused and surprised by seemingly incoherent and inexplicable Iranian behaviour in political interactions.[50]

Historically Iran has been considered the crossroads between Asia and Europe, East and West. Not only people, but also goods as well as beliefs and cultural norms have passed through the country for centuries. This unique geographical location led to what may be termed 'the crossroad effect' – one which is both stabilizing and enriching to the country and one which leads its people to be hospitable and highly self-conscious towards foreigners in general.[51] But this effect has also exposed the country to foreign interference and invasion, not least following the discovery of petroleum resources.

Many observers of contemporary history argue that Iranian politics are marked by a high degree of paranoia as well as mistrust, insecurity, and factionalism.[52] Such observations can, however, be enriched by the argument that political paranoia in Iran exists as a mode of expression and a style, and that such a style can be justified by history. For example, it can be said that Iran's experience of imperial domination by foreign powers – first Russia and Britain and later the USA – has determined the formation of the country's political landscape over the last two hundred years.[53] During that period, the imperial powers left the country with deep scars resulting from their direct and influential role in staging, among a handful of other events, three disastrous wars in the first half of the nineteenth century, the subsequent capitulations in the treaties of Golestan, Turkmanchai, and Paris, the 1901 D'Arcy oil concession, and more importantly three military coups in 1908,

1921, and 1953.[54] It was perhaps the last of these incidents, financed and orchestrated by foreign powers to topple Mosaddeq, which most severely aggravated the culture of mistrust and xenophobia. This single event had a remarkable impact on the decision-making process and management of the petroleum industry and, over the past several decades, has created great sensitivity and caused this sector to be highly politicized.

After the Revolution, the petroleum industry underwent major changes which reveal how concerns about foreign intervention were manifested in government policy making. One important change was the Revolutionary Constitution which prohibits participation of any foreign entities (individual or corporate) in the oil and gas sector.[55] A few years after the Iran–Iraq war when the country was in need of large amounts of capital for the reconstruction and development of its petroleum sector, Iran's Parliament approved the opening of its industry to foreign investment. Despite taking a more moderate stance towards foreign participation in the petroleum industry, fears of outside intervention were manifested in adopting the buyback contractual regime which maintained the country's sceptical approach towards foreign investors (see Chapter 4).

Iranian negotiating behaviour is strongly influenced by negotiators' fears of being exploited or deceived by foreign partners; the negotiators themselves may even be concerned that they themselves are accused of compromising the national interest.[56] Some international executives who have negotiated with Iran say that its negotiators insist on deals that leave the foreign partners with little profit and frequently seek to renegotiate provisions of a contract after it has been concluded and ratified.[57] Some sources even believe that the impact of domestic political factors on the industry is as destructive as international sanctions. US administrations have reportedly claimed that, even without actually imposing sanctions on Iran, the mere threat of imposing sanctions coupled with 'Iran's reputedly difficult negotiating behaviour have combined to slow the development of Iran's energy sector.'[58]

The tendency to consider all information about the oil and gas industry as secret also stems from the same political concerns about foreign intervention. It originally goes back to the post-nationalization era when there were concerns that foreign companies' access to the industry's information could undermine the nationalization process. Treating the industry's information and contracts as extremely confidential has not always had positive outcomes, as in some cases it has led to mismanagement and institutional corruption.

## Politicization of the petroleum industry: institutional structures and responsibilities

To a significant extent, the politicization of the petroleum industry (which has created a great degree of mistrust within powerful institutional structures) stems from deep concerns about the likelihood of the sector being exploited and manipulated either by foreign or internal forces, hence the resulting sensitivity which rightly reflects the profound importance of the industry in the livelihood and national prestige of Iranians. The politicization phenomenon has also been exacerbated by the revolutionary political mindset which can be characterized as an opaque political structure and as parallel bodies of power with overlapping monitoring and supervisory capabilities, which have also played a key role in creating a complicated rentier system and growing systematic corruption (see introductory chapter).

As mentioned above, the direct and indirect foreign interference in the petroleum sector which caused nationalization, de facto denationalization, re-nationalization, revolution, and a major war, also caused a striking lack of trust within both the Shah's and the post-Revolutionary eras.[59] Before the Revolution, NIOC was established to end the Iranian oil contracts signed with foreign companies, in order to reduce the significance of foreign players in Iran's oil industry.[60] NIOC was only a business-oriented company and did not directly engage in foreign political activities and diplomacy-related policies and decisions.[61] The industry's policies and the politics affecting it were entirely in the hands of the Shah, who personally handled most major foreign and international issues relating to Iran's oil diplomacy, from decisions within OPEC to relations with foreign companies and governments.[62]

With the overthrow of the Shah and the coming to power of an ideologically anti-western, revolutionary regime, the politicization of the industry intensified dramatically. There were criticisms that the Shah's extensive reliance on foreign powers had led to the latter's dominance over the oil industry and cheap sales of national wealth. Hence throughout the course of the Revolution, the issue of national distribution of the oil and gas was central to the revolutionary motto, based on which Ayatollah Khomeini promised the nation that, upon success of the Revolution, he 'will bring the oil money to families' dinner spread (Sofreh).'[63]

Initially started by a direct order of Ayatollah Khomeini cancelling all oil and gas development contracts concluded with foreign companies, the politicization process extended to establishment of the Ministry of Petroleum with its management team directly appointed by the government and strictly supervised by the Parliament.[64] The Ministry of Petroleum was founded not only to enable the Minister to attend OPEC Ministerial Conferences, but also to establish a regular and more active presence of the hydrocarbon sector in the Cabinet and on the country's political scene.[65] Lack of trust, resulting from chronic fear of foreign intervention, has played an important role in the political intervention of multiple institutions in the petroleum industry, causing confusion over decision making in the sector, with many organs claiming authority over the industry. These include: the President, the Ministry of Petroleum, the Ministry of Energy, the Parliament, the Expediency Council,[66] and the Council of Guardians,[67] as well as NIOC, NIGC, and last but not least NIGEC.[68]

NIOC, as the sole executive body in charge of the development of petroleum resources and originally designed to be purely commercial, is highly influenced by its major shareholder, namely the government through the Ministry of Petroleum, which plays an extensive role in its decision making.[69] As a result, decisions tend to be influenced by politics – possibly to the detriment of commercial considerations.[70] The appointment of four petroleum ministers during the Ahmadinejad administration is an example of how political will overrules long-term commercial interests in an industry which requires integrated and sustainable management.

Other organs, such as the Parliament and Council of Guardians, also play their own legislative and supervisory roles over the industry. They can, as they have in the past, exert their influence through opposing the implementation of oil and gas development contracts, or accusing the authorities involved in negotiations of investment contracts of corruption, or refusing to ratify investment bills presented by the government on the basis of inconsistency with national interests or with the provisions of the Constitution. Also, the national petroleum companies' budgets, finally approved only by the Ministry of Petroleum, must now be approved by the Planning Organization and the Parliament; and once the Parliament gets involved, the Council of Guardians also has the right to question the budget – as a legislative act of the Parliament – and to check whether it is consistent with the Constitution and Shari'a law.

On the commercial development side of the industry, three national companies – NIOC, NIGC, and NIGEC – have extensive overlapping responsibilities. NIOC is in charge of all oil and gas resource exploration, production, and development activities (upstream), while NIGC is responsible for domestic transmission, distribution, and sales of natural gas (downstream). The situation became even more complex when, in

2003, NIGEC was established to handle natural gas export projects. The confusion mostly arises when stakeholders are required to deal with responsibilities that are spread across different companies. This is particularly challenging for gas export project development where NIGEC is responsible for provision of research, studies, and planning; NIOC's International Affairs Division is in charge of negotiations; and NIGC is responsible for downstream operational and technical activities.[71] Dealing with this triangular structure, IOCs often complain about confusion over which body they should approach for different stages of project development. Furthermore, as mentioned in Chapter 1, in July 2012, NIOC dissolved NIGEC as one of its subsidiaries, as there were concerns among NIOC officials over a prospective amalgamation of NIGC and NIGEC which, it was suspected, might reduce NIOC's power and influence over the natural gas sector. Hence, in a pre-emptive strike, NIOC announced the dissolution of NIGEC, a decision which reaffirmed the influence of political considerations rather than commercial matters in decision-making processes in the Iranian petroleum industry.[72]

In the policy implementation stage, the same problem of parallel power structures has caused confusion over decision making in the oil and gas industries. The opaque and unique structure of the petroleum organizations, where duplicating and conflicting authorities rule the sector, can make it very difficult for outsiders to understand exactly who has the authority and responsibility to take decisions. For instance, the Ministry of Petroleum, which should be the policy maker of the hydrocarbon sector, is still involved with the day-to-day running of the sector, making it commercially ineffective and highly political.[73] This has also made it inefficient in policy making, and caused delays in the adoption of coherent long-term strategic vision and action plans, which are very much needed for the development of the sector.

Constant interventions from different political bodies, and attempts to accommodate their different views in decision making, have also prevented the country from designing and implementing a comprehensive energy resource development plan which is undoubtedly necessary for a country like Iran.[74] Disagreements between politicians are particularly intense in the natural gas sector, where there have been prolonged debates about whether to give priority to export projects or domestic markets (see Chapter 6).[75] During Khatami's presidency (1997–2005), gas export projects were pursued more actively; by contrast in the Ahmadinejad administration (2005–13), there was explicit reluctance to allow such projects to proceed. Frequent changes in policies towards the natural gas sector have, for example, resulted in the notoriously unstable gas export contract with Turkey, which has seen numerous disputes over price and delivery terms and also reputational damage (see Chapter 1). Unstable policies have also affected a secure and sufficient supply of gas to the domestic market, particularly for reinjection purposes, seriously impacting the country's oil production and revenues (see Chapter 6).

The politicized mindset which overlooks the development of the petroleum sector has also affected the management structure of the industry. After the Revolution, almost the entire senior and mid-level management of the industry were either expelled or forced into exile, or were given early retirement, for fear of their ideological attachment to the monarchy and consequent preference for interactions with western countries.[76] The new appointees were mostly chosen on the basis of political considerations; in other words, Islamic and revolutionary credentials were given greater priority over technical competence and work experience.[77] As a result, any fundamental changes in the management of the industry would face fierce resistance both from within the industry and, more generally, from the various political bodies.

In addition to the drawbacks enumerated above, politicization of the petroleum industry, which initially emerged to protect the industry from foreign influence, has inevitably left a major impact on the growth of systemic corruption in the industry. Parallel institutions and the absence of a transparent, integrated supervisory body, has allowed favouritism and the award of opaque deals to those with close relations with these influential institutions. In addition, the limited channels of trade which have resulted from international sanctions have assisted opportunistic figures – mainly under the facade of the private sector but with direct links to the authorities –to exert a tighter grip on the lucrative opportunities in the petroleum sector. This situation has also justified the extensive involvement of powerful public institutions, such as the commercial arm of the IRGC – Khatam-al-Anbiya Base – in the development of oil and gas projects, raising concerns among independent, private investors, including foreign companies, about the success of their business in Iran in case their commercial interests should clash with these entities, increasing the political risks of doing business in Iran.

## Conclusion

In Iran, history and historical events matter. Some of these events have left deep scars on Iranian memories of foreign involvement in their country, creating a sense of national grievance and victimization.[78] As a result, Iranian politicians, decision makers, and negotiators, when dealing with a foreign entity or a foreign issue, perceive themselves as holding the weaker position, seeing their foreign counterparts as stronger powers with superior political, economic, and commercial capabilities, aiming to force Iran to surrender to unequal and unfair agreements.

More specifically, in the natural gas sector, the opaque management and decision-making mechanism has caused serious administrative and managerial inefficiency and confusion among investors. The large number of institutions, the important roles of non-government actors, overlapping institutional structures, and the importance of personal ties have often led to conflicting polices and uncertain implementation.[79] One of the obvious manifestations of such a confusing mechanism is the government's failure to design and implement a long-term strategic vision for the development of the natural gas industry, in order to enhance transparency and stability and to put an end to the prolonged and ongoing disputes among different institutions on how to allocate natural gas resources optimally (see Chapter 6). Dominance of political considerations in the industry's decision-making processes means that commercial viability is neglected, undermining the industry's profitability and operational efficiency. The resulting mismanagement and corruption, along with political uncertainties and favouritism, have all led to an unstable business environment in which the private sector has concerns about making investments. This has had a major impact on the government's ability to attract investment capital and technology – which are badly needed for substantial gas development, particularly for export projects.

## CHAPTER 3

## THE IMPACT OF US AND INTERNATIONAL SANCTIONS ON OIL AND GAS DEVELOPMENT

### Introduction

For nearly two decades sanctions have been an integral part of Iran's economy. Although no comprehensive study has been conducted on the exact impact of sanctions, available evidence shows that they have played a major role in weakening both the economy and the oil and gas industry. Since the mid-1990s, the oil and gas industry has been subject to extensive unilateral, multilateral, and international sanctions. Initiated by the US government, sanctions were later broadened both in terms of their coverage and international support, aiming at forcing the Iranian government to halt its allegedly hostile foreign policy and bring its nuclear programme under full international scrutiny to prove its peaceful purposes.

In this chapter, sanctions regimes, their effectiveness, and implications on oil and gas development will be reviewed.

### US unilateral sanctions

Relations between the USA and Iran deteriorated sharply following the 1979 Islamic Revolution. US foreign policy towards Iran underwent a dramatic shift as the revolutionary momentum opposed US policy in the Persian Gulf. During the era of the Shah, Iran was considered a close ally of the USA, spending vast sums of petrodollars to purchase military goods from the USA to protect the security of the region in the power vacuum resulting from the departure of British forces in 1971. In return, the US government helped the Shah to remain in power during a relatively long period of political and economic turmoil.

After the Revolution, antagonism between the two countries began following the 1979–80 Tehran hostage crisis in which US diplomats were held hostage for more than a year by a group of Islamist students. In a direct response to the crisis, President Carter imposed the first series of economic sanctions on Iran, while also freezing $12 billion worth of assets in the USA and placing a temporary ban on all imports from the country.[1] Even after the hostage crisis, the US government continued to deploy punitive measures against Iran, to alter what it regarded as unacceptable political and military behaviour, alleged support of terrorism, and, later on, the development of its nuclear programme. During the Reagan administration, sanctions continued to prevent the country from receiving arms under the US Arms Export Control Act[2] and prohibit imports of crude oil and all other Iranian imports to US markets.[3] US unilateral sanctions were further expanded by the Clinton administration where two Executive Orders banned the participation of all US firms in the development of the Iranian petroleum sector, and broadened the scope of sanctions to encompass a total trade and investment embargo on the country.[4] Sanctions, however, did not prevent European and Asian companies from filling the gap left by US companies in the petroleum sector, resulting in an evident 'loop-hole' which notably undermined the effectiveness of the US unilateral sanctions. As a result, the US Congress expanded the coverage of sanctions, through enactment of the Iran–Libya Sanction Act (ILSA), which included foreign companies investing in Iran's oil and gas sector, thus targeting the most vital segments of the country's economy.[5]

### The Iran Sanctions Act (ISA)

The Iran Sanctions Act (ISA) has been a crucial component of US attempts to isolate Iran's access to non-US foreign investors' capital and technology for the development of its petroleum resources.[6] ISA followed an earlier March 1995 Executive Order, barring US companies' investment in the Iranian energy industry. The Act originated from the 'Iran Foreign Oil Sanctions Act', proposed by Senator Alfonse D'Amato in 1995 to sanction foreign firms' export to Iran of energy *technology*.[7] A revised version passed the Senate in December 1995 imposing sanctions on *investment* in Iran's energy sector.[8] Being aware of the country's needs to attract substantial foreign investments for the development of its old oilfields and the underdeveloped natural gas sector, the Act was designed to prohibit foreign entities (companies and individuals) from investing more than $20 million in one year in its energy sector. Non-compliance with this legislation would entail drastic financial penalties, ranging from denial of Export–Import Bank loans and credit guarantees, to denial of licences for US export, and US government procurement prohibition.[9] The definition of 'investment' in ISA also includes not only equity and royalty arrangements, but also any contract that includes responsibility for the development of the petroleum sector.[10] As such, banks and international financial institutions which assist energy investment, and refining and gasoline procurement activities, were subject to sanctions under ISA.

### Extra-territoriality of US unilateral sanctions

When enacted, ISA was heavily criticized for its 'extra-territorial' characteristics, which would authorize US penalties against foreign firms incorporated outside US territory.[11] Although the exercise of extra-territorial jurisdiction was accepted strictly in exceptional circumstances when, for example, there was a threat against international peace and security, most nations refused its application as an instrument of a nation's foreign policy. Not surprisingly, the US attempt to impose its law extraterritorially on the economic activities of companies and economic entities having limited and sometimes no links to the USA, aroused great opposition and criticism among its allies. The EU, for example, strongly opposed ISA and the use of indirect trade and investments sanctions to enforce policy objectives on the international community in an extra-territorial and unilateral manner, which was considered contrary to widely accepted principles of international law. As a result, the EU adopted blocking legislation, in which measures for non-compliance and notifications requirements would be applied to ISA. In practice, it meant that European companies were prohibited from complying with ISA provisions, and that such companies should inform the European Commission if their economic or financial interests were affected by US actions. The EU also threatened to file a complaint against the US government before the World Trade Organization (WTO) which, together with the blocking legislation, pressured the US government to start negotiations with the EU aimed at granting a general waiver for EU investment in Iran. In April 1997, the USA and the EU finally reached an agreement to avoid a trade confrontation over ISA, with the EU committing not to file any complaint with the WTO and the Clinton administration waiving sanctions on the first project which was determined to be in violation of the Act's provisions, namely the $2 billion contract signed in 1997 in which a Total SA, Gazprom, and Petronas consortium were to develop phases 2 and 3 of the South Pars gas field.

### Sanctions trajectory: from resistance to international support

In the early years of the imposition of unilateral sanctions, a lack of support from its allies cast serious doubt about the effectiveness of US unilateral sanctions. The election of President Khatami (1997–2005), a reformist cleric who had promised to implement political and economic reforms, made the imposition of sanctions on companies investing in Iran increasingly unlikely (see the introductory chapter). Despite all economic and political limitations, the Khatami administration managed to promote foreign investment and economic reform as a means to further economic development. His government managed to improve relations with the EU, while taking advantage of the USA–EU confrontation over the US extra-territorial sanctions. The political situation improved to the extent that in the early 2000s, the George W. Bush administration decided to ease trade sanctions with Iran, mostly as a result of the US policy to support the ruling reformist government.[12]

However, the prospect for further improvement in US-Iranian relations did not last long. Following the 9/11 attack, US military intervention in Afghanistan and Iraq to combat terrorism, and faced with new information about Iran's previously concealed nuclear installations, the Bush administration reversed its policy and intensified the political and economic pressure on Iran, while listing the country as a member of the 'Axis of Evil' to justify its hostile policy.[13]

This situation was further exacerbated by the coming to power of a hardline, extremist president in Iran, namely Mahmoud Ahmadinejad (2005–13), whose foreign policies were based on finding and creating external threats to unify the domestic population against a common cause, in order to deflect attention away from internal economic and social problems (see the introductory chapter).[14] His fierce rhetoric and stubborn continuation of the nuclear programme, despite all political and security threats, led to the intensification of sanctions both in terms of scope and numbers, which also helped him to increase the dependence of society on its government as a result of greater isolation and tighter economic conditions. Soon after Ahmadinejad's election, negotiations with the 'E3' trio of European countries (the UK, France, and Germany) which had started in 2000 broke down, and Iran started enriching uranium, violating the suspension agreement negotiated with the E3. The Ahmadinejad government's rejection of a comprehensive proposal, including economic and security incentives for a long-term agreement to resolve outstanding nuclear issues, resulted in the International Atomic Energy Agency (IAEA) Board's finding Iran to be in violation of its Safeguard Agreements and, in 2006, referring the case to the UN Security Council (UNSC).[15]

## Internationalization of sanctions

Iran's failure to submit to the UNSC's interim decision urging the suspension of its nuclear activities caused the UNSC to pass seven resolutions in the period 2006–10, of which four imposed sanctions.[16] The UN sanctions on Iran do not directly place restrictions on the country's energy industry but mostly focus on prohibition of the provision of sensitive and dual-purpose technologies which could possibly be utilized in its nuclear activities. The UN sanctions include:

- a freeze on the financial assets and other economic resources of individuals and entities designated by the UNSC as having ties with Iran's nuclear programme (imposed in 2006);17
- the banning of arms exports from Iran together with restraining member states from sales to Iran of certain categories of heavy conventional arms (in 2007);18
- an intensification of travel bans and financial restrictions on designated Iranian individuals and companies (in 2008);
- the imposition of a complete arms embargo and targeting of the assets of the IRGC and Republic of Iran Shipping Lines (in 2010).19

Applicability of UN decisions to all its member states has made these so-called 'international sanctions', as opposed to US unilateral sanctions, less legally controversial and more practically effective.[20] In other words, UN sanctions brought about a consensus among the international community over potential security threats emerging from Iran's nuclear programme. UN member states' commitments to comply with the Security Council's resolutions unified them to undertake concrete measures in restricting Iran's access to any resources, including indirect revenues gained from the sale of its oil and gas, which could have been used to fund its acquisition of prohibited items and to continue its nuclear activities. Thus, UN sanctions indirectly strengthened the international acceptance and credibility of US sanctions, and provided leverage for the US government to increase pressure on Iran.

## Intensification of US sanctions

Despite the UNSC resolutions and increasing international pressure on Iran, the Ahmadinejad government persistently continued its hostile foreign policy and further progress in the development of nuclear capabilities. As a result, in 2010, the Obama administration and the US Congress, now with greater support from their allies, increased the scope and number of unilateral sanctions. Administered by the US Treasury's Office of Foreign Assets Control (OFAC), Congress passed the Comprehensive Iran Sanctions Accountability and Divestment Act

(CISADA), expanding the authorities of ISA to deter sales by foreign companies of gasoline to Iran. CISADA also amends the definition of 'investment' in ISA to include pipelines to or through Iran and contracts to construct, upgrade, or expand energy projects.[21] Sanctions on pipelines are deemed to prevent Iran from developing its petroleum sector.[22] Sanctions also encompass oil and LNG tankers, and products used in the construction of pipelines that transport oil and gas. The Act further stipulates that sanctions are applicable from the beginning of pipeline construction, and not from the start of oil or gas flow through a finished project.[23] It also made the sales of energy-related equipment sanctionable as long as such sales would need to be structured as investments or ongoing profit-earning ventures rather than simple sales transactions.[24] Exceptions, however, have been granted for the purchase of Iranian natural gas. Sanctions provisions have made it clear that gas purchase is distinguishable from the construction of natural gas pipelines. Payments for purchased gas, however, might still be subject to sanctions due to international banking restrictions in place.

The US government continued to exert pressure on Iran following a report from the IAEA, indicating that Iran might have worked on nuclear weapons-related technology. As a result, the US government issued an Executive Order in November 2011 expanding the authority of ISA to impose at least one of the available ISA sanctions on foreign firms that provide Iran with $1 million or more (or $5 million in a one year period) worth of goods or services that Iran could use to maintain or enhance its oil and gas sector.[25] They were also banned from providing Iran with $250,000 (or $1 million in a one year period) worth of goods or services that could be used to maintain or expand its production of petrochemical products.[26] To increase the pressure, the US Department of the Treasury further strengthened sanctions regulations in February 2012 and extended their provisions to 'foreign financial institutions that knowingly conduct or facilitate certain significant financial transactions with the Central Bank of Iran or a US-designated Iranian financial institution.'[27]

In 2012, the provisions of ISA were further expanded to apply to entities which have owned a vessel that had been used to transport Iranian crude oil, or to have been involved in oil and gas ventures with Iranian participation, but outside Iran and commencing after 2002.[28] The provisions are also applicable to entities that have purchased oil and other petroleum products from Iran. The same measures would also apply to petrochemical products and those companies which conducted transactions with NIOC or the Naftiran Intertrade Company (NICO). The provision of insurance or re-insurance for NIOC or the National

Iranian Tanker Company (NITC) was also subject to the same provisions. Contrary to previous practice, CISADA obliges the administration to conduct investigations when there is 'credible information' about a potential violation, an obligation which did not exist under ISA.[29] As concerns over Iran's nuclear activities mounted, the Obama administration has extensively used ISA provisions to discourage companies from continuing their business in Iran; a practice which had not been seen in previous administrations due to the reluctance to confront allies.[30]

## EU sanctions

The EU reaction to Iran's nuclear development underwent a major shift from an initial opposition to US extra-territorial sanctions, toward support for the latter and imposition of sanctions which, in some cases, exceeded those of the USA. Prior to 2010, the EU tried to take a conciliatory role in Iran's nuclear dispute, hence limiting its preventive measures to enforcing UN sanctions imposed since 2006 instead of imposing independent, direct punitive sanctions. The EU altered its policy only after the UNSC passed its fourth Resolution (UNSC Resolution 1929) in 2010; this was followed by the first round of EU sanctions encompassing trade and investment restrictions in the oil and gas sector, and by prohibition of provisions of 'key' equipment and technologies from use in refining, LNG, exploration, or production plants. This remarkable change in the EU position did not happen in a vacuum of political and international security concerns. The EU policy change was encouraged by concerns that the Iranian nuclear development could contribute to political and economic instability, leading to a potential pre-emptive strike by Israeli forces on Iran's nuclear facilities which might trigger military reaction, directly impacting the international oil market and the global economy.[31] In fact over several years, as Iran's nuclear programme was transformed into a high-profile security issue for the international community, effective and collective measures became increasingly important to EU member states. The failure of the 2003–5 EU diplomatic initiative to negotiate and reach a peaceful solution to Iran's nuclear programme affected diplomatic relations which further deteriorated following the election of Ahmadinejad, whose provocative and inflammatory statements had a direct impact on the maintenance of regional and international peace and security.[32] Since then, the dual policy of conducting negotiations along with imposing sanctions – the so called 'carrot and stick' policy – was central to the EU approach to Iran.[33]

The EU 2010 sanctions included a package of restrictive measures in areas of trade, financial services, energy, and transport, as well as a visa ban and asset freeze.[34] The EU made it clear, however, that these sanctions did not prohibit imports of Iranian oil and gas, nor did they ban exports of gasoline to Iran.[35] But less than 18 months later in December 2011, following the failure of the nuclear negotiations and the attack on the British Embassy in Tehran in November of the same year, the EU announced the toughest ever sanctions – these went beyond those imposed by the US government.[36] Led by France and Britain, the EU embargo prohibits the purchase, transport, and import of Iranian crude oil. The embargo also banned the export of major equipment and technologies used by the oil sector, as well as related financial deals including insurance for shipping oil and petrochemicals out of the country.[37] To minimize the impact on those EU countries most reliant on Iranian oil, existing contracts were allowed to continue until 1 July 2012, due to concerns over the impact of sanctions on oil prices and the subsequent implications for the already fragile EU recovery from the 2008 economic crisis.[38] These sanctions froze the assets of Iran's Central Bank in Europe, and banned trade in gold and other materials with the Central Bank, causing dramatic volatility in the country's foreign exchange market.[39]

Less than a year later, in October 2012, EU member states approved a third package of sanctions, banning imports of natural gas and prohibiting financial transactions between European and Iranian Banks. It also included bans on the construction of oil tankers for Iran, the supply of shipping for the transport or storage of oil and petrochemical products, and flagging and classification services for Iranian oil tankers and cargo ships. The EU ban on gas imports, although believed to be a rather symbolic political gesture, given the fact that the EU has never imported gas from Iran, was very important as it made clear that future and planned pipeline projects would be restricted.

### The impact of sanctions on the development of the oil and gas sector

In the mid 1990s and despite US sanctions, the first major petroleum contract was signed with the US Conoco company (a subsidiary of the Dupont Cooperation), for development of two offshore oil and gas fields in the Persian Gulf worth $550 million. Following the enactment of ISA and possible criminal liability arising from conducting business in Iran, Conoco withdrew from the Sirri A and E projects. When Conoco withdrew, it was replaced by Total and Petronas, and these companies were never held in violation of ISA despite investments of $600 million in the project. Eni's $3.8 billion investment for the development of the South Pars gas field also progressed despite the US threat of sanctions. The company signed a new five-year buyback contract for the development of Darkhovin oilfield worth around $1 billion. The USA continued threatening companies such as BHP Billiton Ltd and Canadian Sheer Energy Company with the imposition of sanctions, when speculation surfaced over their involvement in the development of Foroozan, Esfandiar, and Balal oilfields.[40]

During this period, as sanctions became tougher, primarily as a result of UN actions and the EU policy shift from conciliation to condemnation, their effectiveness started to evolve. Beyond concerns over their actual implementation, sanctions caused reluctance among major companies to invest and operate in Iran's energy sector, due to rising political risks, and operational costs compared with other petroleum-rich countries offering more attractive conditions to foreign investors.[41] Major international companies, such as Royal Dutch Shell, Total, and Repsol pulled out of key petroleum projects and declined to make further investments, or resold their investments to other companies.[42] In July 2008, Total and Petronas, the original South Pars investors, withdrew from the Pars LNG project, announcing that investing in Iran at a time of growing international pressure over its nuclear programme was 'too risky'.[43] Japanese companies also reduced their participation in the development of the massive Azadegan oilfield and later in 2010 completely withdrew from the country.[44] In 2011, US sources estimated that Iran's investment loss in the energy sector had been around $60 billion resulting from companies withdrawing from projects or refusing to make additional investments in new projects.[45] This figure is significantly higher if revenue losses resulting from imposing sanctions on the sale of oil are taken into account.

In response to the withdrawal of major IOCs, Iran turned to Chinese, Indian, Russian, and some eastern European companies, including those from Hungary, Belarus, and Romania, to fill the gap. Chinese companies were particularly active in the development of oil and gas fields such as Northern Azadegan, Yadavaran, Garmsar, and phase 11 of South Pars. They also showed great interest in developing phase 12 of South Pars, which was initially promised to Indian companies in 2009. There were also talks with the Chinese on the possibility of replacing Indian companies in the gas export project to Pakistan. According to Garver (2010, China committed substantial investment to Iran's oil and gas sector, including $30 billion in 2009 alone.[46] The

**Table 3.1:** Energy firms ending business with Iran (2009–2010)

| Country | Company | Action |
| --- | --- | --- |
| France | Total | Ended investments in Iran |
| Germany | Linde | Stopped all businesses |
|  | Schlumberger | Exited Iran in 2013 |
| India | Reliance | Stopped sales of refined products; will not import crude oil from Iran |
| Italy | Eni SpA | Ended investment in Iran |
| Japan | Inpex Corp. | Exited from the Azadegan oil field |
| Kuwait | Independent petroleum Group | Stopped sales of refined products |
| Malaysia | Petronas | Stopped sales of refined products |
| Netherlands | Royal Dutch Shell | Ended investment in Iran |
| Norway | Statoil | Ended investment in Iran |
| Spain | Repsol | Abandoned negotiations over development of phases 13 and 14 of the South Pars gas field |
| Switzerland | Vitol | Committed to not supply refined petroleum products to Iran |
|  | Glencore | Committed not to supply refined petroleum products to Iran |
| Turkey | Tupras | Cancelled contracts to supply gasoline to Iran |
| United Kingdom | BP | Stopped supplying jet fuel to Iran Air; halted a BP–NIOC joint venture in the Rhum gas field |
| International | Trans-Adriatic Pipeline | The pipeline will not be used to transport Iranian gas to Europe |

Source: Katzman (2012).

ability of Chinese companies to successfully fill the gap left by European companies did not take long to discover. Long delays in completing the development of projects to which Chinese companies had committed, reaffirmed the scepticism of some energy experts about their technical capacity and experience, particularly in technologically complex projects such as LNG trains, through which Iran had planned to emerge as a major gas exporter.[47]

The policies of Chinese companies in relation to compliance with international sanctions were unclear. Although China, along with Russia, to a large extent rejected US sanctions, they did not hesitate to vote for three rounds of UN sanctions.[48] Moreover, despite the announcement of interest in further investment, delays in projects, such as the development of North Pars, South Azadegan, and Yadavaran, were said to be partially due to 'logistical difficulties experienced as a result of sanctions on technology and financial transactions.'[49] Whether due to lack of expertise or sanctions, Chinese companies are also facing difficult times in Iran. In August 2012, for example, the Chinese CNPC company withdrew from a project for development of phase 11 of South Pars, suspending a $5 billion development contract.[50] In February 2014, CNPC also received an ultimatum from Oil Minister Zanganeh, requiring it to complete its long-delayed South Azadegan oil field (jointly with Iraq), or face cancellation of its contract and expulsion of its staff.[51]

Withdrawal of international companies also provided opportunities for some domestic companies to participate in the development of energy projects. This provided unique opportunities for IRGC-linked or controlled companies to acquire a large share in development of the sector, regardless of their technical and technological competence (see Chapter 2). Perhaps an additional undesirable consequence of sanctions was that they allowed military and radical forces to obtain and then maintain a strong grip on economic activity in major sectors, including oil and gas, thereby increasing the risks for private sector investors if they return to Iran and enter into competition with such entities.

The impact of international sanctions is not confined to the departure of foreign companies from Iran. The 2012 sanctions drastically affected Iran's oil exports. The sharp fall was a result of the EU embargo on purchases of oil from Iran, and of decisions by others around the world to reduce their oil imports in order to obtain waivers from US sanctions. Iran's oil production dropped from 3.706 million bbl/day in 2010 to 2.817 million bbl/day in July 2012, reducing its export capacity from 1.9 million bbl/day to 900 thousand bbl/day.[52] In October 2012, IEA reported that Iran's crude oil deliveries had further fallen to an estimated 860 thousand bbl/day. By the end of 2013, oil exports had slightly increased – thanks to the interim agreement reached in Geneva in November – reaching slightly above 1 million bbl/day but still far below 2011 levels. Restrictions on access to the international banking system also continue to make it difficult to receive payments for oil exports. As a result, the practice of customers paying in their own currencies, or using goods in exchange for oil, is likely to continue unless an agreement leads to the easing or removal of sanctions.

**Table 3.2:** Top energy buyers from Iran and agreed reductions 2011 & 2013 (bbl/day)

| Country/Bloc | 2011 average | 2013 average |
|---|---|---|
| European Union (particularly Italy, Spain, and Greece) | 600,000 | Negligible (no Iranian oil has entered key Rotterdam refinery since February 2012) |
| China | 550,000 | 420,000 |
| Japan | 325,000 | 200,000 |
| India | 320,000 | 200,000 |
| South Korea | 230,000 | 130,000 |
| Turkey | 200,000 | 120,000 |
| South Africa | 80,000 | Negligible |
| Malaysia | 55,000 | Negligible |
| Sri Lanka | 35,000 | Negligible |
| Taiwan | 35,000 | 10,000 |
| Singapore | 20,000 | Negligible |
| Other | 55,000 | Negligible |
| Total | 2,500,000 | 1,087,000 |

Source: IEA & CRC calculations (2013) cited in Katzman (2014).

Sanctions on sales of oil have reduced the government's revenues substantially. In 2011, Iran received some $100 billion of petroleum export revenues, which were the only major source of hard currency.[53] The decline in oil exports, however, reduced revenues by more than 60 per cent to around $35 billion in 2013.

### Sanctions and natural gas projects

Natural gas exports, whether through pipeline or LNG, have also been affected by sanctions. The Peace Pipeline to export Iranian natural gas to Pakistan and India faced great opposition from the US government. Although failure to finalize the deal can, to some extent, be attributed to concerns over the security of the pipeline, the price, India's and Pakistan's inability to finance or attract financing for the project (see Chapter 1), and the US government's pressure on these two countries to suspend participation, have also played a major role.

US and EU sanctions also excluded Iran from all pipeline projects for export of gas to European markets. Before being abandoned in favour of TAP in 2013, the Nabucco pipeline was initially planned to be a major route for export of Iranian gas to European markets. Despite many years of negotiations, Iran was finally removed from the project in the wake of intensifying international sanctions.

The exception is, however, exports to Turkey on which, despite US objections, no sanctions were imposed. This is mainly due to the fact that each country was responsible for the construction of its section of the pipeline, and hence the project was not considered an 'investment'.[54] Also the USA did not impose sanctions on the basis that Turkey imports gas from Turkmenistan that transits through Iran.[55] Moreover, considerations about Turkey's energy security and reducing its reliance on Russian gas made the US government hesitant to impose sanctions on that country.[56] The passage of CISADA in 2010, however, bans any investment, construction, expansion, and upgrading of natural gas export pipelines from Iran, which makes it highly unlikely that such US concessions would be granted to any other countries interested in importing Iranian gas. Following the EU sanctions imposed in November 2012, even the gas exported to Turkey has come under scrutiny in the light of the EU ban on imports of Iranian gas to European markets. Although Iran has never directly exported gas to the EU, there is speculation that Iranian gas is mixed with the gas from other exporting countries and delivered to European markets through Turkish pipelines, an assumption that cannot be proved and has been rejected by the Turkish government.

International sanctions have also rendered Iran unable to develop LNG projects. The impact of sanctions on LNG projects has been considerably greater than on pipeline projects. Although the original version of ISA did not apply to the development of LNG, CISADA specifically includes such projects in the definition of petroleum resources, thereby making investment in LNG projects (or in the supply of LNG tankers) subject to sanctions.[57] Since the withdrawal of major IOCs, all projects have stalled and three have been cancelled (see Chapter 1). National and Chinese company initiatives to develop LNG projects have reportedly failed, as the LNG technology is patented by US and European firms, access to which is strictly prohibited.

## Conclusion

There is little doubt about the high costs of the sanctions imposed on Iran's economy as a whole and its oil and gas sector in particular.

Although its longstanding response to sanctions has been defiance and resistance, the post-2010 sanctions have bitten so hard that even the Iranian authorities started admitting that their impact was severe. A few years before, there had been hope that if Iran improved its investment regime and offered more concessions, the country could minimize the impact of sanctions by engaging smaller non-OECD companies. This hope, however, proved to be wrong, particularly for the development of oil and gas resources, as these companies lacked the required expertise and technologies, or were threatened and prosecuted by the USA or the EU for breaches of sanctions regulations.

As a result of international sanctions and the prohibition on investments and transfer of technologies, almost all natural gas projects defined and started after the mid 1990s could not be fully developed or were cancelled or abandoned. The South Pars gas field, for example, which was initially planned to become fully operational by 2015, has only 11 out of 24 phases on line, and some of the phases are not producing gas at full capacity. All LNG projects and some major pipeline export projects, such as those to Asian and European markets, were also cancelled or suspended as a result of increasing international pressure, making the prospect of Iran becoming a major international gas player in the near future almost impossible. Therefore, if the current status of sanctions continues, or intensifies even further if Iran fails to reach a deal with the international community, it is very difficult to see any major development of the gas industry, and further deterioration seems more likely.

The prospect for sanctions on the Rouhani government might be different. Rouhani's election as Iran's president in June 2013 was a clear sign of growing public dissatisfaction about political and economic conditions, and placed pressure on the regime to pursue policies of conciliation with the West (see introductory chapter).

Rouhani's election has revived hopes for a peaceful settlement of the nuclear dispute, with possible removal or easing of sanctions. In November 2013, an interim agreement was reached in Geneva following intense negotiations between P5+1 and Iran's representatives, based on which further expansion of Iran's nuclear programme would be halted in exchange for temporary and modest sanctions relief.

To the surprise of many, this interim deal received broad international support, indicating political and diplomatic momentum among the world's powers to settle Iran's nuclear crisis. Although sanctions on investment in the energy sector had not been eased through the interim nuclear deal at the time of this book's completion in mid-2014, reports suggested that, despite the threat of existing sanctions, major international companies had already started negotiations and were planning their way back into Iran on the assumption that sanctions would soon be lifted.

Hardliners in both Iran and the USA are actively pursuing radical mandates, which makes speculation over the scope and timing of any final agreement very difficult. The sanctions are a complex, inflexible, and rigid set of measures which are driven and imposed by various political elements in the USA and elsewhere, making them difficult to lift or ease. Assuming that negotiations succeed in reaching a final agreement, there is speculation that the removal may become as lengthy as the 10 years it took to remove UN sanctions in post-Saddam Iraq.[58] If parties manage to reach a final deal within the set deadline, however, it is unlikely that removing sanctions would take such a long time. First, Iran's political and economic situation is different from that of other countries subject to sanctions – such as Iraq, Libya, or Syria. There is a comparably stronger political and economic system in Iran, and more importantly there are high security measures which are rigorously implemented throughout the country which make it a relatively safe and stable place for foreign investment. Second, numerous attractive investment opportunities are available in Iran which make it very difficult to continue banning foreign companies from investing in the country if agreement is reached and Iran fulfils its commitments. Thirdly, the unprecedented political determination of Iran's leadership and its counterparts suggests that the likelihood of reaching a final agreement in a short period of time is high, which itself suggests that all parties are committed to comply with the terms of an agreement – part of which is removal of sanctions.

While removal of US sanctions due to Congressional opposition might take a longer period of time, there is more optimism about the possibility of EU sanctions removal and a return to the early 2000s, when Iran had closer diplomatic and trade relations with the EU. Therefore, sanctions relief may be achieved temporarily in the case of a US presidential exemption (if Congress rejects permanent removal) and is more likely to be granted by EU countries.

Sanctions removal can release blocked funds in international banks and restart flows of investment and technologies which can increase gas production capacity. Increases in production can be translated into reduction of imports and adequate supply to the domestic market, with reduced concern about supply cuts. This also means an increase in gas reinjection and enhancement of oil recovery which will have a direct impact on growth in government revenues. With regard to export projects, while it is highly unlikely that any LNG projects will recommence development in a short period of time, even after sanctions removal, the increase in gas production could lead to a considerable increase in exports through pipelines within five years, using existing infrastructure.

# CHAPTER 4

## INVESTMENT REGIME IN THE OIL AND GAS SECTOR

### Introduction

The development of Iran's massive oil and gas resources requires a substantial amount of capital investment which the country has so far failed to attract, mainly as a result of US and international sanctions (see Chapter 3). But there are arguments that, had the country offered a more attractive legal and fiscal framework, it could have been more successful in circumventing sanctions and attracting foreign investors.

The post-Revolution foreign investment regime has, to a large extent, been influenced by constitutional limitations which are themselves affected by historical events which have restricted participation of foreign entities in development of sensitive sectors such as oil and gas (see Chapter 2). It was in response to these restrictions that, back in the mid 1990s, the government introduced buyback contracts for the development of hydrocarbon resources. Although this was a contractual framework, alien and unfavourable to industry players, it was an important step towards opening doors to foreign investors after many years of isolation and self-reliance.

This chapter examines Iran's oil and gas investment regime and starts with a historical review of contractual frameworks since the discovery of oil in the early 1900s. It continues by reviewing buyback contracts and critiques of their efficiency and attractiveness. It also addresses the Rouhani government's initiative to abandon buybacks in favour of a more attractive contractual framework, known as the Iran Petroleum Contract. While the discussion continues to review other laws and regulations perceived to be important for the attraction of foreign investment, it answers the question of whether regulatory and contractual reform is in itself sufficient to ensure the long-term presence of foreign investors in the country.

### A historical review of oil and gas contractual frameworks

Contracting for the exploration and development of oil and gas fields in Iran can be traced back more than a century to the well-known

D'Arcy concession. As explained in Chapter 2, the initial exploration and development of petroleum resources, fully controlled by a foreign entity that possessed capital, know-how, and expertise, was based on concessions. The foreign company had an extensive and exclusive right to control resources in the area covered by the concession agreement against a royalty paid to the government. The government's role in these projects, and consequently its share in the profits, was quite insignificant compared with that of the foreign company.

Following the nationalization of the oil industry in 1951 and the enactment of the 1957 Petroleum Act, Iran concluded various types of contracts with foreign companies, including production sharing agreements and service contracts, to secure a larger share of profit for itself and a more influential role for NIOC. The 1957 Petroleum Act granted to NIOC the required authority to enter into agreements with domestic and foreign companies, with the aim of expanding as rapidly as possible the operation of research, exploration, and extraction of petroleum throughout the country and the continental shelf.[1] Deteriorating economic and political conditions in the aftermath of oil nationalization and the international oil embargo on Iran, forced the government to adopt a more moderate approach in which private foreign investment was encouraged, while opportunities were also provided for a more proactive role for NIOC.[2]

In 1974, a new Petroleum Act was passed by the Parliament imposing significant limitations on the participation of international oil companies in upstream oil and gas operations. The first traces of buyback contracts can be found in the 1974 legislation; these appear as 'service contracts' which were introduced as the prevailing contractual regime for the development of the hydrocarbon sector.[3] The Act prohibited contracts or ventures that would offer ownership of reserves to foreign entities. Article 3 of the Act emphasized the nationalization of the petroleum resources and dictated that any activities in respect of exploration, development, production, and operation must be exclusively carried out by NIOC. As a result, the government was no longer authorized to engage in production-sharing agreements, and for the first time in the country's history, the provisions of the 1974 Petroleum Act led to formation of 'risk-service contracts'.[4]

As reviewed in Chapter 2, following the 1979 Revolution, all existing oil and gas agreements were revoked and the Revolutionary government assumed full responsibility for controlling and developing the oil and gas industry. Iran then pursued an ideologically isolationist path that emphasized self-sufficiency and independence from foreign investment.[5] The government actively shaped the country's overall

economic policy through a legal framework with the explicit prohibition of foreigners' presence in the petroleum sector.[6] The enactment
of the 1987 Petroleum Act also reaffirmed the restrictions already in
place, highlighting the overall mood of xenophobia and pessimism
towards foreign involvement which had intensified during and after
the Iran–Iraq war.

In the early 1980s, the government only offered agreements which
used the services of oil companies under turnkey or EPC contracts.
In these contracts, the scope of the project was precisely defined and
prices were fixed for all materials and services to be rendered by
contractors.[7] However, as the budget for the projects would have to be
allocated through public funds, the government had to struggle seriously
to provide the required capital, due to the shortage of foreign currency
as a result of the war. Also the rigidity of the agreements made it very
difficult to accommodate any changes in the contractual and fiscal
terms which would directly affect project viability. The first solution to
these problems, whose terms were within the restrictive boundaries set
by the Act and the Constitution, was to obtain short- to medium-term
loans to finance projects. In 1988, the Parliament also authorized the
government to conclude up to $3.2 billion worth of agreements with
competent foreign companies for the development of the Pars and
South Pars gas fields, provided that all costs would be recovered by
the output of these projects. Based on this mechanism, international
companies were required to provide funding and complete the project
as NIOC's contractor, while the risk of any shortfall in production was
borne by NIOC.[8]

Substantial damage inflicted by the war, however, forced the government to urgently seek capital investment and technology to reconstruct
its petroleum industry and maintain government revenue through oil
exports. As there was strong legal opposition to foreign investment,
both in the Revolutionary Constitution and in the 1987 Petroleum
Act, the Ministry of Petroleum and NIOC had to present a solution
which, while being in full compliance with the provisions of the law,
would provide a sufficiently attractive contractual framework to enable
and promote foreign investment in the petroleum sector. The proposed
solution was buyback contracts.

## Origin and background of the Iranian buyback contracts

The legal and contractual regime in the Iranian petroleum sector is
highly influenced by the country's history. The experience of foreign

dominance of the country's petroleum resources (see Chapter 2) led to the adoption of severe restrictions on foreign companies and investors.[9] Shari'a law also played a major role in the establishment of a post-Revolution regulatory system with the ownership, control, and management of mineral and petroleum rights, all governed by the Shari'a principles.[10] According to the Ja'afari school of Islamic law,[11] private property of minerals is not lawful, and nor is extraction except as a part of the state's commercial activity.[12] The theory stems from a broader Islamic notion that recognition of private ownership of natural resources will be against the public interest, as it will lead to corruption and an unfair distribution of such wealth.[13] These provisions have also been explicitly reflected in various articles of the Constitution and the Petroleum Act of 1987.

### The Constitution

Restrictive provisions concerning the involvement of foreigners in the development of the hydrocarbon sector can be found in various articles of the Constitution. As a matter of general economic and financial principle, Article 43 of the Constitution bans foreign economic 'domination' of the country's economy. Article 45 stipulates that the disposition of public wealth and property, such as 'mineral deposits', should be solely in the hands of the government, as should (according to Article 44) the ownership of all large-scale and 'mother industries'.[14] A broad interpretation of these articles implies that oil and gas reserves are state-owned and only the government can and should administer public assets; the private sector is only granted a supplementary role in the economic activities of the state.[15]

The issue of involvement of foreigners in economic activity is more specifically addressed in Articles 81, 82, and 153. Article 81 stipulates that granting concessions to foreigners for the formation of companies or institutions dealing with commerce, industry, agriculture, services, or mineral extraction, is absolutely forbidden. But the Article, according to the Council of Guardians' advisory opinion, does not restrict the establishment of foreign companies' branches in Iran. Furthermore, following ratification of the Foreign Investment Promotion and Protection Act (FIPPA), restrictions on registration and incorporation of foreign companies were abolished, and the establishment of subsidiaries of foreign companies with 100 per cent foreign ownership became possible.[16]

Most controversies over participation of foreign investors in the petroleum sector arise from the provisions of Article 153, which places a total ban on the conclusion of agreements that would result in foreign control over natural resources, economic resources, military affairs, and other strategic sectors. Hence, by implication, the Article asserts, for example, that in the petroleum sector there are no rights for IOCs to own equity or book reserves – a restriction which has caused most criticism of the buyback regime.[17]

Article 82 forbids the employment of 'foreign experts except in cases of necessity', and then only subject to parliamentary approval. The Article is complemented by the provisions of the Law of Maximum Utilization of Technical, Engineering, Production, Industrial, and Executive Potential (1997), which requires utilization of at least 51 per cent local content in development projects. The Article also requires parliamentary approval for the transfer of property to foreigners, without which such transfers are prohibited.

## The Petroleum Act 1987

The Petroleum Act of 1987 was ratified when the country was involved in the war with Iraq and there was a growing sensitivity about foreign investment. Consequently, the new petroleum law placed major restrictions on involvement of foreign companies in the petroleum industry. Article 2 of the Act reaffirms the provisions of the Constitution by providing that petroleum resources are part of the public domain, which belongs to the Iranian people and remains at the disposal and control of the government.[18] The Act banned any form of direct foreign investment in the oil and gas sector and required that all activities should be carried out under the control and supervision of the Ministry of Petroleum. According to Article 5, the involvement of local and foreign individuals and companies in the petroleum sector was only permitted provided that they enter into contracts with the Ministry of Petroleum or its affiliated companies. Article 6 envisages that all capital investment required for petroleum projects should be proposed by the Ministry of Petroleum and be included in the annual budget. This Article, in practice, put major restrictions on the amount of capital which could be invested in the petroleum sector.

## The Budget Acts and Five-Year Development Plans

The buyback contract was first introduced in the 1993 Budget Act and the Second Five-Year Development Plan (1996–2000). According to the Budget Act, NIOC was authorized to enter into contracts with IOCs up to the value of $2.6 billion, provided that:[19]

- no equity shall be granted to the contracting party to the oil whether produced or in the ground;
- instalments shall be paid exclusively from exports of resultant outputs of the project, and therefore no guarantee shall be provided in terms of any shortfall in production;
- utilization of Iran's existing potential in designing, engineering, construction, and installation shall be maximized;
- transfer of technology shall be accomplished through joint-venture agreements between local and foreign companies; and
- a minimum of 30 per cent of Iranian content shall be included.

In order to comply with the provisions of the Constitution, the Budget Act remained reluctant to envisage any guarantee by Iranian banks or state enterprises for recovery of costs and profits in the event of production decline or decrease of oil and gas prices.[20] Although the concept of a buyback contract was first created in the Budget Act 1993, it was not until the Budget Act 1994 that the term 'buyback' was first mentioned, authorizing NIOC to conclude up to $3.5 billion worth of investment for the development of Assaluyeh gas refinery and South Pars gas field.[21]

The first orchestrated attempt to introduce buyback contracts to the international investment market was during a specially held conference in London in July 1998, at which Iran offered more than 40 onshore and offshore fields under the buyback formula to foreign oil and gas companies.[22] The first buyback contract was signed with American-based Conoco Oil Company, but this was later cancelled as a result of ISA (the Iran Sanctions Act).[23] The French company, Total, subsequently replaced Conoco and entered into an agreement with NIOC for development of the Sirri A and E offshore oilfield, with expected rates of return of 20 and 23 per cent, respectively.[24] In the period between 1998 and 2013, 14 exploration contracts and 20 buybacks were concluded between NIOC and foreign investors, considerably less than the number of projects that the Iranian authorities had offered in the first place.[25]

The permission granted for foreign investment in oil and gas projects through buyback contracts was extended in the Third, Fourth, and Fifth Five-Year Development Plans. Articles 125 and 126 of the Fifth Development Plan (2011–15) explicitly introduce buyback contracts as the main contractual method for attraction of foreign investment in the petroleum industry. The Plan also envisaged other financial sources, in addition to buyback contracts, for development of Iran's hydrocarbon sector. These sources were planned to circumvent the impact of international sanctions and included: domestic and international bonds, Islamic finance, investment by national banks, national development funds (including the establishment of an Iranian expatriates' joint investment fund), a designated bank of the oil and gas industry, and exploitation of NIOC's internal fund.[26] However, as sanctions became increasingly burdensome, the possibility of taking recourse to these methods vanished amid strictly limited access to international financial institutions, and lack of interest from international banks.

### Legal and fiscal terms of buyback contracts

The Iranian buyback contract has been categorized as a 'risk-service contract'[27] in which the IOC agrees to develop an oil or natural gas field, and then to hand it over to NIOC once production starts. The IOC in return will be repaid at a level based on certain percentages of production at the field on an agreed-upon rate of return. Once the contractor has been fully repaid, it no longer has any share in the project.

The buyback framework has undergone an evolutionary process to offer more incentives to the foreign investors. Before the signing of early contracts, such as those signed for the development of Sirri oilfield and some of South Pars phases, exploration activity had already been carried out and the economic viability of the project was proven. For this first generation of buybacks, IOCs were invited to tender and to provide a Master Development Plan (MDP)[28] based on the data and information which had been collected during the exploration stage. The fiscal structure of buyback contracts features different stages of expenditure including: capital cost (Capex), non-capital cost (non-Capex), operating cost (Opex), and bank charges. Capital costs include the direct cost of development operations, which are recoverable up to the agreed-upon ceiling. Thus, any costs incurred by the IOC which go beyond the ceiling will not be reimbursed. Indirect costs are the funds paid by the IOC to the government for projected taxes, social security charges, customs duties, and other levies. Operational costs cover the IOC's expenses during the project operation, prior to handing it over to NIOC. There is no cap on Opex which are all fully recoverable. Finally, bank charges include the cost of financing the project, are calculated on the basis of the London Interbank Offered Rate (LIBOR) plus an extra agreed-upon interest percentage.[29] All these costs are recoverable provided that: firstly, the objectives of the contract as stipulated under the MDP materialize; secondly, the authenticity of the costs is verified by NIOC or an international auditor; and thirdly, that costs are correctly categorized in accordance with the accounting procedure annexed to the contract.[30]

In addition to costs, a remuneration fee is also envisaged in buyback contracts; this is generally a fixed amount agreed upon by the parties, to be paid to the IOC as a reward for its investment and risks.[31] The fees recoverable by the IOC are paid through allocation of a certain portion of outputs of the projects, which is usually around 50–60 per cent. Since the IOC has no rights to the oil or gas in place, or the oil at the wellhead and export point, NIOC either sells the oil and gas to the IOC itself or to a third party.[32]

The buyback provisions also include a requirement that the lands and purchased assets for the purpose of project development should be the sole property of NIOC. The operating company is also obliged to use at least 51 per cent local content – to give local companies a competitive advantage. In comparison with other petroleum development contracts, conventional buyback contracts have a shorter life, about seven to ten years, with a possible extension for an additional five years as an 'investment recovery period'.

Buyback contracts are reportedly more popular for the production of oil than gas, which is a more challenging commodity to commercialize.[33] In buyback contracts for the development of gas, there is normally no specific price per unit and the buyback contract only stipulates the agreed-upon remuneration and internal rate of return.[34] Also, as natural gas development is different from oil (in the sense that it requires an integrated value chain from production to the end-users) there are uncertainties over the possibility, and indeed the necessity, of extension of the contracts to downstream production activities, particularly LNG.

### Buybacks second and third generations

Since their introduction as Iran's sole contractual regime for development of upstream oil and gas resources, buyback contracts have received much criticism from both IOCs and the officials of NIOC. The authorities, particularly after Rouhani's election, did not hesitate to openly criticize buyback. In an interview, Mehdi Hosseini head of the Contracts Revision Committee, openly admitted that buybacks are a one-sided regime which only serve the interest of the Iranian counterpart, and leave foreign investors with no incentive to participate in the development of the country's oil and gas fields.[35]

Buyback contracts have been criticized on several grounds, including their fixed rate of return, short-term participation of IOCs in the development of the field, and impossibility to book reserves. This criticism, combined with the Iranian government's determination to improve the investment climate, brought about creeping changes in the legal and fiscal structure of buybacks. In December 2009, Iran signed a buyback contract with China's Sinopec, whose terms were perceived as a notable improvement.[36] The contract was signed for development of Yadavaran field and offered better terms of investment, including:[37]

- a better payback period, which was reduced to around four years (almost half that of earlier buyback contracts);
- a rate of return, which increased to 14.98 per cent (from its previous 10–12 per cent) with no risk, embedding a premium of 3 per cent compared with older contracts;
- for the first time, flexibility towards potential cost escalation was envisaged in the contract, significantly reducing investment risks.

One of the major changes in the new model was a more flexible and realistic approach toward cost calculation of projects. There were concerns, however, that, despite these new provisions, the actual practice of authorities and the clauses in the final draft of buyback contracts may not fully reflect the intended flexibility of the new provisions.[38]

A set of incentives was also introduced in the new buyback models to encourage better performance by the IOCs. These incentives include:

- an alternative ceiling on the rate of return if actual quarterly production exceeds the production profile envisaged in the MDP; and
- payment of additional percentages of the remuneration fee if the IOC increases the local content beyond the mandatory percentage.[39]

More significantly, this new generation of buyback contract envisages the possibility of extending the term of the contract for full recovery to as long as 12–15 years. Such provisions could provide great relief for contractors who have been facing the risk of expiry of their contract before completing cost recovery, as was the case in the old model where amortization could not continue beyond the expiry of the contract.[40]

The new buyback model also envisaged the continuation of the Joint Management Committee (JMC) from the project's inception and beyond, in order to have the IOCs' managerial expertise onboard throughout the life of the contract. In addition, it required the establishment of sub-committees for technical, administrative, financial, and legal matters affecting the development of the project at different stages of exploration, appraisal, and development, enabling both IOCs and NIOC to better evaluate the project's optimal development.[41]

The new contractual and fiscal terms introduced in the buyback contracts never had a chance of being included in any new oil and gas contracts with western IOCs, as a result of international sanctions and the consequent lack of interest from investors.

## The new upstream contractual regime: a flexible framework to offer greater incentives

The reform of Iranian upstream oil and gas contracts came at the top of Zanganeh's agenda immediately after he was appointed as oil minister in summer 2013. Noting that in the prevailing competitive environment in the Middle East, better contractual terms should be offered to attract foreign investors, and being aware that buybacks had failed to achieve this goal, Zanganeh established and authorized the Contract Revision Committee to design and present a new contractual framework which, while being attractive to foreign investors, would also serve national interests. In parallel with extensive diplomatic efforts to solve the nuclear dispute with the international community, the new upstream contractual regime will, according to Iranian officials, be competitive with contracts offered by other countries in the region.

The new model is being drafted following a comprehensive analysis of upstream petroleum contracts in more than 30 countries. The model reportedly resembles Iraq's Technical Service Contracts (TSCs),[42] although according to Iranian officials, it offers more lucrative legal and fiscal terms to attract long-term participation of oil companies in the recovery process of the country's oil and gas industry. In Iraq, for example, for the development of giant fields such as Rumaila, the federal government has offered a fixed margin based on a predetermined development plan; a practice that the authorities believe will not work in Iran. Therefore, in contrast to the restrictive approach in buybacks, in the new model, the government is looking for longer-term commitments, as long as 25–30 years, in which foreign companies can have an active presence in the operation and maintenance of fields, while Iranian companies will also thrive. The new contracts are unique to Iran and do not follow the structure of any already established framework such as PSAs or TSCs; hence the term 'Iran Petroleum Contract' or IPC.

In drafting the new model, the Revision Committee has put great emphasis on a long-demanded win–win framework in which investors' risks and rewards are proportionate. In the new models, the different phases of a field's development – namely exploration, development, and operation – are integrated and awarded under a single contractual package. The rate of return on investment will be proportionate with the progress made in each phase of the field's development and, for the first time since buybacks, the Central Bank will guarantee the returns. NIOC can form partnerships for crude oil and gas production with international companies to manage the project, provide financing, and maximize oil and gas recovery. Companies conducting exploration projects will be remunerated for their work with a share of the output. Moreover, international companies will act as the sole operator of exploration blocks and will be responsible for the risks involved in those projects, although NIOC may also act as a technical partner in the development process.

In buyback contracts, taxes did not play an effective role in the control of the contractor's income. In fact, the accrued taxes paid by the contractor would be reimbursed to it under non-capital costs. In IPCs, a tax rate of around 30–35 per cent is planned. Also, Signature Bonuses, absent from buybacks, will be included in the new model. Investors will be offered an increased incentive to improve their cost savings, as no longer will any interest be paid on their investment costs, as was the case under buybacks. In practice, under the new model the investor has to reduce investment costs and improve operational efficiency, because its profit depends on long-term production and efficient operation, using the latest technologies and know-how.

To encourage investors, greater remuneration will be offered for the development of smaller and mature fields, joint-fields, and riskier exploration and production projects such as those in deep water. According to Mehdi Hosseini, fees paid to international partners will be linked to international oil prices and based on a sliding scale; this means that the development of riskier fields will attract higher remuneration rates.[43] The new contract will also include incentives for extending the life of fields and enhancing recovery rates. Enhanced oil recovery (EOR) projects form one of the most important categories of project for which the new models are expected to attract substantial capital and technology. In addition, future partners can recover all development costs linked to an exploration project at the start of production, and if they do not find oil or gas in a block, they will be offered exploration rights in nearby areas.

The reservoir's ownership as asserted by the Constitution is not transferable and belongs to the nation. But in the new model, ownership of the produced oil by foreign companies is said to be possible and they can report future revenue for valuation purposes.[44] The right to book reserves, which has been the main reason behind Iran's reluctance to offer PSAs, is also envisaged under special conditions and is negotiable – as long as it does not entitle the investors to claim reserve ownership, and is for the development of fields in which the risks involved are so high that the government has to offer better terms.[45] Such projects, for example, include ageing joint-fields, Caspian Sea deep water drilling, and exploration projects in less rich hydrocarbon regions.[46] Under buybacks, the ownership of petroleum, whether in place or produced, was not possible irrespective of how challenging the development of the field might have been. The changes in the new model are also in line with the new legislation put forward by the previous government and ratified by Parliament to make buybacks more appealing to foreign investors. For example, Article 125(3) of the Fifth Development Plan authorizes the oil ministry to conclude development and production contracts for the development of joint-fields, which by implication means that the production phase could be incorporated into buybacks, allowing ownership of production to be transferred to the operator.

At the time of writing, the launch of the new model was planned to take place at a conference in London in November 2014.

## The foreign investment regime

Despite all the criticism of buyback contracts, they were relatively successful in attracting foreign investment to the hydrocarbon sector before the imposition of sanctions. In the early stages of opening up its petroleum sector to foreign companies in the late 1990s, Iran attracted more than $8 billion worth of foreign investments. As shown in Table 4.1, the aggregate value of investment contracts with international companies since 1999 is over $70 billion.

The intensification of international sanctions since 2006, together with a lack of improvement in the contractual and investment regime, slowed down investment and caused all major IOCs to pull out of Iran or decline to make further investments. As a result, Iran lost billions of dollars worth of investment – either for agreements which it had entered into, or relating to contracts it could have concluded. Although some of these investments were taken up by Asian and east European companies (as shown in Table 4.1) many such replacement deals failed to progress due to unfavourable terms, or lack of technical capacity of the investor, or reconsideration by the investors of the risks of US sanctions (see Chapter 3).[47]

**Table 4.1:** Major proposed investments in Iran's energy sector (1999–2011)

| Date | Field / Project | Investors | Value |
|------|-----------------|-----------|-------|
| Feb 1999 | Doroud (oil) | Total/ENI | $1 billion |
| Apr 1999 | Balal (oil) | Total/Bow Valley/ENI | $300 million |
| Nov 1999 | Soroush and Nowruz (oil) | Royal Dutch Shell/Japex | $800 million |
| Apr 2000 | Anaran Bloc (oil) | Norsk Hydro & Statoil/ Gazprom & Lukoil | $105 million |
| Jul 2000 | Phases 4 & 5, South Pars | ENI | $1.9 billion |
| Mar 2001 | Caspian Sea oil exploration | GVA Consultants | $225 million |
| Jun 2001 | Darkhovin (oil) | ENI | $1 billion |
| May 2002 | Masjed Soleyman (oil) | Sheer Energy/CNPN | $80 million |
| Sept 2002 | Phases 9 & 10, South Pars | LG Engineering and Construction | $1.6 billion |
| Oct 2002 | Phases 6–8, South Pars | Statoil | $750 million |
| Jan 2004 | Azadegan (oil) | Inpex 10% stake. CNPC agreed to develop north Azadegan | $200 million (Inpex stake); China $1.76 billion |
| Aug 2004 | Tusan Block | Petrobras | $178 million |
| Oct 2004 | Yadavaran (oil) | Sinopec | $2 billion |
| Dec 2006 | North Pars Gas Field | China National Offshore Oil Co | $16 billion |
| Feb 2007 | LNG tanks at Tombak Port | Daelim ( S. Korea) | $320 million |
| Feb 2007 | Phases 13 & 14, South Pars Investors pulled out | Royal Dutch Shell/ Repsol | $4.3 billion |
| Jul 2007 | Phases 22–24, South Pars | Turkish Petroleum Company (TPAO) | $12 billion |

**Table 4.1:** *continued*

| Date | Field/Project | Investors | Value |
|------|---------------|-----------|-------|
| Dec 2007 | Golshan and Ferdowsi onshore and offshore gas fields and LNG plant | SKS Ventures, Petrofield Subsidiary (Malaysia) | $15 billion |
| 2007 | Jofeir Field (oil) | Belarusneft/ Naftiran | $500 million |
| Feb 2008 | Lavan Field | PGNiG (Poland) | $2 billion |
| Apr 2008 | Kish gas field | Oman | $7 billion |
| Jun 2008 | Resalat oil field | Amona (Malaysia), joined by CNOOC and COSL | $1.5 billion |
| Jan 2009 | North Azadegan | CNPC | $1.75 billion |
| Mar 2009 | Phase 12, South Pars | Indian firms (ONGC, Oil India Ltd, Hinduja and Petronet); Sonanagol (Angola) and PDVSA (Venezuela) | $8 billion |
| Oct 2009 | South Pars– Phases 6–8 gas sweetening plant | G and S Engineering and Construction (S.Korea) | $1.4 billion |
| Nov 2009 | South Pars: phase 12, part 2 and 3 | Daelim (part 2) and Tecnimont (part 3) | $4 billion |
| Feb 2010 | Phase 11, South Pars | CNPC | $4.7 billion |
| Dec 2011 | Zaagheh oil field | Tatneft (Russia) | $1 billion |

Source: Katzman (2012).

The Rouhani government's initiative to reform the upstream contractual framework, along with the more investor-friendly laws and regulations which have been enacted during the last 10 years, has improved the prospects for foreign investment. Some of this legislation will be reviewed in the next section.

### The Foreign Investment Promotion and Protection Act (FIPPA)

The Foreign Investment Promotion and Protection Act (FIPPA) is considered a remarkable move by the reformist government of Khatami, aiming at reforming and improving the old and inefficient investment regime and its supporting regulatory framework.

FIPPA came into force in 2002 after a long disagreement between Parliament and the Council of Guardians over its ratification. As explained in Chapter 3, the law making process in Iran is complicated. The legislative process requires all approved Parliamentary bills to be verified by another clerical body, the Council of Guardians, based on the provisions of Shari'a and the Constitution. In the case of rejection of a bill by the Council of Guardians and Parliament's insistence on the bill's final ratification, a third body, known as the Expediency Council, adjudicates between them. The latter body has ultimate authority to approve provisions which have already been considered unconstitutional by the Council of Guardians for the sake of the national 'Maslahat'. (The concept of 'Maslahat', which is generally translated as 'expediency', is a political manoeuvring tool employed to deem certain actions legal for the sake of overall national interest, despite being officially illegal.) The Expediency Council is the sole authoritative body in Iran which can resort to 'Maslahat' to overcome deadlocks on key policy issues which are recognized as unconstitutional or against Shari'a law. Therefore, the approval of FIPPA, although recognized as unconstitutional, created a precedent in favour of the possibility of future changes in the Iranian legal framework if the national interest so requires.

FIPPA maintains most of the provisions of its predecessor, the 1956 Law for the Attraction and Protection of Foreign Investment (LAPFI). However, it goes beyond this and provides protection for investment schemes not covered under the latter. FIPPA provides protection for virtually all activities of foreign investors, whether in the form of direct investment or through non-equity participation; it also covers civil partnership, build, operate and transfer (BOT) schemes, and service contracts – such as buyback agreements.[48] In practice, FIPPA provisions make possible foreign direct investment (which is only permitted for economic activities conducted by the private sector) either through direct equity participation in the share capital of a company to be established, or by obtaining equity in an already established company;[49] or as foreign investment through a contractual framework, be it a joint-venture, BOT, or buyback.

The Act's permission for foreign investment – within the framework of civil partnership and buyback arrangements in all sectors – is in direct conflict with the Constitutional provisions, which strictly prohibit private sector involvement in strategic industries such as the oil and gas sector and related exploration, production, and export activities.[50] Not only do the provisions of FIPPA permit foreign participation in strategic industries, but they also remove all restrictions on the percentage of foreign shareholdings (Article 2.b.1.2). By implication, this solves the problem of foreign ownership restrictions by indicating that so long as a foreign investment project does not place more than a certain percentage of the relevant economic sector under its control, foreign ownership in a single project is admissible. The interpretation of Article 44 of the Constitution by the Expediency Council in 2004 also supports the provisions of FIPPA by permitting the private sector to participate in downstream oil and gas activities, while excluding direct participation of the private sector in upstream activities.

FIPPA may be criticized for its failure to provide a clear dispute settlement method or to introduce international regulation for competitive tendering; yet it is a modern and efficient legal framework for investment promotion and investor protection. By obtaining an 'investment licence' from the Organization for Investment and Economic and Technical Assistance of Iran (OIETAI), FIPPA also ensured that the investors' capital and profits will be convertible and transferable, creating a strong sense of security and assurance. In addition, it has shortened the bureaucratic processes involved in foreign investment and improved transparency and business planning.[51]

FIPPA provisions can specifically cover investments in LNG projects where the Iranian legal and regulatory framework lacks the required governing legislation. Article 2 of FIPPA requires foreign investors to apply for an investment licence (which would permit the admission of foreign investment for production activities in such projects) from OIETAI. A foreign investor seeking to participate in the development of an LNG project can be admitted through a joint venture, BOT, or a buyback contract – especially, in the case of the latter, when the project is incorporated with upstream activities.

The fact that Iranian regulations have not explicitly classified LNG operations as upstream or downstream activities can have implications for the method of investment. If an LNG project is an integrated part of an upstream activity, then investments should be made through a joint venture, BOT, or buyback.[52] Such a contractual arrangement has to be made in partnership with a state company, which is usually NIOC. Since the establishment of NIGEC in 2003, the latter has been also responsible for natural gas downstream operations and exports of gas, both LNG and pipeline. Therefore, an agreement for the development of an LNG project should be concluded between NIGEC/NIOC and the foreign investor. In the four major LNG projects offered to foreign investors in the early 2000s, the joint venture arrangement was the most common mechanism used.[53]

## The Law on International Commercial Arbitration

International investors are increasingly concerned that a dispute with the host state will be referred to domestic courts, with the risk of a biased and unfair judgement. Therefore, inclusion of an arbitration clause in the investment agreement is of utmost importance for investors. However, host states are reluctant to confer to a foreign tribunal the right to adjudicate over the country's domestic affairs, particularly when it concerns the development of the oil and gas sector which is generally considered a matter of sovereignty and national security.

Iran is no exception to this trend. According to Article 139 of the Constitution, settlement of claims related to public and state property, or the referral of such claims to arbitration, should be subject to the Council of Ministers' approval and Parliament must be notified. It further adds that in cases where the other party to a dispute is a foreigner, and in significant domestic issues, the ratification of Parliament is also mandatory. Accordingly, as is also envisaged in the draft of buyback contracts, the settlement of any disputes arising from investment in the petroleum sector may be referred to arbitration. A problem arises when prior approval is required from the Council of Ministers and Parliament for referral of a dispute to an arbitration tribunal. In practice, if a dispute arises between NIOC and an IOC, the latter may refer the case to arbitration while NIOC is seeking approval from the Parliament and Council of Ministers which, in case of rejection, may abort the dispute settlement process. Although referral of a dispute by IOCs to an arbitration tribunal or a domestic court has rarely occurred, there are concerns that it may impose considerable risks upon foreign investors when negotiating and concluding investment deals with NIOC.

To improve dispute settlement and reduce uncertainties in the event of a dispute, the Government adopted legislation on international arbitration known as 'The Law on International Commercial Arbitration' (LICA) in 1997. Although there are shortcomings in the provisions of this law, it closely follows the model law adopted by the United Nations Commission on International Trade Law (UNCITRAL) on International Commercial Arbitration.[54] The Law provides for the establishment of an arbitral tribunal based on widely adopted international procedural codes.

In addition, FIPPA, though criticized for not taking a concrete stand on the vital issue of dispute resolution, has reaffirmed the possibility of recourse to arbitration if a Bilateral Investment Treaty (BIT) between Iran and the investor's state is in existence. Article 19 of FIPPA provides that, if disputes between the government of Iran and foreign investors are not settled amicably through negotiations, such disputes should be referred to domestic courts – unless another method for settlement of disputes is provided in the law relating to the mutual investment agreement being entered into (BIT) with the respective government or foreign investor.

Over the past two decades, Iran has signed more than 60 BITs with other countries – these include almost all European countries and the respective states of major IOCs.[55] Iran's BITs provide for settlement of disputes through arbitration, meaning that if a different method of dispute settlement is provided for in a BIT between Iran and the home country of the foreign investor, that method should be followed. The BITs that Iran has signed include a dispute settlement clause for arbitration under UNCITRAL Arbitration Rules, or arbitration at the International Centre for the Settlement of Investment Disputes (ICSID). To further strengthen the country's international investment dispute mechanism, Iran joined the New York Convention on the Recognition and Enforcement of Foreign Arbitral Awards (1958) in 2001,[56] guaranteeing recognition and enforcement of awards in Iran and virtually worldwide.

In addition to the dispute resolution mechanism, BITs are also designed to offer fair and equitable treatment through banning arbitrary or discriminatory measures; they also guarantee national and most-favoured-nation treatment to foreign investments.[57] BITs also offer protection to foreign-owned assets from state expropriation and nationalization, limiting the right of the host state to exceptional circumstances where a state expropriates foreign property on the grounds of national interest.

## Other regulations

### Registration and operation of foreign firms

As a result of Article 81 of the Constitution – which strictly forbids the granting of concessions on the formation of companies and institutes to foreigners in the fields of commerce, industry, agriculture, mining, and services – there was a general perception that the establishment of Iranian companies by foreigners, as well as the registration of branches and representative offices of foreign companies, was impossible. The resulting uncertainty made the then Prime Minister Rajai submit an inquiry to the Council of Guardians, requesting a legal interpretation. The Council clarified the fact that foreign companies which have concluded contracts with Iranian public entities may register branches of their companies in Iran according to Article 3 of the Act of Registration of Companies.[58] The government subsequently presented a bill to Parliament to legalize registration of branches and representative offices of foreign companies in Iran, which led to ratification of the Law on Registration and Operation of Foreign Firms in 1997. A decade later, in 2008, a new directive came into force allowing the Tehran Company Registration Bureau to register companies in mainland Iran which were up to 100 per cent foreign controlled, without any need to obtain a foreign investment licence. Prior to this new directive, the operation of foreign companies had only been possible through a joint partnership with an Iranian entity and with a maximum 49 per cent share for the foreign partner.

### Patents, industrial designs, and trademarks

IOCs' concern over protection of their patents in the process of technology transfer to Iran was addressed in 2008 by ratification of the Law on Registration of Patent, Industrial Designs, and Trademarks. This law replaced the Trademarks and Patents Registration Act of 1932 and is considered the most important regulation with respect to protection of trademarks and industrial property rights in Iran. The law envisages full protection of IP rights and prohibits any unauthorized use of invention, trademark, or industrial design by anyone other than the owner. With regard to trademarks, the exclusivity right also extends to the use of marks that resemble the registered trademarks and that could lead to public confusion or deception.[59] The law, however, envisages an exception to the exclusivity of the patents where the government, 'for the sake of national security, health, and economy' may seek to use a patented invention in an unauthorized way.[60] As the scope of such an exception is not clearly defined by the regulator, it can be considered a serious loophole in the law through which the government can, based on its own interpretation of national security and economic considerations, infringe an investor's patent rights.

### Free Economic Zones

The Law on the Administration of Free Trade Zones (FTZ) passed the Parliament in 1993, granting special rights to foreign investors in FTZs. Iranian FTZs seek to attract capital investment through offering special economic incentives and facilities. Article 12 of the Law envisages exemptions for foreign investors from the requirements of the Labour

Law, the payment of the social security and insurance premium, the issuance of residence and work permits, and taxation of investment income. With the approval of the Board of Ministers, the importation of goods produced in the free zones to the mainland are also exempted from payment of all or part of customs duties and commercial profit tax. There are also special provisions which grant credit guarantees and assure repatriation of investment capital. The initiative was also followed up through setting up 'Special Economic Zones' to facilitate transit of goods, and to improve supply and distribution networks, through granting the same special benefits, including exemption from levies and import/export taxes.[61] The Pars Special Economic Energy Zone (PSEEZ) is an example of these special economic zones; it was established in 1998, to offer special privileges to foreign investors investing in the development of oil and gas activities in the South Pars region, including LNG and petrochemical projects.

## Is the contractual and regulatory reform sufficient?

A review of academic literature and industry's common practice shows that the reform of legal and regulatory frameworks to improve the investment environment is necessary but not sufficient. Supporters of legal reform and its role in promoting development have come under attack from those challenging the assumption that law plays a significant causal role in economic development.[62] Implementing reforms in the legal system of a country does not necessarily bring about desired developments. As an empirical study by Perry (2000) shows, in the context of international economic activities (such as foreign direct investments) although neo-institutional economic theory predicts that foreign investors will be attracted to states with 'effective' (that is: stable, accessible, predictable, and clear) legal systems, 'there is little empirical evidence to suggest that they are so attracted.'[63] Wälde (2005) also argues that there is no evidence proving that a developed and effective legal framework can be considered a necessary condition either for economic development or for a growth in international investment.[64] He rejects the general assumption that very large investment projects – like those typical in the oil and gas industry – would be carried out 'on the basis of a developed, comprehensive, favourable, and stable system of law.'[65] He presents the Persian Gulf region as an example where some of the world's largest oil and gas investments have been carried out, 'without any basis in a developed system of law, but mainly on the basis of legally problematic state–investor agreements.'[66]

In discussions about the role of legal reform in economic development, distinctions have been made between substantive and institutional law. Scholars like Dam (2006) strongly reject any correlation between substantive law and improvement of the rule of law, and maintain that 'no degree of improvement in even global "best practice" substantial law will bring the rule of law to a country that does not have effective enforcement.'[67] In other words, it is the rule of law, or enforceability of the law, which provides confidence to investors and attracts foreign capital, and that to a great extent depends on the host state's policies toward investment and economic development. In fact, it is the state's choice of policy, which is manifested in positive law, that makes the enforceability of a contract, or protection of investment, possible. Therefore, in the hierarchy of factors influencing promotion and protection of investments, government policies stand above laws and regulations.

To a significant extent, policy and the policy-making process itself is influenced by social, political, historical, and economic factors. Political instabilities and uncertainties resulting from the influence of any of these factors can undermine the enforceability of law, no matter how advanced. In the case of Iran, complicated, opaque, policy making mechanisms, and the resulting concerns about who is the ultimate decision maker, have caused serious damage to the perception of the country as a safe investment environment. As explained in Chapter 2, politicization and exertion of influence by multiple parallel institutions have created serious confusion and uncertainty, and have made the country's investment environment extremely unpredictable. Unless improvements are made in the policy making process, and in the state's determination to establish the rule of law and guarantee its enforceability, attempts to reform the legal system may not achieve the expected result. To fulfil the goal of regulatory reforms, the government has to enhance the role of governance institutions which, as a result of the syndrome of politicization, have been weakened causing mismanagement, corruption, and failure to enforce the law.

## The role of governance institutions

In a report by the World Bank in 2014, Iran was ranked 152 out of 189 countries for ease of doing business.[68] The report took into account criteria, such as property protection and contract enforcement, to evaluate the efficiency and effectiveness of the bureaucratic and institutional governance of the examined countries.

Governance institutions are identified by some scholars as a leading element in any country's investment climate. Aysan et. al. (2007) explain that as investment decisions are mainly driven by profitability motives and their forward looking nature, 'good' governance institutions can reduce the uncertainty, and promote the efficiency, required for improving bureaucratic performances and predictability, and ultimately reduce the cost of doing business.[69] In the majority of the resource-rich countries of the MENA region, including Iran, the concerns and uncertainties related to the application of the rule of law as a result of the discretionary power of the host state, are more challenging than that of adopting a modern, investor-friendly legal framework. In the regulatory process, what matters is the way the law works, not how it is formulated. The host state's governance structure, including the judicial system, must be reasonably stable, transparent, and predictable and it should not be 'corrupt'.[70] The lack of an efficient administrative and judicial capacity in most resource-rich countries of the region has caused significant transaction costs and corruption, creating a negative atmosphere around secure and profitable trade and investment in these countries.[71] Corruption – widespread among these countries – weakens property rights, deprives investors of available compensation for risk-taking, and increases uncertainty about potential investment returns, directly impacting incentives to invest and in turn dampening economic growth.[72] For example, Mauro (1995), through (subjective) indices based on surveys of investors, proved that higher corruption is associated with lower investment and growth.[73]

In addition, consistent and non-discriminatory application of law is a crucial factor in creating trust. Property rights and security of contract constitute powerful disciplinary constraints on the behaviour of both the host state and investor, 'but only when they are consistently enforced.'[74] The protection of property rights and the enforcement of contracts are two major elements of economic development, endogenous to underlying political bargains and institutions.[75] A sound judiciary system is the key to enforcement. Better-performing, independent courts have been shown to lead to a more rapid growth of small, as well as larger, companies.[76] As Haggard and et. al. (2007) put it, 'a vicious circle of enforcement inefficiency' will, first of all, make the judicial system 'a non-dependable institution' diminishing investors' confidence; secondly, it will increase production costs by diverting resources into rent seeking; finally, and most importantly, it will introduce distortions that will constitute barriers to long-run growth including: monopolies, restriction on entry, protectionism, misallocation of government spending, and private expropriation of assets through managerial malfeasance.[77]

The investment risks and uncertainties in Iran mostly stem from its weak, non-transparent, and (to a large extent) corrupt governance institutions. Iran has a poor record on enforcement of contracts and on fair protection of property rights, which are of utmost importance to investors. Corruption and rent-seeking attitudes are widespread both in the judicial and administrative institutions, particularly when dealing with oil- and gas-related matters where the financial interests at stake are enormous.[78] Such weak and inefficient governance institutions will not be able to meet the level of protection required by foreign investors. In other words, regardless of any reform in the country's regulatory and contractual regime, as long as enforcement bodies do not operate independently and effectively, and in the light of concerns about changes of policy caused by interventions of multiple political powers, the prospect for 'long-term', large scale participation of foreign investors remains dubious.

## Conclusions

For about two decades since Iran's decision to open up its oil and gas sectors to foreign investors, buyback contracts were the only contractual means for upstream development of hydrocarbon resources. Despite all criticisms, buybacks initially managed to attract a considerable amount of investment. But increasingly stringent US and international sanctions, and the failure of buybacks to adapt to the evolving circumstances, made them so unattractive that international oil companies claimed that even if sanctions are removed, they are not willing to invest under such contracts. Noting these shortcomings, the Rouhani government undertook initiatives to design a new contractual model which will offer better investment terms compared with buybacks and with development contracts offered elsewhere in the region. The new model, which does not follow the structure of any other existing contractual framework, is designed to offer various incentives based on flexible terms which vary depending on the fields for which the contract is concluded.

The reforms of the contractual framework, combined with the already existing laws and regulations, have revived hopes among stakeholders for a better, more investor-friendly, environment. The reforms can be particularly attractive for the development of natural gas resources, where an integrated contractual system is needed to cover development activities in different segments of upstream and downstream operations over a long period of time. The flexible terms of the new contract, and its emphasis on integration of all development activities under one contractual system, can be especially attractive to investors interested in export projects where the disconnection between upstream development and downstream activities had previously caused serious operational challenges. The government's willingness to offer flexibility in its future contractual arrangements with IOCs is likely to be particularly important for the development of joint-fields such as South Pars, from which Qatar has been producing gas for many years.

However, although these new changes are very important, and should be given credit for their role in returning Iran's oil and gas sector back to the international spotlight, they might not be sufficient for the country to establish long-term, mutually beneficial business relations with foreign companies. Empirical evidence shows that improvement in the rule of law and its enforceability is more important than reforms in substantive law in attracting investors. To a large extent this depends on effective and efficient operation of governance institutions (which are in charge of protecting the legitimate interests of investors), and on promotion of the rule of law. In Iran, particularly during the eight years of the Ahmadinejad presidency, governance institutions, including the judiciary and bureaucratic administrations, have been severely weakened and strongly influenced by rent-seeking, politically driven incentives, leaving them with little capacity to perform their role of just and fair protection and enforcement of investors' rights.

Therefore, while effective, long-term improvement of the investment environment needs reform of the legal and regulatory framework, more importantly it requires substantial structural reorganization in which the policy-making process is stable and transparent, and the systematic mismanagement and corruption are curbed, by enhancing the effectiveness of governance institutions. This is very important in natural gas projects, particularly those related to exports, where long-term, stable relations are a major requirement for success. In such projects, investment costs and financial interests are so large that, unless investors are confident that projects will not be exposed to unstable policy-making, they are likely to consider the risks to be too great.

# CHAPTER 5

# ENERGY SUBSIDIES AND THEIR REFORM

## Introduction

Iran's domestic consumption of natural gas has grown remarkably in the last 30 years, reaching 161 bcm in 2012 – a nearly 1600 per cent increase since the 1979 Revolution.[1] Low energy prices charged nationwide, due to government subsidies, have been one of the major impediments to controlling and rationalizing domestic consumption, turning the country into the third-largest gas consumer in the world after the USA and Russia.[2] As reviewed in Chapter 1, except for relatively small exports to Turkey, almost all the gas produced is consumed domestically plus those imports from Turkmenistan needed to fill the domestic deficit. Like most of the oil-exporting countries in the region, Iran has also had a long history of subsidizing the consumption of petroleum products. In 2010, the IEA reported that Iran had the highest share of fossil fuel consumption subsidies in the world, equivalent to almost 23 per cent of the country's GDP, and amounting to nearly $80 billion.[3] Although political and social considerations, including public support and concerns over disadvantaged groups, are usually put forward as reasons for subsidizing energy consumption, subsidies are economically costly and rarely serve the interests of the targeted groups.

This chapter addresses the issue of subsidies in Iran's energy market and evaluates their impact on the development of the gas sector. It also examines the extent to which the 2010 energy subsidies reform controlled the growth rate of domestic consumption, and whether the reform has improved the prospects for the gas industry.

## A short history of subsidies in Iran

Subsidies can be traced back four centuries, when ruling governments used them as a means to protect citizens from domestic and international economic volatility. During the Safavi and Qajar dynasties, ruling governments tended to indirectly subsidize food by offering tax exemption or supplying free seeds to farmers.[4] The first precedent in the government's direct intervention in supply and demand of food goes back to 1932 when, in compliance with Parliament's legislation, the government committed itself to buy cultivated wheat and store it in silos to minimize the impact of an ongoing famine.[5] For many years, governments continued to offer financial aid to the agricultural sector through either purchasing products at higher prices if supply exceeded demand, or selling them cheaper to consumers in the event of demand increase.

Following stable food subsidies, similar policies were introduced in the energy sector after World War II. Although during the 1960s the aggregate amount of subsidies paid by the government for essential commodities remained negligible (around IRR1.6 billion, equivalent to $20 million), it substantially increased following the 1970s oil price shock and reached IRR111 billion (equivalent to $1.4 billion) in 1976.[6] Rising oil prices and the continuously growing expectations of the population for enhancement of living standards made financing subsidies on such a large scale increasingly difficult.

After 1979, as a part of the 'revolutionary social compact', the government further expanded price controls.[7] As the policy was applied nationwide, it was widely perceived as a basic citizenship right, something that had been earned and deserved.[8] Soon after the Iran–Iraq war, in order to minimize economic hardship, the government introduced rationing in the form of subsidies for energy, basic foods, medicine, and utilities. Meanwhile, the policy of population growth, which had almost doubled the population from 34 million to around 60 million after the war, inflicted further heavy pressure both on national production and budgets.[9]

The challenges resulting from subsidies and their negative impact on the economy were first addressed in the First Five-Year Development Plan (1991–5). According to that plan, subsidies of essential commodities should target low-income groups, with the aim of gradual elimination. It was in the Third Development Plan (2001–5) that the regulator explicitly highlighted the importance of targeting, particularly energy subsidies, with several aims: rationalizing consumption of subsidized products and preventing their smuggling; promoting and encouraging investment and supporting domestic production of subsidized products; reducing benefits for wealthy households and increasing the subsidies for low-income families; and finally, providing resources for development of infrastructure and creating jobs.[10] The issue of energy subsidies was also addressed in Article 3 of the amendment to the Fourth Development Plan (2006–10), in which the government was obliged to prepare and present to Parliament a bill for revision of energy prices on an annual basis.[11] It was only several years later that the government took the required initiative to address the issue of energy subsidies and the urgent need for their reform decisively.

## An overview of domestic natural gas pricing

Domestic energy prices have been historically set by the government. Since the commercialization of natural gas in the early 1960s, the government has actively pursued a policy of promoting consumption through low prices. This precedent dates back to 1960 when the first transmission pipeline was inaugurated, delivering Gachsaran gas to Shiraz. In 1961, the first commercial consumer, namely Namazi Hospital in Shiraz, received gas at IRR0.8/cm,[12] 20 per cent below the price of the available alternative fuel, namely fuel oil.[13] In 1966, in order to encourage gas consumption in the industrial sector, the government adopted a consumption-based pricing policy in which pricing had a reverse correlation with volume; this meant that consumption of more than 0.85 mmcm of gas (30 mcf) would be charged on the special discounted rate of IRR1/cm, compared with IRR1.25/cm for any volume below that threshold.[14] Following the expansion of the natural gas network to other regions, the same pricing pattern was followed, being based on gas consumption in all sectors, including households, commercial, and government premises, with prices below the 'general tariff' category.

Not until 1968 were factors such as geographical location and consumption volume, or the consumer categories of public sector, industrial sector, and power plants, taken into account in gas pricing. (See Table 5.1)

**Table 5.1:** Natural gas pricing based on consumption volume and sector (1968)

| Category | Monthly Consumption Rate (cm) | Tehran (IRR/cm) | Public Sector (IRR/cm) | Khoozestan[15] (IRR/cm) |
|---|---|---|---|---|
| Public | <1000 | 2.2 | 2.0 | 1.9 |
| | 1001–10000 | 2.0 | 1.8 | 1.7 |
| | >100001 | 1.8 | 1.6 | 1.5 |
| Industry | 0–20000 | 1.2 | 1.1 | 0.8 |
| | 20001–200000 | 1.1 | 1.0 | 0.7 |
| | 200001–2000000 | 1.0 | 0.9 | 0.6 |
| | >2000000 | 0.9 | 0.8 | 0.6 |
| Power Generation | - | 0.65 | 0.55 | 0.60 |

Source: Nasr Esfahani (2008).

Pricing remained unchanged until the Islamic Revolution after which, in the period 1982–90, a new system based solely on consumption categories – households, commercial, industrial, and power generation sectors, was adopted. One of the advantages of this mechanism was that lower gas prices were charged for industrial and manufacturing sectors as a part of a state support scheme for industrial growth and economic development.

**Table 5.2:** Natural gas tariffs (1982–1990)

|   | Category | Price ( IRR/cm) |
|---|----------|-----------------|
| 1 | Household | 5 |
| 2 | Commercial | 5 |
| 3 | Industry | 2 |
| 4 | Power Generation | 2 |

Source: Nasr Esfahani (2008).

In the 1990s, facing growing concerns about rising consumption levels, the government, decided to gradually increase prices and include a consumption volume index in the formula. In 1997, in order to moderate peak household demand, a hybrid mechanism was introduced which varied depending on the season, with higher tariffs in the cold months of the year.

In 1998, a geographical index was also added to the formula and consequently the country was divided into seven geographical regions. Tariffs further increased in 2002, 2004, and 2006 after which a new gas pricing mechanism, based on a 'consumption pattern', was adopted; this mean that, depending on the region, tariffs for volumes within certain thresholds were fixed while additional volumes attracted extra charges.[16]

Despite these efforts to bring domestic market growth under control through gradual price increases, there was no evidence to suggest that the government had been successful in even controlling the upward consumption trend, let alone reversing it. As a result, pressure for gradual elimination of subsidies gained political momentum, despite concerns about its political and social complexities.

## Political and economic objectives of energy subsidies

Governments usually justify energy subsidies by putting forward the numerous social, political, and economic benefits derived from providing these goods and services to citizens. In this policy context, energy subsidies are given to alleviate energy poverty, promote economic development, and create jobs by providing access to affordable energy services. The ultimate aim is to enhance welfare protection or social equity. Subsidies are also implemented as a means of protecting the income of citizens, especially the vulnerable and the poor, from high fuel costs. Producers and manufacturers also benefit from subsidies provided by the government in relation to their costs, enabling them to supply cheap goods to end users.[17] In addition, energy subsidies are introduced to support industrial development and boost employment. Energy-intensive industries (such as cement, fertilizers, and petrochemicals) particularly benefit from energy subsidies as these provide cheap feedstock, lower energy input tariffs, and guaranteed purchase prices. Moreover, subsidies are aimed at improving access to modern and cleaner forms of energy – such as electricity and natural gas. The process is particularly accelerated by the expansion of infrastructure (such as natural gas networks in rural and remote areas), through direct subsidies for initial household connections to grids, and by encouraging fuel substitution in power generation.[18]

Besides all the economic benefits, in Iran and other resource-rich countries with a similar political system, subsidies are generously provided to reduce risks of political and social unrest (such as those seen across the Arab world in 2011) by providing cheap goods and services to citizens. As Victor (2009) argues, from a political point of view, the cheapest fuels are mostly provided by governments that do not face 'popular referenda', a political move also called the 'populist paradox'.[19] For these governments, artificially low prices are considered a rent distribution mechanism, as a result of which they give up the potential rent they would receive from higher prices either in domestic or international markets, for the sake of protecting their political existence.[20]

## Critiques of energy subsidies and justifications for their reform

Since the early 2000s, and as a result of the upward trend of oil prices, the Iranian government has found it increasingly difficult to continue energy subsidies, while facing numerous critiques as to their efficiency and effectiveness. Subsidization policy is known to be less distorting in a low-oil price environment, when prices are relatively stable and close to production costs. As energy prices rise, however, subsidies place an increasing burden on government finances. The challenge was particularly hard for the Iranian authorities as rising oil prices post-2009 coincided with mounting international sanctions.

Low prices caused wasteful consumption, particularly in the residential and commercial sectors, as there were no incentives or pressure for efficient use of energy. There is a similar lack of efficiency in power generation where, in gas-fired plants, 3 kwh of electricity is produced for each standard cubic metre of gas; by international standards this means that 16 per cent of the gas is wasted.[21] Low prices have also discouraged industrial sectors from upgrading old and inefficient capital stock as the return on investment is not sufficiently attractive. High costs in the downstream energy sector, resulting from operational inefficiencies, have sometimes also encouraged further energy subsidization, making state-owned companies like NIGC, or state-owned power plants, fall short of adequate sources of funding to expand production capacity or run their business efficiently.

Subsidies are also criticized for mis-targeting end-users. The fact that subsidies disproportionately benefit the top income groups demonstrates that they are an extremely costly method of protecting the welfare of poor households.[22] According to the Independent Evaluation Group (IEG) of the World Bank, the bottom 40 per cent of the population in terms of income distribution receives only 15–20 per cent of the fuel subsidies in developing countries.[23] This means that lower income groups incur substantial welfare losses, as their low consumption levels do not absorb low energy prices to the same extent as high-income households.

Moreover, fossil-fuel subsidies have had an adverse impact on the investment resources available for the development of energy infrastructure. In a state-dominated economy like Iran where competition does not exist and the economy is heavily subsidized by the state, investors are usually required to sell a portion of the energy produced at low prices to domestic markets, which substantially reduces their return on investment. Hence, in the absence of offsetting compensation payments to companies, subsidies reduce energy companies' incentives to invest. In 2005, the IEA reported that cheap gas prices in the Middle East and North Africa are considered to be the main reason for lack of success in developing gas projects.[24] The same argument is also put forward by Marcel (2006), who argues that to attract foreign investment, the first important step is to deregulate, then eliminate domestic energy subsidies and release more capital for investment in the petroleum industry in order to enhance production.[25] Thus, the larger the subsidies for petroleum products, the less are the funds available for capital investment for further development of the industry.

The challenge of reduced financial resources caused by subsidies has also placed a burden on NIOC, as the budget for its subsidiaries is allocated only after the share of subsidies is deducted from the total amount of oil and gas revenue deposited at the treasury by NIOC, leaving inadequate funds for the development of the company's projects.

Even if prices are liberalized, however, and the profitability of the business becomes more certain, investors may still not be allowed into the gas sector. The issue of a reliable supply to end users is a national security matter, as a result of which the participation of the private sector may be considered risky. For example, the Rouhani government, immediately after taking office, ordered the removal of NIGC and its subsidiaries from the list of companies that had been planned to be privatized. Oil Minister Zanganeh also opposed any plan to transfer gas processing plants to the private sector, due to the sensitive and important role they play in the production, export, and supply of gas.[26]

Subsidies are also criticized for their impact on gas exports. The inefficient use of gas resulting from low prices has hastened resource depletion and reduced the amount of gas available for export. Low regulated prices, and consequent artificially high demand, have led to increasing dependence on imports from Turkmenistan, while the domestic gas shortages resulting from low prices have forced the government to respond by curtailing or cutting-off exports, inflicting serious long-term financial costs and, perhaps more importantly, reputational damage. Subsidies have also distorted price signals and, in doing so, have also distorted the allocation of resources, causing serious confusion amongst politicians about which options would yield the highest economic return (see Chapter 6). Thus in addition to wasteful consumption, subsidies may lead to investments that do not reflect relative scarcities of resources.[27]

Last but not least, for many years subsidized fossil fuel consumption has been considered an underlying cause of environmental problems, such as air pollution. In 2006, the Energy–Environment Review (EER) estimated that without price reform and policy intervention, the cost of environmental damage would grow to $12 billion, or 6.6 per cent of nominal GDP, by 2019.[28] Phasing out subsidies would create energy conservation incentives and, most importantly, encourage investment in energy-efficient capital stock, thereby moderating the increase in demand.[29]

## Energy subsidies reform

The urgent requirement for subsidies reform became a matter of absolute political consensus in the late 2000s as the status quo was agreed to be costly, wasteful, unfair, counter-productive, and altogether unsustainable.[30] With around 1 per cent of the world's population, Iran consumed around 5 per cent of global gas production in 2012 and was ranked as the third-largest gas consumer in the world after the USA and Russia.[31] Per capita natural gas consumption was 2.5 and 1.5 times bigger than India and China respectively, and more than twice that of Germany, Europe's most industrialized country.[32] According to the IEA, during the sharp oil price rise of 2008, subsidies cost the government an unprecedented $120 billion.[33] A year later the drastic, though short-lived, fall in oil prices also hit hard the country's ability to finance subsidies.[34]

**Table 5.3:** Fossil fuel consumption subsidies ($ billions)

| Fuel | 2007 | 2008 | 2009 | 2010 |
|------|------|------|------|------|
| Oil | 36.56 | 53.78 | 29.20 | 40.92 |
| Gas | 18.78 | 32.03 | 24.12 | 25.49 |
| Coal | 0 | 0 | 0 | 0 |
| Electricity | 9.22 | 15.19 | 11.31 | 14.43 |

Source: IEA (2011).

During the same period, tighter economic sanctions increasingly isolated the economy, significantly reducing the oil revenues on which the budget was largely dependent.[35] Not surprisingly, the resulting explicit and implicit fiscal costs to the government's budget were so immense that urgent government action was required. These difficulties strengthened politicians' willpower, which played a key role in the initial success of the reform plan. In 2010, after several failed attempts by previous governments, the Ahmadinejad administration undertook what the IMF called 'one of the boldest economic makeovers ever attempted in the oil-rich Middle East to reform energy subsidies.'[36]

Noting their acute economic impact, the government finally submitted the reform bill before Parliament in September 2008; in this bill, objectives such as promotion of standards of living, equal distribution of wealth, control of fuel smuggling, enhancement of the country's oil and gas export capacity, and reduction of waste and rationalization of consumption were put forward as the main drivers of the reform.[37] Although there were major disagreements between the government and the Parliament over some procedural and substantive aspects of the bill, including the price increase threshold and the aggregate revenue to be gained from price increase, the **Subsidies Reform Act** was finally passed in January 2010, with an expected implementation from the beginning of the Iranian New Year (21 March 2010). Concerns over political unrest, however, particularly during the aftermath of the controversial presidential election in June 2009, together with instability in the foreign exchange market and double-digit inflation, postponed actual implementation until December 2010. The reform was planned to be implemented within a five-year period overlapping with the country's Fifth Five-Year Economic, Social, and Cultural Development Plan from 2011 to 2015.[38]

### The Targeted Subsidies Reform Act

The Targeted Subsidies Reform Act (henceforth the Reform Act) calls for a *gradual* increase of energy prices within a five-year period (2011–15). Retail prices of petrol, diesel, fuel oil, kerosene, and liquefied petroleum gas (LPG) are required to increase to no less than 90 per cent of Persian Gulf free on board (f.o.b) prices. Natural gas retail prices are also envisaged to increase to at least 75 per cent of average export prices (after deduction of transmission costs and export taxes). In order to manage future price volatility, the Reform Act also authorized the government to absorb up to 25 per cent of the f.o.b Persian Gulf price increases (relative to f.o.b Persian Gulf prices of 2010 when the Reform Act came into force) through further subsidization, without changing the consumer price. Note 3 of Article 2 envisages minimum and maximum revenue of IRR100 thousand billion and IRR200 thousand billion (approximately $10 and $20 billion) from price increases in the first year of the reform.[39]

As many citizens consider low energy prices an entitlement, the government faced major challenges in countering potential social unrest. Thus, to compensate the nation for higher energy prices, the law authorized payments to the population of a maximum of 50 per cent of the fiscal revenue from the price increase in the form of in-cash and in-kind payments, bearing in mind each family's level of income; and improving the social security system through, for example, setting up a national health insurance scheme, creating employment, and offering low-interest rate mortgages.[40]

The Reform Act also designated payment of a 30 per cent share of the revenue from price increases to support industries and producers through subsidies of interest on loans for the adoption of new energy-saving technologies, and credit lines to reduce the impact of higher energy costs on cash-flows.[41] The remaining 20 per cent was allocated to the government to cover subsequent increases in its costs and to improve its infrastructure.[42]

## The implementation of the subsidies reform plan

In the first year, the implementation of the reform plan was hailed as a success as it did not entail serious public unrest or major inflationary impact.[43] To the surprise of many, the reform received an overall public acceptance which the IMF attributed to an exemplary design, and encouraged other countries introducing similar reforms to take lessons from Iran's experience.[44] In its 2013 special report on subsidies reform, the IMF noted that the Iranian reform was well planned, highlighting the plan's clear objectives, its compensating measures, and its timetable, preceded by an extensive public relations campaign.[45] This was reportedly due to the 'excellent' communication strategy and extensive public relations campaign which educated and familiarized the nation with the reform process, including the negative impacts of the subsidies, energy price rises, and envisaged benefits.[46] The cash payment to every citizen, prior to the effective date of reform (though access to deposits was frozen until the day when energy prices were increased), was also a decisive factor in its initial success.[47] The process was very simple and citizens only needed to file applications to receive compensation. The Iranian banking system was also swiftly upgraded to handle direct cash payments to the beneficiaries' accounts, in addition to the 16 million new accounts which were opened to handle the nationwide cash transfers.

The actual timing of the reform also played a crucial role in its initial success. Consideration was given to the lowest energy consumption period of the year, with less personal travel, air conditioning demand, and completion of the harvest season. The controversial presidential elections in 2009, during which the Iranian government showed the public that it was willing to use force to put down unrest, also gave the government more confidence to implement the reform.

Before the start of the reform, and in order to control the inflation rate, the authorities adopted several policies to stabilize the exchange rate. The Central Bank governor frequently made public statements, reassuring people of the country's strong international exchange and gold reserves, and rising oil prices, which would provide the treasury with sufficient inflows of foreign exchange.[48] Moreover, administrative policies were adopted to prevent producers and retailers from increasing the prices of staple commodities in anticipation of the reform, in addition to publicly advertising measures for direct distribution of many of the basic staples and commodities to counter panic buying.[49]

The Reform Act, however, and the government's implementation of it, was much criticized by both politicians and experts. In the Act itself, many crucial points remained unclear, including the level and frequency of price adjustments for fuels, the definition of those eligible for compensation payments, and the amount and duration of those payments. This left the door open for the government to implement the Act based on its own interpretation which, in many respects, was not in compliance with the overall objectives of the plan.

As explained above, in order to control inflation and minimize the resulting economic pressure on the population, the Reform Act stipulated a *gradual* increase in prices. It failed, however, to stipulate the *rate* at which prices should increase every year to reach international market levels (for oil and oil products) and export prices (for natural gas) by the end of the five-year implementation period. It also failed to address the issue of price volatility in international markets and the resulting challenge of how to pass the prices through to the population if they were to increase substantially.

In practice, the government insisted that the price increase had to be meaningful in order to effectively reduce energy demand.[50] As a result, it took the 'shock therapy' approach and substantially increased prices in order to counter excessive energy consumption, and to ensure an increase in real fuel prices in the light of the annual inflation rate, the increase in international prices, and exchange rate depreciation.[51] Its approach, unsurprisingly, encountered serious opposition from members of Parliament who were expecting a gradual price increase (of around 20 per cent/year). The Parliament criticized the government for creating an uncontrollable rate of inflation through such a sudden and dramatic price rise (for some energy products, such as diesel, prices increased to around 80 per cent of international prices in 2010).[52]

The Reform Act also authorized in-cash and in-kind payment to families (representing a maximum 50 per cent of the revenue resulting from price increases) giving due consideration to their average income. Cash transfers allowed consumers to have choices, while the cost to the budget was known with greater certainty than had been the case for generalized subsidies; they were also targeted at low-income families.[53] The Act, however, did not establish a method or set a benchmark on which to evaluate the relevant level of income of families, nor did it specify the exact amount of monthly cash payments to be redistributed. As Iran has never had an effective and systematic database of household income, the government faced major difficulties in identifying the target groups, and hence had to announce that all Iranian nationals were eligible to receive monthly cash payments of IRR455,000 (equivalent to around $45 at the 2010–11 exchange rate). This even entitled those Iranians living abroad to apply for and receive cash payments.

In the first year of the reform, from December 2010 to December 2011, the cash payment to 73 million Iranians cost the government around IRR33,000 billion (equivalent to $3 billion) every month. Despite the government's revenue of around IRR300,000 billion (equivalent to $30 billion) from the price increases in the first year of the reforms, which far exceeded the total annual gain of $10–20 billion as stipulated by the Act, the actual public cash payment in the corresponding year was approximately IRR450,000 billion (equivalent to $44 billion).[54] In order to cover the IRR150,000 billion (equivalent to $14 billion) deficit, the government, in addition to taking loans from the Central Bank, almost fully distributed the 30 per cent and 20 per cent shares of industry and government (see the final paragraph of the section 'The Targeted Subsidies Reform Act' above). It also used tax revenues, and the development funds of the Ministries of Petroleum and Energy, to pay for the monthly cash hand-outs.[55]

The rate at which the government increased the prices in the first reform phase, and its intention to further increase them in the second phase, raised concerns among members of Parliament over whether the government would exceed the price rise ceiling as envisaged in the Act. As a result, in April 2012, Parliament placed a ban on implementation of the second phase of the reform, although this was later lifted in early 2014 as President Rouhani took office.

### The impact of the subsidies reform on the natural gas sector

Since its implementation, the subsidies reform plan has had diverse impacts on the economy as a whole and on the petroleum sector in particular. The reform process, while relatively successful in its first year, had a drastic economic impact on the country in the second and third years, which overlapped with the intensification of international sanctions in January 2012. Subsidies reform had particularly acute impacts on the development of the natural gas industry. Despite substantial price increases in the first phase of the reform, the government fell short of the required revenues to allocate to natural gas projects, as a result of expensive cash hand-outs and international sanctions.

In the first year of the reform, the gas sector was subject to some of the highest price increases, of 100–300 per cent depending on the sector. As shown in Figure 5.1, the smallest price increase was implemented in the public sector, from IRR690 to IRR1000/cm, and the maximum price increase targeted the transportation sector (from IRR80/cm to IRR2600/cm) (Figure 5.1 and Table 5.4).[56]

In the household sector, one of the major gas-consuming sectors, a

**Table 5.4:** Natural gas tariffs in different sectors

| Sector | Sub-Sector | | Price (IRR/cm) | | | | | | |
|---|---|---|---|---|---|---|---|---|---|
| | | | | | | 2010 | | 2011 | |
| | | | 2005 | 2007 | 2009 | *First 9 months of year* | *Last 3 months of year* | *First 7 months of year* | *Last 5 months of year* |
| Household | | Residential premises | 80 | 113 | 81.9 | 132 | 527 | 1200 | 700 |
| Public | Cat.1 | Commercial | 200 | 250 | 250 | 280 | 871 | 2000 | 1000 |
| | Cat.2 | Sport, education, religious premises | 70 | 90 | 90 | 120 | 600 | 1000 | 600 |
| | Cat.3 | State premises | 200 | 690 | 690 | 720 | 1000 | 2000 | 1000 |
| Industry | Cat.1 | Industrial units | 139 | 159 | 158.5 | 188.5 | 700 | 700 | 700 |
| | | Power generations | 29 | 49 | 49.3 | 79.3 | 800 | 800 | 800 |
| | | Petrochemical complex feedstock | 40 | 60 | 158.5 | - | - | 700 | 700 |
| | | Petrochemical plants | 90 | 110 | 161.7 | - | - | 700 | 700 |
| | | Agriculture | - | 159 | 168.2 | - | - | 1000 | 600 |
| | Cat.2 | Transportation (CNG stations) | 60 | 80 | 80 | - | - | 2600 | 2600 |

Source: NIGC (2011).

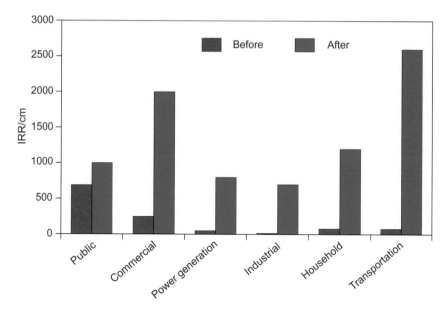

**Figure 5.1:** Average natural gas price increases in 2010 (IRR/cm)

Source: Iran Energy Balance (2012).

**Table 5.5:** Post-reform household natural gas prices (2010 and 2014)[57]

| Tier | Consumption Range (cubic metre) | IRR/cm (during 5 cold months) 2010 | 2014 | IRR/cm (during 7 non-cold months) 2010 | 2014* |
|------|------|------|------|------|------|
| 1 | 0–45 | 300 | 400 | 700 | 800 |
| 2 | 46–95 | 500 | 600 | 900 | 1000 |
| 3 | 96–145 | 700 | 800 | 1200 | 1300 |
| 4 | 146–195 | 900 | 1000 | 1600 | 1700 |
| 5 | 196–245 | 1100 | 1200 | 2000 | 2100 |
| 6 | 246–295 | 1600 | 1700 | 2200 | 2300 |
| 7 | 296–345 | 1900 | 2000 | 2500 | 2600 |
| 8 | 346–395 | 2200 | 2300 | 2800 | 2900 |
| 9 | 396–445 | 2500 | 2600 | 3000 | 3100 |
| 10 | 446–495 | 2800 | 2900 | 3200 | 3300 |
| 11 | 496–545 | 3200 | 3300 | 3400 | 3500 |
| 12 | >545 | 3500 | 3600 | 3500 | 3600 |

\*   The IRR100 increase in 2014 gas prices is due to an increase in gas consumption taxes.

Source: NIGC (2011) and NIGC (2014).

multi-tier tariff structure was adopted in which tariff rates varied on the basis of consumption and season (see Table 5.5).[58] Surprisingly, despite the sharp rise in prices, there was no major resistance to payment of bills, as the increase in prices would be compensated by the government's cash hand-outs and less wasteful consumption. The government had also shown that it would seriously follow the strategy of gas cut-offs or fines for those who had not paid gas bills.[59]

The country was divided into five geographical regions in which tariffs varied depending on temperature.[60] The use of the multi-tier tariff mechanism played a significant role in moderating the impact of the price increase on, particularly, poor households[61] (Table 5.6).

Despite the Act's provisions for annual increases in the price of energy (including that of natural gas), prices did not increase further after their first spike in 2010–11 until March 2014. As a result of the Ahmadinejad government's mismanagement of the reform plan and Parliament's subsequent ban on the implementation of the second phase of the reform (which had been planned to entail further price increases) energy prices remained unchanged until March 2014, when the Rouhani government received the green light from Parliament to increase prices.

Subsidies reform, along with international sanctions, was central to Rouhani's presidential campaign. He promised to continue the implementation of the reforms according to the law, while minimizing their economic and social impacts. To that end, his administration redefined the reform policies and submitted a bill alongside the 2014–15 budget bill to Parliament; there was a major policy shift on energy price increases, cash redistribution, and the scheme of financial aid to industries in the bill. In February 2014, as a part of the budget review, Parliament approved the bill, obliging the government to start the second phase of the subsidies reform – which envisages a considerable rise in energy prices and elimination of 30 per cent of the cash payment to recipients in higher income groups. The Rouhani government began partial implementation of the second phase of the reform in March 2014, with natural gas tariffs for household and public sectors increasing by 20 and 30 per cent, respectively. Industrial tariffs increased by around 43 per cent reaching IRR1000/cm.[62]

In gas, like other energy sectors, there were expectations that potential savings from reduction of domestic consumption could increase the country's export capacity. It was also predicted that the revenue yielded from the export of energy products could support a virtuous cycle of investment that would further increase production and subsequently enhance export capacity.[63] In practice, however, natural gas price increases

**Table 5.6:** Post-reform household gas prices in different geographical regions (IRR/cm)

| Consumption Level | 1 | 2 | 3 | 4 | 5 | 6 | 7 | 8 | 9 | 10 | 11 | 12 |
|---|---|---|---|---|---|---|---|---|---|---|---|---|
| Region 1 | Up to 300 | 301–400 | 500–401 | 600–501 | 700–601 | 800–701 | 900–801 | 1000–901 | 1100–1001 | 1200–1101 | 1300–1201 | >1300 |
| Region 2 | Up to 250 | 350–251 | 450–351 | 550–451 | 650–551 | 750–651 | 850–751 | 950–851 | 1050–951 | 1150–1051 | 1250–1151 | >1250 |
| Region 3 | Up to 200 | 300–201 | 400–301 | 500–401 | 600–501 | 700–601 | 800–701 | 900–801 | 1000–901 | 1100–1001 | 1200–1101 | >1200 |
| Region 4 | Up to 150 | 250–151 | 350–251 | 450–351 | 550–451 | 650–551 | 750–651 | 850–751 | 950–851 | 1050–951 | 1150–1051 | >1150 |
| Region 5 | Up to 76 | 76–150 | 250–151 | 350–251 | 450–351 | 550–451 | 650–551 | 750–651 | 850–751 | 950–851 | 1050–951 | >1050 |
| Price (IRR/cm) | 300 | 500 | 700 | 900 | 1100 | 1600 | 1900 | 2200 | 2500 | 2800 | 3200 | 3500 |

Source: NIGC (2011).

did not have a major downward impact on domestic consumption. According to NIGC's annual report, in the first year of the reform, overall gas demand grew by 9 per cent, with the household sector experiencing a growth rate of 10 per cent.[64] The increase in household consumption was a result of further expansion of the national grid and connection of more households to the network (see Chapter 1).[65] In the second year of the reform, however, household consumption fell around 10 per cent, which consequently encouraged the diversion of gas to the industrial sector, particularly power generation, with the aim of reducing the risk of power cuts.[66]

Hence, considering the growing number of gas end-users and an extensive natural gas substitution policy in power generation, it is not surprising that there was no major reduction in consumption (despite the substantial price increase in 2010), and that gas supply interruptions were seen during cold winters (for example 2013–14).

In terms of export capacity, although the export volume to Turkey almost doubled, reaching 9.1 bcm in the first year of the reform, the increase can hardly be attributed to the subsidies reform.[67] A 4 per cent increase in the country's production (an additional 5 bcm) was a major driver in the increase in export capacity in that year.

Furthermore, the country has not been successful in injecting the capital investment needed for development of the gas industry. Based on the Fifth Five-Year Development Plan (2011–15), the country should produce 1.3 bcm/day of gas, which requires an investment of $6 billion/year.[68] A major part of this investment was expected to come from elimination of subsidies, which was also put forward by the government as one of the main objectives of the reform. As mentioned above, from the $30 billion of revenue that the government gained from the energy price increase in the first year of reform, 30 per cent ($9 billion) was intended to be spent on the industrial sector, including natural gas development projects. But as the government was very much concerned about potential social unrest, this was redistributed among the population instead, leaving the government with no source of funding to support infrastructure projects, particularly those in the natural gas industry.[69] In the same way, when news about the bankruptcy of NIGC surfaced in autumn 2013, blame was laid at the door of the cash payment scheme, for swallowing revenues which should have been allocated to the gas industry.[70] The scheme was held responsible by Oil Minister Zanganeh for the 'tragic and sorrowful' problems it had created for the development of the petroleum industry. He lamented the fact that the former president's administration dipped into the treasury of NIOC and its subsidiaries to pay monthly cash handouts, and urged restructuring of the subsidies reform plan to reduce government pressure on NIOC's annual budget.[71]

## Conclusion

Energy subsidies were first introduced as a means of financial support for the poor, but they rarely met this objective and encouraged wasteful consumption of scarce resources. Being aware of these problems, the government undertook bold economic reforms in 2010 to address the growing burden of subsidies on the country's treasury, particularly in the aftermath of the 2009 oil price rise, which made financing the energy subsidies increasingly challenging.

Despite relative success in the first year of the reform, the process faced major difficulties in subsequent years as a result of government mismanagement and the intensification of international sanctions, causing Parliament to ban the implementation of the second phase, for fear of further exacerbating economic problems and causing social unrest. Prices of energy products, despite the provisions of the Subsidies Reform Act (which called for increases on a gradual basis over a five-year period), were subject to a single substantial increase, leading to high inflation, increased costs of production, and subsequent bankruptcy of a large number of manufacturing companies. The nationwide cash payment policy, adopted to minimize the impact of price rises on households, turned into a black hole which soaked up all the revenues gained from the price increase, plus the portion of development funds earmarked for NIOC, NIGC, and their subsidiaries. Despite the substantial price increase in 2010, growing inflation and devaluation of the national currency, which further accelerated as a result of international sanctions in 2012, allowed a large part of the subsidies to creep back into the economy. The devaluation of the currency resulted in average gas prices (based on 2013 US dollar equivalents) dropping from $1.5/MMBtu in 2010 to $0.73/MMBtu in 2013, casting serious doubt on the overall success of the first phase of subsidies reform. The energy price increase remained confined to the first year of the reform, and further increases were suspended until early 2014.

In the natural gas sector, subsidies reform seems to have caused more harm than good. The reform not only failed to allocate additional investment funds for development of natural gas projects, but also used a large part of NIOC's and NIGC's budgets for cash payments to citizens. To the surprise of many, reports of NIGC's bankruptcy, with debts of over IRR100 thousand billion (or around $5 billion), surfaced in 2013, the subsidies reform plan being blamed for the company's inability to meet its financial commitments in the face of government failure to pay its budgetary allocation.

Available data on natural gas consumption suggest that price reform did not have a major impact on reducing gas demand. In almost all sectors, except households, consumption continued its upward trend, although at a slower rate. This was partly due to the policy of domestic market expansion, according to which gas is planned to reach every single Iranian. In the light of this policy, and as a result of limited production capacity, subsidies reform is unlikely to play a major role in the substantial development of natural gas export capacity before 2020 (either by reducing domestic consumption or by increasing investment revenues). As consumption and production are currently growing at almost the same rate, the pre-reform challenges (which include shortages of gas for oilfield reinjection, dependence on gas imports, and difficulties in meeting its export commitments) are likely to persist. Natural gas price reform can, however, have a positive impact on moderating the previous rate of demand increase and on encouraging more efficient use of gas resources. But if Iran is to become a major gas exporter, it must substantially expand its production capacity.

Also, despite subsidies reform, comparatively low gas prices are unlikely to attract private investors, including IOCs, into the development of downstream projects; the absolute price level is not yet high enough to remunerate investment, and is unlikely to reach that level in the short to medium term. Investment in the upstream sector for gas export purposes can also face challenges, as a large share of the produced gas may have to be allocated to the domestic market if the government fails to substantially increase the country's overall gas production capacity. In addition, general concern about security of supply to the domestic market will also reduce the possibility of foreign companies replacing state-owned companies such as NIGC in downstream activities – which include processing, transmission, and distribution of gas. This is despite the fact that new investors might run these activities more efficiently.

# CHAPTER 6

## NATURAL GAS ALLOCATION POLICY AND PRIORITIZATION CHALLENGES

### Introduction

The allocation of natural gas resources to the domestic market, reinjection, or export has been central to numerous political debates in Iran. Usually, in a gas-rich country, natural gas is consumed across a wide range of sectors in domestic markets and, where production capacity is sufficiently high, gas can also be allocated to export markets. In the period 1998–2005 when production was growing strongly, there was little concern about Iran's ability to supply gas to domestic and export markets. Its ambitious export plans, however, were hard hit by a combination of production shortages and domestic market growth, forcing the country to increase its gas imports from Turkmenistan and interrupt exports to Turkey at times of peak domestic demand. As discussed in Chapters 1, 3, and 5, production capacity has been increasingly constrained as various projects have been delayed, postponed, or cancelled, mainly as a result of the intensification of US and international sanctions. Also, low prices and political bias in favour of domestic consumption inflated the size of the country's gas market and has consequently reduced availability for exports, despite strong support for the latter among some experts and officials. This has caused a prolonged debate among Iranian politicians and decision makers about the overall economic, political, and social benefits of allocating gas resources to export or domestic markets, which has itself played an important role in mismanagement, and further postponement or cancellation of natural gas projects.

Since the recommencement of gas exports in the early 2000s, extensive opposition has been directed by some members of Parliament towards the government's gas export policy, arguing that gas exports do not serve the long-term interests of the country. They justify their arguments on the basis of rising oil prices, rapid decline in oil production, and the growing need for job creation and revenue generation. These opponents, mainly from the Parliamentary Energy Committee, urge the allocation of the country's vast gas resources to oilfield reinjection and development of petrochemical and gas-based industries.[1] Supporters of exports argue that, with its vast resources, favourable geopolitical situation, and proximity to regional and international markets, Iran possesses the attributes to become a major player in the international gas trade, which would subsequently increase its revenues and strengthen its bargaining power in the international political arena. Closer examination of both sides' arguments shows that they have given little consideration to the county's political and economic conditions, and the realities of global energy market developments.

The study of optimal allocation of gas resources would have not been as pressing as it is today had the country produced sufficient volumes of gas to allocate to both domestic and export markets. Conducting a thorough precise analysis of Iran's gas allocation options requires numerous technical, political, and security considerations to be taken into account. Lack of data and statistics do not allow this type of detailed economic evaluation. Such an analysis can only be carried out by means of a quantitative framework, embracing extensive numerical and sensitivity analyses. It should include econometric analysis and, ideally, an economic model of domestic and international energy markets. Therefore, the scope of this chapter remains confined to a descriptive analysis of economic, political, and social benefits of different uses of gas, shedding light on important variables which need to be taken into account in order to develop allocation policies.

## Optimal allocation of gas resources: the importance of economic and welfare maximization

The issue of optimal allocation of resources gains its importance from growing concerns about the adequacy of natural resources to meet the needs of all beneficiaries. Economic development, to a large extent, depends on the use of resources, whether in the form of a stock of primary material or as a flow of primary energy required as an input in the production process.[2] Utilization of, particularly, depletable and exhaustible resources such as natural gas, can have a profound influence on a society's production capacity and its level of welfare. Therefore, it is important that these resources are available and accessible over a long period of time, and in a manner which maximizes net benefits from their utilization. Additionally, the depletable, exhaustible character of most energy resources adds to the importance of their optimal allocation.[3] The extraction of these resources reduces the remaining stock and affects economic gains and sustainability. Therefore, scarcity is a major element in optimal resource allocation, meaning that when a resource is scarce and/or inadequate to meet the needs of all markets, its optimal allocation helps governments to minimize the resulting adverse distributional effects, and to maximize economic returns by allocation to the most economically attractive end-users. In the reallocation process which can result from obstacles to the development of energy resources, some users may be deprived while others are given priority. As such, effective allocation of natural resources should entail the identification of significant short-term and long-term objectives, which can range from economic growth and national welfare to sustainable development and social equity.

While the previous paragraph has reviewed general arguments pertinent to the optimal allocation of natural resources, so huge are Iran's gas resources that such considerations are not of paramount or immediate importance (as they are for the majority of other countries). The key point for Iran is the lack of immediately available production capacity, rather than total resource availability. This lack of production capacity highlights the importance of how to allocate resources in an optimum manner. It has caused domestic market sectors (including oilfield reinjection) and export markets to compete against one another for access to supply. As each of these options entails different levels of economic, social, and political benefits, and because production capacity is insufficient to meet the demand of all options, those options which maximize welfare gains and yield the highest social benefit should be given priority.

Nevertheless as discussed in Chapter 5, distributional objectives often lead to major economic and allocation distortions and inefficiencies. Therefore, striking a balance between economic efficiency and social equity should form a major part of a government allocation policy; this has, unsurprisingly, proved to be a challenging task. As Allsopp and Stern (2012) argue:

> ... the transition from distorting to less distorting ways of meeting distri-butional objectives is vital in the allocation of resources, though this has proved to be very difficult in nearly all countries.[4]

These challenges mostly arise from uncertainties that put at risk the effectiveness of government allocation policy. These uncertainties can include a wide range of issues such as: concerns about political and economic stability; concerns over extraction costs and rates of return which systematically vary over time with depletion of resource deposits; uncertainties about future values of depletable resources, future prices, and future extraction costs; and, last but not least, the possibility of technological breakthroughs which can change almost all energy market calculations.[5] Undoubtedly the Iranian government is not unusual in facing such difficulties,[6] but as discussed above, the duty of economic and welfare maximization supported by economic, political, and social factors obliges it to design and implement an allocation policy which, given future uncertainties and, arguably, past failures, maximizes the economic and social benefits from the allocation of resources.

## The political debate about natural gas allocation options

Prolonged political disagreements among politicians about how to allocate gas resources optimally have seriously affected the government's ability to design and implement an effective policy. Political debates are mostly conducted between exponents of radical views – those who either completely rule out the exports option, reasoning that, for example, the country's old oilfields are in dire need of gas reinjection, and those who believe that the country's gigantic gas resources cannot easily and quickly be translated into huge production capacity to boost export potential.

There are also moderate arguments in support of gas exports, such as the claim that in an international political context exports, particularly through pipelines, can be positively linked with Iran's overall security:

> ... regardless of the economic viability of export projects.[7]

After the Revolution, and despite termination of the only gas export project to the USSR,[8] Iran began:

> ... to recognize the strategic value of gas exports and realize that an aggressive gas export policy was a very important tool in energy diplomacy.[9]

Russia was observed as a successful case in promoting powerful energy diplomacy, convincing policy makers that:

> ... creating a bilateral or multilateral dependence via gas pipelines could be regarded as an energy strategy that would promote Iran's regional and international political advancement.[10]

In other words, they believe that gas exports, particularly through pipelines, would inevitably promote national security by increasing Iran's international bargaining power.

Iran's policy of taking political advantage from establishing gas export links with regional and international markets came into existence in the early 1990s, as the country began to face increasing political and economic pressures from the US government. As the USA tried to implement a stronger containment policy against Iran, and weakened the country by isolating it from the international political and economic arenas, the government increasingly used energy export policy to neutralize or minimize the impact of US attempts to influence other countries' positions vis-à-vis Iran. As reaffirmed by Soudani, a former member of the Iranian Parliament, natural gas export is a 'necessary' policy in the light of intensifying international sanctions against the country, irrespective of its economic profitability.[11] Hence, many politicians believe that by making importing countries dependent on Iranian supply, Iran will gain the required capacity to dominate these countries in future negotiations and decision-making processes. For example, supporters of natural gas exports believe that Turkey's opposition to the intensification of international sanctions and its unwillingness to cease cooperation with Iran is a result of its gas import reliance on the latter.[12]

In addition, proponents of this policy believe that gas exports, particularly through LNG, would entail significant economic advantages, including foreign investments, state-of-art technologies, and employment. They argue that by diversifying market opportunities, gas exports would boost revenue generation and improve the country's participation in international markets.[13] These views are also encouraged by the country's geopolitical position – centrally located among the world's major oil and gas producers, sharing land and sea borders with 15 neighbouring countries. It has a relatively strong economy (though hard hit by international sanctions and economic mismanagement in the past few years), with a large skilled workforce and well-developed infrastructure. Moreover, the country is on the eastern border of Europe and western border of Asia, offering the potential for large-scale exports of natural gas both to EU markets, and to the growing energy markets in East Asia and beyond.

On the other side of the debate, however, stand gas export opponents, some with radical and some with more moderate views. The former group argues that regardless of the country's production capacity, natural gas resources should be allocated to the domestic market and reinjection purposes and, in the event of potential surplus capacity, gas should remain in the ground for future generations.[14] They base their argument on the fact that the consumption of gas enhances standards of living, and its utilization in power generation frees up a larger share of petroleum products for export. They also argue that reinjection of gas into old oilfields increases oil production which, in the light of high oil prices, can entail significantly higher economic returns for the country, while the reinjected gas can be utilized in the future. Some more moderate opponents, however, argue that, given limited production capacity and considering the prevailing requirements for fulfilling the growing domestic market and reinjection needs, Iran will not have enough gas to allocate to export markets and therefore, it should not expand export capacity.

## Natural gas allocation options: challenges and opportunities

A factor which particularly distinguishes Iran from other gas-rich countries such as Qatar is the multiplicity of options available for the allocation of gas resources, each of which can yield significant economic and social benefits for the country. These options range from huge domestic consumption and reinjection to export through pipeline and/or LNG and the development of value-added industries. In this section, these options will be studied and the challenges and opportunities resulting from each option will be examined.

### *Domestic consumption*

Regardless of the debate about allocation of gas for export or reinjection, there is a consensus among Iranian politicians that priority should be given to secure and adequate supply of gas to the domestic market, which consists of household, commercial, and power generation sectors. These sectors combined constitute around 65 per cent of Iran's domestic consumption of natural gas, around 95 bcm in 2012.[15] They play a significant role in the country's economic development and welfare enhancement. As discussed in Chapter 1, post-Revolutionary gas policy predominately focused on the development of the domestic market which, as of 2012, supplied gas to more than 55 million Iranians – around 95 per cent of the urban and 54 per cent of the rural population.[16]

The development of transmission and distribution systems accelerated in the 1990s following the discovery of the South Pars field, after members of Parliament required the government to extend the distribution networks to small towns and villages within a five km radius of the transmission network. In the Fourth Five-Year Development Plan (2006–10), this threshold increased to 15–20 km, which literally covered all towns and villages in the country. While members of Parliament argue that supplying gas to the rural population would enhance its standards of living and free up distillate and other petroleum products for export, there is little evidence suggesting that this policy has met these objectives. First of all, extending the distribution network to villages, sometimes as small as five households, has placed a huge financial burden on government budgets. According to an official from NIGC's Planning Department, depending on the number of households in a village, and its distance from the transmission network, a connection can cost as much as IRR200 million to IRR400 million, equivalent to $8,000–$16,000.[17] Secondly, petroleum products consumption in rural areas is not as high as in urban areas, or in the power generation sector; hence one should not expect a significant decrease in overall petroleum products consumption from substitution by gas in rural areas. Equally important is the missed opportunity for development of renewable sources of energy – such as installation of solar panels for heating water in rural areas – which could have cost the government considerably less than expanding distribution pipelines to rural areas.[18] The extensive expansion of domestic networks has also been criticized on safety and security grounds; in the event of earthquakes for example, particularly in large cities like Tehran, there is a huge risk of severe, large-scale explosion. Furthermore (and according to the same NIGC Planning Department official), because of inability to control and monitor the total gas flowing through 35,000 km of transmission and 236,000 km of distribution networks, every year around 10–12 bcm of gas go 'missing' due to leakages in the network, or theft.[19] This is also known as 'lost gas'.

Despite all the critiques, and as a result of MPs' pressure on NIGC, domestic gas supply policy is moving forward in high gear. It should be stressed that the political willpower behind the policy is, unsurprisingly, much stronger than economic and/or welfare considerations, and there is speculation in the industry that MPs, in order to win more votes at Parliamentary elections, promise gas supply to their constituents, forcing extensive development of the network after their election.

As mentioned above, household and commercial sectors are generally given absolute priority in domestic supply policy. In competition with other sectors, such as power generation and industry, it is the latter whose gas supply will be cut or reduced in the event of gas shortages, for example during cold winters. The consumption of natural gas has been extensively promoted in power generation since the mid-1990s in order to maintain oil export availability and reduce the air pollution resulting from burning fuel oil. In 2013 more than 40 power stations were connected to the natural gas grid. In the period 2005–10, consumption in power plants increased from 35 to 45 bcm. In 2011, however, due to shortage of supply and delays to the South Pars phases, consumption fell to 38.9 bcm (a 13 per cent decline). According to

NIGC, from 2010 to 2012 increased fuel oil use in power generation resulted in \$28 billion of foregone export revenue.[20] NIGC has also reported that, had not Iran replaced fuel oil consumption by natural gas in power generation, the country would by now not only be consuming all its oil exports domestically, but also be importing around 3 million bbl/day to meet electricity demand.[21]

With regard to the economic evaluation of allocation to domestic markets, studies show that in gas-rich countries, where there is a network in place, the economic benefit of substituting fuel oil and petroleum products with natural gas is very high. A study by Razavi (2009), almost a year before Iran's energy price reform, showed that the netback value of gas consumption in the residential sector was \$12/MMBtu.[22] He stressed that in countries like Iran, where there is an extensive gas network in place, the netback value of gas used in the residential and commercial sectors is significantly higher than that of other options, particularly exports.[23]

In his study the economic benefit, or netback value of gas use, is estimated based on the economic cost of the replaced fuel, while adjustments are made to take account of differentials in many factors, including capital and operating costs, thermal efficiency, and the cost of fuel processing and delivery. Natural gas consumption in domestic markets requires extensive transmission and distribution grids which, when combined with the exploration and development costs, require substantial up-front investments. The IEA projected that, in the period 2011–20, exploration–development and transmission–distribution costs for additional production of around 70 bcm would reach \$18 billion and \$12 billion, respectively.[24] One should not forget, however, that the large volume of condensate, produced along with gas, can fully compensate the costs of gas production and development. The IEA's projection also showed that in the same period, the long-run average incremental cost (LRAIC) of gas supply would be \$0.73/MMBtu at the city gate[25] which, taking into account the additional distribution cost involved in reaching customers, was significantly higher than the pre-reform average gas price of \$0.35/MMBtu (see Chapter 5).[26]

In the allocation of gas to domestic markets, non-economic arguments are more important than economic ones. Although the domestic market, with the possible exception of power generation, remains unprofitable due to low prices and rates of return on investment, the market is expanding at an astonishing rate thanks to the support of MPs and the government's universal connection policy (described above). In Iran, as in many other petroleum-rich countries, political and social considerations pertinent to consuming gas in domestic markets play an important role in allocation policies. In almost all energy-rich countries in the MENA region, equity and distributional issues are silent on economic efficiency arguments over optimal resource allocation.[27] Thus, it is not surprising that politicians and decision makers are under immense pressure to prioritize the allocation of low-priced gas to domestic markets in order to meet social equity objectives, even though higher revenues could have been earned had the resources been allocated to other options, and even though these policies do not achieve social equity objectives (see above). This policy also serves the interests of the political elite by maintaining their popularity and hence their grip on social and political power.

### Natural gas reinjection into oilfields

Natural gas reinjection was introduced in the mid 1970s as a method of enhancing rates of recovery at oilfields. Enhanced oil recovery is defined as the additional production of oil and gas resulting from the introduction of artificial energy into the reservoir.[28] In practice, it includes water flooding, gas injection, and other operations involving fluids or gases.

Oil reservoirs usually experience three production periods during their life time: early rising production, plateau production, and decline. The majority of Iranian oil fields are at the end of plateau production or the beginning of the decline period.[29] Current oil recovery rates are approximately 25–30 per cent, meaning that 25–30 per cent of oil is recovered, while 70–75 per cent remains in the ground until enhanced oil recovery (EOR) methods are utilized. Although limited studies are available on the secondary recovery rate for the country's oilfields, laboratory simulation reports show an approximate rate of 5–7 per cent.[30] Technical analysis in comparative studies does suggest that gas reinjection into fractured carbonate reservoirs – which account for around 90 per cent of Iranian oilfields – is technically more effective and economically more viable than other EOR methods such as water and $CO_2$ injection.[31]

Natural gas reinjection has been one of NIOC's top priorities. The company has been obliged by multiple Five-Year Development Plans to increase natural gas reinjection into oilfields in order to protect the hydrocarbon resource rights of future generations and to preserve the national wealth, which plays an important role in long-term investment plans in the petroleum sector and strengthens the country's economy by increasing revenues from crude oil exports. The vital importance of enhancing oil recovery rates had been manifested in a Fatwa issued by late Supreme Leader, Ayatollah Khomeini, urging preservation of oil resources by any means possible.[32]

Despite all the emphasis on the political and economic importance of gas reinjection, the government has never succeeded in achieving the planned level of gas reinjection (Table 6.1). It was only in 2001 that the actual reinjection volume was close to the planned volume – thanks to the start of production from South Pars phases – suggesting that reinjection planning has been unrealistic.

**Table 6.1:** Natural gas reinjection 1995–2012 (mmcm/day)

|  | *1995* | *1998* | *2001* | *2004* | *2007* | *2010* | *2011* | *2012* |
|---|---|---|---|---|---|---|---|---|
| Planned Injection | 101 | 130 | 90 | 137 | 145 | 150 | 150 | 190 |
| Actual Injection | 54.6 | 67.4 | 75.4 | 80.0 | 87.7 | 88.4 | 86.0 | 77.7 |

Source: Iran Energy Balance (2012).

In the absence of a precise analysis on the exact gas volumes needed for reinjection, different figures have been given by experts as to how much and over what time period gas is needed for reinjection purposes. According to a study conducted by Ranani et.al. (2008), in order to compensate losses resulting from the delay in natural gas reinjection and the decline in oilfield pressure, 350 mmcm/day of gas is required for reinjection in order to recover 45 billion barrels of oil throughout the production life of designated oilfields.[33] The Fourth Five-Year Development Plan (2006–10), however, required an average reinjection of 150 mmcm/day. The actual average reinjection by the end of the Fourth Development Plan in 2010, was only 88.40 mmcm/day which was almost half the volume stipulated by the Plan (see Table 6.1). According to the Fifth Five-Year Development Plan (2011–15), crude oil production capacity should increase to 5 million bbl/day by 2015. This would require an increase in the oilfield recovery rate of 1 per cent, which will require an increase in gas reinjection of more than 200 mmcm/day (or 73 bcm/year) which is highly unlikely to materialize.

*Strategic importance of natural gas reinjection*

The importance of natural gas reinjection is reflected in the role it plays in oil production levels, particularly in the light of high oil prices which can boost the country's sources of revenue and strengthen its political and strategic power – or energy diplomacy – regionally and internationally.

Iran's economy is highly dependent on oil revenues. In 2013, oil revenues accounted for 80 per cent of export, and 60–70 per cent of total government revenues.[34] In 1976–77, average oil production exceeded 5.5 million bbl/day with maximum production of more than 6 million bbl/day.[35] But, since the 1979 Revolution, a combination of war, limited investments, international sanctions, and a high rate of natural decline in mature oilfields has made those production levels impossible. The average production capacity of each of the 300 oil wells drilled before the Revolution was then around 25,000 bbl/day. After the Revolution, albeit with production from more than 1000 oil wells, there was a dramatic decline to around 3,000 bbl/day per well by 1998. According to some reports, an estimated 300,000–600,000 bbl/day of crude production capacity is lost annually due to decline in mature fields.[36] The decline rate has caused serious challenges, particularly for light crude production from onshore fields. Two-thirds of this production comes from three fields: Ahwaz-Asmari, Karani, and Agha Jari which have been producing oil for more than six decades and are declining at a rapid rate.[37]

Although Iran has maintained its oil production capacity since the early 2000s as a result of South Pars condensate production, gas reinjection is needed to prevent further decline.[38] Despite massive natural gas resources, the country's ambitious development policies, both in domestic and international markets, and the consequent growing demand, have put serious strains on natural gas supply for

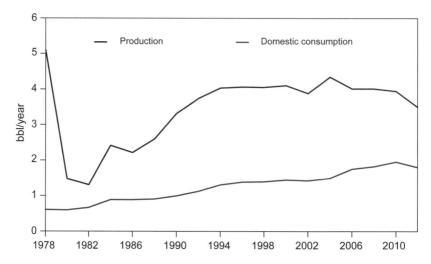

**Figure 6.1:** Iranian oil production and consumption, 1978–2012 (bbl/year)

Source: Iran Energy Balance (2012).

reinjection purposes. In 2009, the Parliament Research Centre warned that, at the current depletion rate, Iran would become an oil importer by 2015.[39]

*The economic evaluation of reinjection projects*
Detailed economic evaluation of reinjection projects, like almost all depletable natural resource development projects, requires extensive econometric analysis which is not possible due to lack of data and goes beyond the scope of this book. For this reason, the issue will be addressed in a qualitative and descriptive economic analysis.

An important factor in the economic evaluation of reinjection projects is the time during which the production rate can be enhanced. It is impossible to assess the economics of a reinjection project merely on the volume of gas needed for reinjection and the amount of oil recovered thereafter. In such projects, costs and returns should be evaluated throughout the operating period, and only when compared with the current value of the project can their economic efficiency be estimated. To estimate the costs of reinjection projects, two methods can be used:[40]

- first, project costs include those of gas production, primary processing, transportation to oilfields, and reinjection. In this method, the condensate production accrued as a result of gas fields development can be added to the project's revenues.
- second, development costs of the downstream operation are calculated independently from that of the upstream sector. In this method, gas is supplied to reinjection projects at a specific price per unit, in which its intrinsic value (including the costs of production and transportation to the oilfield) is included.

An advantage of the second method is that in addition to evaluating the economic efficiency of reinjection, it also provides a comparative cost–benefit analysis of allocating the gas to domestic and export markets. In both methods, in addition to the value of the recovered oil, the value of the gas stored in the oilfield (70–80 per cent is assumed to be recoverable once the oil has been extracted), can be calculated as the benefits of the project.

The economics of reinjection projects can be profoundly affected by the prices of the oil and gas, and the physical characteristics and behaviour of a reservoir. Continuing high oil prices since 2009, and significantly low costs of natural gas field development in comparison with development costs elsewhere, have made reinjection projects highly profitable. Therefore, as long as oil prices are at levels around $100/bbl, the economic viability of reinjection projects will remain intact unless prices plummet, which is not expected in IEA oil price scenarios.[41]

To take the Agha Jari reinjection project as a case study, the field is one of Iran's largest oilfields, where production first came on stream in 1939. Production from Agha Jari reached its peak in 1973, producing around 1,023,000 bbl/day. However, before its gas reinjection project became operational in 2010, the field's production hardly exceeded 100,000 bbl/day. Since the start of gas reinjection, oil production has risen slightly and is estimated to reach 300,000 bbl/day by 2025. In 2013, gas was reinjected to Agha Jari field at the rate of 17 mmcm/day, while its full reinjection requirement is said to be around 40 mmcm/day.[42]

According to NIGC, an estimated volume of 70 to 110 cm of gas is required to be reinjected into the oilfields to add one barrel of oil production capacity.[43] If the price of Iran's natural gas export to Turkey in 2012, which was around $500 mcm, is set as a benchmark, the country earns $0.5/cm from exporting gas while reinjection of the same volume accrues revenue of $0.9 to $1.4 at average oil prices of $100/bbl in 2013. Although profitability also depends on the investment requirements of these options, which are briefly discussed below, the reinjection of gas, even after deducting reinjection costs, is more profitable than exporting gas.[44]

In order to reach more accurate estimates on the cost–benefit analysis of reinjection, the economic loss resulting from the declining production

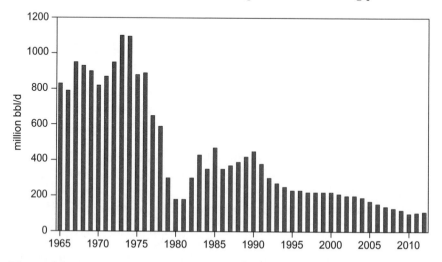

**Figure 6.2:** Agha Jari oil production 1965–2012

Source: Data collection by author.

rate of oilfields should also be taken into account. The statistics over Iran's oilfield annual decline rate are varied. While NIOC reports an average annual production decline of 4 per cent,[45] the US Energy Information Administration (EIA) has suggested a significantly higher average depletion rate of 10 per cent.[46] In our analysis, the calculation based on a NIOC average depletion rate of 4 per cent presents an optimistic scenario, according to which Iran loses 152,000 bbl/day of its production capacity per year, causing an aggregate export revenue loss of around $5.5 billion/year at an average oil price of $100 bbl.[47] Based on a pessimistic scenario of 10 per cent depletion per annum, the aggregate production loss will be 380,000 bbl/day, causing an annual export revenue reduction of $13.8 billion. With the country's domestic oil consumption growing at an average of 5 per cent per annum (equivalent to 2 per cent of the country's current oil production), and taking into account the 4–10 per cent decline in production rate mentioned above, an average 76,000 bbl/day of export capacity per annum will be lost, which, combined with the losses resulting from the depletion rate, can be translated into losing between $8.5 and 16.5 billion of revenue per year.

**Table 6.2:** Agha Jari reinjection project initial cost estimates (2003)

| Infrastructure | Cost ($ million) |
|---|---|
| Construction of 512-km, 56-inch pipeline | 650 |
| Transit route compressor stations | 450 |
| Reinjection compressor stations | 300 |
| Reinjection wells drilling | 120 |
| Total | 1,520 |

Source: Hajarizadeh (2004).

In any comparison between the reinjection and gas export options, however, it is also important to take into account the initial investment cost and operation and maintenance expenses. According to NIOC, the largest gas reinjection project in the Middle East, namely Agha Jari oilfield reinjection, cost around $2.1 billion (inclusive of the gas field development costs) which, albeit relatively higher than the initial estimated cost (see Table 6.2), was significantly lower than the cost of export projects, whether pipeline or LNG, based on cost estimates of recently developed projects (see the next section).[48]

### Pipeline and LNG exports

Iran's post-Revolution gas export projects, arguably with the exception of gas exports to Turkey, did not proceed as initially planned (see Chapter 1). As shown above, the economic benefits of exporting gas may not be as lucrative as reinjection projects, but using gas exports as a strategic means to improve the country's energy diplomacy and bargaining power has been put forward as a justification for lower economic returns. But since Iran's first serious attempt in the early 2000s to become a major gas exporter, many political, geopolitical, economic, and technological changes have occurred which require further consideration to justify new gas export plans.

Firstly, and most importantly, Iran's natural gas production has been outpaced the growing domestic consumption in the last few years. Owning vast gas resources is a necessary but not sufficient condition to become a substantial gas exporter. Many other conditions (reviewed in previous chapters) are needed to turn resource potential into actual export capacity. One may argue that Iran, thanks to its massive gas resources, will 'at some point' produce enough gas, find customers, and build sufficient export infrastructure to become a major gas exporter. But, a review of the Iran–Turkey gas export project shows that this approach has not been successful and has left the country with serious financial and reputational damage.[49] In addition, successful gas exports require long-term policy consistency and adherence to contractual terms while minimizing political and economic risks and uncertainties – conditions which, as shown in Chapters 2 and 4, have been lacking in Iran.

Even if Iran succeeds in substantially increasing its production capacity, it needs to take into account emerging risks and challenges which did not exist when it restarted export projects in the early 2000s. The first challenge is the rising cost of export infrastructure, particularly for LNG. Capital-intensive, highly specialized equipment is required for liquefaction and transportation. In the 1980s, building a liquefaction plant cost around $350/mt, a figure which fell in the 2000s to $200/mt as technology improved.[50] However, in 2013, some LNG facilities are estimated to cost as much as $3,200/mt.[51] One reason is that the price of steel, which LNG projects use in large quantities, has increased dramatically. In 2005, the total investment for building an LNG plant in Iran was estimated at around $1.5–2.5 billion, depending on capacity required. Today, it can cost as much as $15–20 billion to build a 10 mt/year LNG plant, to which the cost of ships must be added.[52]

Another challenge is that substantial development of export infrastructure, in the light of current changing dynamics of regional and international gas markets and uncertainties among investors about natural gas prices, is complicated, requiring an in-depth analysis of the long-term viability of such projects, particularly for a country like Iran with extensive domestic market needs. The discovery and development of shale gas in the USA has changed many market equations; it has created a 'glut of gas supply' in North America, causing prices to plunge and diverting large volumes of LNG to other markets.[53] The IEA has suggested that unconventional gas can put pressure on conventional gas suppliers and on traditional oil-linked pricing mechanisms:

> ... by diversifying sources of supply, tempering demand for import (as in China), and fostering the emergence of new exporting countries (as in the USA).[54]

Despite many obstacles to shale gas outside North America,[55] there is growing optimism that, through further advancement of production technologies, shale gas development can play an increasing role in global gas development. The IEA believes that China (and to a lesser extent India) with sharply rising gas consumption will emerge as a major shale gas producer by 2035.[56] The process will probably accelerate as gradual changes in gas pricing will help to improve incentives for exploration and development of unconventional gas in these countries.[57]

In addition, the emergence of the USA as a potential LNG exporter, in addition to new export projects in East Africa and Australia, will greatly increase global LNG trade in the late 2010s and 2020s. Furthermore, a proportion of this new LNG will have no commitment to a specific market, loosening the long-term structure of LNG sales-and-purchase contracts, and weakening any foreign policy and influence rationale for this trade (see below). The trend has changed the behaviour of leading LNG suppliers, such as Qatar, forcing them to look for alternatives to the US market.

All exporters are seeking to conclude long-term contracts with Asian markets, which have traditionally paid the highest prices for LNG, but in the light of significant additional supplies, and the emergence of short-term LNG trade, there is increasing resistance in Asia to the traditional oil-linked price formula and discussion of a change to market or hub-based prices.[58] Therefore, more price flexibility may be expected from major gas exporters, particularly LNG sellers, with years of experience and strong positions in international markets. But uncertainty about future international gas price mechanisms may undermine the profitability of export projects based on an expectation of linkage to crude oil prices in excess of $100/bbl. Also, short-term trading of LNG, including switching cargoes between markets, might be challenging for a country like Iran, which has no previous commercial experience in LNG, and limited (relatively unsuccessful) pipeline experience.

Over the past decade pipelines, like LNG projects, have also been subject to sharply rising costs of construction, operation, and maintenance. The cost of projects depends on production and transmission costs, the length and capacity of the pipeline, transit charges, and pipeline route specifications. The cost for construction of the Peace Pipeline to Pakistan and India (see Chapter 1) was initially estimated at around $4.5 billion, but as construction was delayed for several years, the cost is expected to rise to as much as $7 billion.[59] Another example is the planned export project to Iraq and Syria which, according to NIGC, is estimated to cost around $10 billion.[60] With investments in the billions, and possibly the tens of billions of dollars, a secure buyer should exist and be willing to sign a long-term sale and purchase agreement. But while project costs are increasing rapidly, revenues may not increase at the same rate. The EIA estimates that the average revenues from Iran's natural gas exports during the period July 2011–June 2012 were approximately $10.5 million/day, or about 5 per cent of the estimated $231 million/day in revenues from crude oil and condensates exports over the same period.[61] In 2010, natural gas exports accounted for less than 4 per cent of Iran's total export earnings, while crude oil and condensates accounted for over 78 per cent, implicitly highlighting the importance of gas reinjection into oilfields.[62]

Like LNG exports, pipeline market characteristics can also be challenging. In addition to the security and political risks involved in projects like the Peace Pipeline, one should not expect significant economic and political returns from the markets of countries such as Armenia – with limited expansion potential and considered to be under the influence of Russia.[63] More promising markets, such as those in Europe, are not easily accessible for a new entrant like Iran, particularly in light of the dominance of Russia (which would strongly oppose any competition from a new supplier) in this market. Iran would have been in a stronger position had it managed to successfully accomplish the gas export projects it had planned in the early 2000s. Back then, its current major rivals, Russia and Qatar, were in much less strong positions. The break-up of the former Soviet Union in the early 1990s had caused 'immediate and continuing problems' in the Russian gas trade, where refusal and/or inability to pay had resulted in huge debts to suppliers and periodic cutbacks.[64] Qatar was also a new entrant at that time; the development of its natural gas resources had faced technical and infrastructure problems, and other obstacles, including political challenges in the ruling family in the mid 1990s, and the second Gulf war which had interrupted many development projects in the region.

*Effectiveness of gas export as a means of energy diplomacy*
As reviewed above, in the consensus among export supporters, the political objective of establishing long-term regional and international gas trade relations far outweighs the economic and commercial returns. After the Iran–Iraq war, reconstruction challenges and the requirement to accelerate social and economic development to meet the expectations of a young population, pushed politicians towards expansion of foreign relations, with a focus on expanding trade and attracting investments for the development of mutually beneficial state-to-state relations and integration into the global economy (see introductory chapter). In the field of energy, this was translated into recognizing the need for regional cooperation, not because of any improvement in relations between regional neighbours, but because of the extremely low level of such interdependence.[65] Regional and international gas trade was perceived by Iranian governments, particularly the Khatami government, as a means of energy diplomacy to counterbalance international political challenges, particularly international sanctions (see introductory chapter).

However, one should challenge the success and effectiveness of Iran's energy diplomacy in the current state of political and diplomatic relations with the outside world. For example, in the case of the Peace Pipeline, besides the prolonged political tension between India and Pakistan, the countries seem to be reluctant to embrace the economic and political risks of establishing long-term gas trade relations with Iran, in the light of increasing international sanctions. Even the most promising export project (namely Iran–Turkey gas export) has been put under threat by EU sanctions on imports of Iranian gas to European markets (see Chapter 1). Perhaps the most acute case demonstrating the unproductive nature of energy diplomacy in a hostile diplomatic environment was the imposition of sanctions on the sale of Iranian crude oil which, despite all the risks and concerns about its potential adverse impact on oil prices in the aftermath of the financial crisis and crippling recession, went ahead and, to the dissatisfaction of many, was implemented successfully.

History has proved that energy diplomacy will become sterile where it is used as a means of manipulation, antagonism, and blackmail. Taking countries like Russia as a role model in implementing political leverage through energy diplomacy, or as it has been put by the media, 'energy blackmailing', has not proved to be a successful policy.[66] First of all, assuming that Russia's energy policy can be shown to be of a blackmailing nature, it has been a failed policy creating a dynamic that has undermined trust and at times created counterproductive outcomes with Russia's energy trading partners.[67] One direct consequence of such a tactic, which could potentially undermine Russia's interest in Europe's gas market, was the swift reaction from EU member states towards adopting a policy of diversification of sources of supply (though these arguably failed to materialize) in order to reduce energy dependence on Russia, hence mitigating their vulnerability. Therefore, using energy as a foreign policy instrument can be as repellent to the importer as it can be attractive to the exporter.[68]

Secondly and more importantly, one ought to distinguish between the use of energy as a diplomatic tool and as a weapon of blackmail. The history of economic relations among nations proves that cooperation, mutual dependence, and reciprocity in trade potential and commercial opportunities, are the underlying elements in sustaining successful trade and economic ties. In addition, any monopolistic and exploitive approach towards trade developments, where for example a country, due to its superior economic capability, perceives itself to be in a position to misuse its power for political leverage or to exert economic pressures on other countries, is doomed to fail. Such an approach is widely believed to be one of the underlying causes of the First and Second World Wars.[69]

Therefore, if Iran wants to monetize its vast energy resources as its mainstay in the region and perhaps in the world, a major shift should be made in its foreign politics. Energy resources can be used as a tool to strengthen commercial engagement by offering mutually beneficial investment projects to foreign governments and world-class companies. This can open up access to capital and state-of-art technologies, while at the same time offering security of energy supply to investors. The resulting interdependence or mutual cooperation would inevitably impact Iran's diplomacy. This will not only secure a more influential position for Iran in international gas trade, but also mitigate current and future resentment and antagonism.

Given Iran's post-Revolutionary relations both within the region and with the international community, the rebuilding of trust and mitigation of antagonism may take many years, and will depend on the regime's overall foreign policy. Improvements since the election of President Rouhani, particularly in foreign policy, have illuminated prospects for better and mutually beneficial relations with neighbouring countries and the international community. But what particularly matters in long-term gas exports is the stability and sustainability of such policies, the lack of which during the Ahmadinejad administration put the country on the verge of global isolation, inflicting on it numerous economic and reputational costs.

## Development of value-added industries

The policy of developing value-added industries, as opposed to oil and gas exports, goes back to the Shah's era when, following his direct order, the first petrochemical plant was constructed in the early 1970s to produce value-added petrochemical products from gas which, up until then, had been flared. This policy was pursued more rigorously after the Revolution and was promoted, albeit in a more radical fashion by opponents of exports, to stop export projects. In the petroleum-rich countries of the MENA region, noticeably Iran and Saudi Arabia, the use of oil and gas to develop value chains is considered of great importance in the promotion of industrialization and diversification.[70] In a famous rhetoric addressed to government authorities, the Supreme Leader, Ayatollah Khamenei, lamented that:

> Generating wealth through selling exhaustible resources like crude oil does not equate to development. We have been selling raw materials and this is self-deception. We have fallen into this trap and we should admit that this is a trap for our nation.[71]

The next section discusses gas-based, value-added industries, specifically petrochemicals, and the possibility of GTL (gas-to-liquids).

### Petrochemical industry

Petrochemicals have become a major industry in Iran. Low-priced[72] and abundant feedstock, geographical advantages, a growing domestic market, and favourable export and fiscal policies make this industry attractive to domestic and international investors. In 2010, the country was the second-largest producer and exporter of petrochemical products in the Middle East after Saudi Arabia.[73] With the beginning of the South Pars gas field development in 2001, the National Iranian Petrochemical Company (NIPC) initiated plans for multiple, large-scale petrochemical plants, such as the Amir Kabir Petrochemical Company. The intensified inward-looking approach of the Ahmadinejad administration further encouraged expansion of the petrochemical industry, increasing the number of operational and planned petrochemical plants to more than 20.[74]

In 2010, petrochemical production capacity reached 51.1 mt/year while actual production was 28.392 mt, of which 10.5 mt was consumed domestically – equivalent to $6.8 billion of sales revenues – and 17.8 mt was exported, generating an income of $11.5 billion.[75] According to Figures 6.3 and 6.4, in 2010 exports increased 26 per cent in volume and 25 per cent in value compared to those of 2009. The growth both in volume and value of exports continued in 2011, reaching 18.2 mt and $14.6 billion, respectively. However, in 2012, as a result of intensification of international sanctions prohibiting sales of petrochemical products, the export value dropped to $12 billion, an 18 per cent decline from the previous year, and further plummeted to $4.84

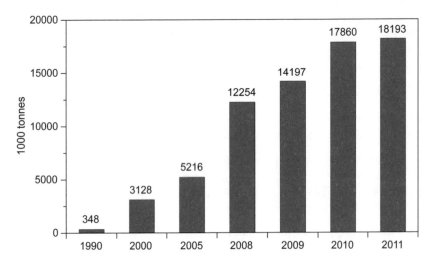

**Figure 6.3:** Iran's petrochemical exports (1000 tonnes)

Source: NIPC Annual Report (2012).

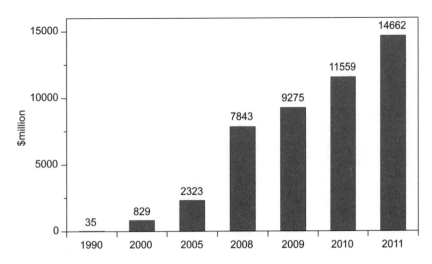

**Figure 6.4:** Iran's petrochemical exports ($ million)

Source: NIPC Annual Report (2012).

billion in the first half of the current Iranian calendar year (starting from 21 March 2013).[76] The removal of petrochemical products from the list of international sanctions following the Geneva interim deal in November 2013 has increased exports which are likely to return to 2012 levels by the end of 2014.

Despite the two-year decline in exports and production as a result of international sanctions, officials remained optimistic about further development of petrochemical capacity. According to Oil Minister, Zanganeh, Iran has the capacity to increase revenue from petrochemical exports to $40 billion/year, for which an investment of $70 billion is required in the next five years.[77]

As in other sectors, there are many challenges facing the development of the petrochemical sector. In addition to international sanctions and lack of capital and technology, weak economic growth, international competition, and slower growth in Iran's major export market, China, have undermined the country's target of reaching a capacity of 65 and 100 mt/year in 2015 and 2025, respectively. Equally important is the possibility of further feedstock shortages (resulting from slow development in the upstream sector), technological failure, and defective equipment causing postponement and/or cancellation of projects.[78]

However, despite all these difficulties, development of the petrochemical industry can economically be very rewarding, not only because of the reasons mentioned above, but also because of the linkage between prices for the majority of petrochemical products and oil prices – a

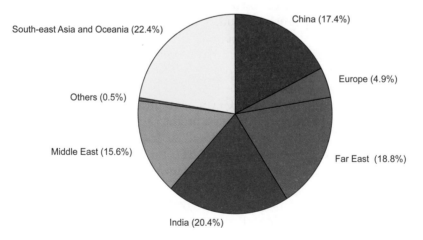

**Figure 6.5:** Percentage shares of Iran's exports of petrochemical products to different markets (2010)

Source: NIPC Annual Report (2011).

linkage which has substantially increased product prices since 2009. By way of comparison with export projects, around 17 per cent of 143 bcm of total gas consumed in 2011 – equivalent to 24 bcm – was used in the petrochemical industry, yielding around $12 billion of revenue; whereas exports of 8.4 bcm of gas generated around $3 billion worth of revenue. The cost of construction of petrochemical plants, depending on the location, specifications, and capacity, varies between $0.5 and 1 billion. For example, the construction cost of Ilam Petrochemical Complex, which started in 2010 and is expected to come on stream by the end of 2014, is estimated around $1 billion, indicating lucrative investment returns.[79]

### Gas-to-Liquids (GTL)

Developments of Gas-to-liquids (GTL) projects have received favourable attention from a broad range of officials and energy experts as another means of monetizing Iran's natural gas resources.[80] GTL projects are developed in countries with favourable geographical characteristics and abundant gas resources or 'stranded resources', meaning reserves located remotely from consumption markets or clusters of small reserves.[81] Concerns about geographical and geopolitical risks, restrictions in some regions on developing pipelines and LNG plants, and the growing divergence between the prices of oil and natural gas have also incentivized gas-rich countries and investors to diversify into GTL projects.

GTL is a process for converting natural gas into synthetic oil, which can then be further processed into other hydrocarbon-based products. It has a long history starting from 1926 when two German chemists (Fischer and Tropsch) produced the first Synthetic Liquid Hydrocarbons (SLH) from syngas (a mixture of carbon monoxide and hydrogen).[82] The technology was first developed on an industrial scale in 1944 when, during the Second World War, Germany found it increasingly difficult to access conventional oil and refined product supplies for its naval fleet.

Iran's first GTL plant was proposed to Iran by Shell in 1999, for which an agreement was signed with NIPC for construction of a 75,000 bbl/day GTL plant near Assaluyeh. However, after three years of negotiation, disagreement over the contractual terms, gas prices, and political and economic pressures resulting from international sanctions, led to the project being cancelled. When Shell built the project (known as Pearl GTL) in Qatar in the 2000s, a substantial increase in costs – from $5 billion to around $18 billion[83] – cast serious doubts about the economic feasibility of GTL projects.[84]

Iran's subsequent attempts to develop large-scale GTL projects with the cooperation of Sasol of South Africa and domestic companies, using European technologies, failed. The country's GTL capacity has not gone beyond a pilot plant inaugurated in Tehran in December 2012. But with serious uncertainties over GTL investment and construction costs, and an inability to access the required technologies due to international sanctions, the prospect for development of any large-scale GTL projects seems very remote. However, if in the future more certainty is achieved with regards to GTL project construction, factors such as: the low prices which can potentially be allocated to such projects, a favourable geographical position, a cheap labour force, and, more importantly, the current trend for natural gas prices to be de-linked from oil, may combine to increase the attractiveness of GTL plants for potential investors.

## Conclusion

Iran has ambitious plans to develop its natural gas markets, both domestically and internationally. The country's limited production capacity, however, has made it unable to meet both domestic and export commitments. Although it has been a modest exporter of gas since the early 2000s, exports are exceeded by imports. Natural gas allocation policies have been subject to much discussion among politicians and energy experts. However, no in-depth economic study has been conducted which would enable a clear conclusion about the economic return from each of the gas allocation options. While this chapter acknowledged that such an analysis is not possible due to a lack of data, it has nevertheless tried to shed some light on the challenges and opportunities for allocating gas to different markets.

Iran's gas export policy has been driven by political, rather than economic, objectives. Establishment of regional and international gas trade relations has been perceived by politicians as a diplomatic and political means to strengthen the country's geopolitical position. A review of gas export projects, however, shows that the country has not been successful in achieving its political objectives through gas exports. And that such a policy is misconceived, since a major component of it, cooperation and reciprocity based on mutual interest, has been lacking.

Today, when discussing the prospects for gas exports, it is important to carefully examine the current political and economic conditions surrounding and affecting Iran's economy as a whole and its petroleum sector in particular. The title of 'largest gas owner in the world' has made many Iranian and foreign observers 'illusional' about its export capabilities.[85] Setting strategic policies requires a fact-based understanding of the natural gas industry. Lack of reliable data, transparency, and the disconnection between upstream activity and downstream objectives, makes any assessment of the cost and potential for development almost impossible. Moreover, export facilities require huge capital investment and modern technologies, access to which is extremely limited in the light of international sanctions. If the current circumstances continue (meaning limited production capacity, a growing domestic market, and prevailing international sanctions) reinjection of gas into oilfields should be given top priority after meeting domestic market demands. This can be followed by the development of value-added industries, including petrochemicals. In this situation, and in the absence of political improvement, binding the country to additional export commitments will not only cause serious economic and reputational damage, but could also jeopardize national interests. In this scenario, it is impossible to see Iran becoming a major gas exporter, even if this does not mean that the country must remain a major gas importer.

However, if the confrontation between Iran and the international community eases, paving the way for sustainable, constructive cooperation, one could imagine Iran having a greater share in regional gas trade, with LNG exports being a longer-term possibility. But the option of significant development of gas export capacity is only realistic following a substantial increase in gas production capacity, combined with measures to control domestic demand growth. Any substantial increase in Iran's production capacity, even if sanctions are lifted within a relatively short period of time after a final agreement is reached, is unlikely to materialize prior to 2020. Even if this happens, *substantial* development of export capacity could only occur after 2025 – for LNG beyond 2030 – because the negotiation of export contracts, construction of required infrastructure, and marketing of gas requires a lead time of 15 years. Therefore, even if the required political conditions are met, Iran may only become a major international gas player after 2030.

# CONCLUSION

## IRAN'S GAS INDUSTRY – OPTIMISM, SCEPTICISM, AND POTENTIAL

### Introduction

This chapter summarizes the findings of previous chapters and offers thoughts on the prospects for Iran's natural gas industry up to 2020 and beyond.

This book has provided a full picture of the industry as it stands in 2014 by examining the factors which have had an impact on its development since the Islamic Revolution of 1979. It has tried to answer the question of why, despite owning the largest gas reserves in the world, Iran has not only failed to play a major role in the international gas trade, but also has turned into a net gas importer to fulfil its growing domestic market needs. Our study identified many reasons for this situation, the most important of which were: US and international sanctions; politicization of the petroleum industry; lack of an attractive investment regime; subsidies and a growing domestic market; and natural gas allocation complexities. These reasons, along with their impacts on the development of the natural gas industry, are summarized in this chapter under five themes while additional thoughts are also offered on the impact of optimistic and pessimistic outcomes for each of these themes on the industry. The chapter concludes by highlighting the potential impact of gas development on domestic and international markets to 2020 and beyond.

### US and international sanctions

US and international sanctions have been the most important factor underlying Iran's failure to substantially develop its gas resources. The progressive sanctions have severely limited Iran's access to international financial institutions and strictly prohibited foreign companies' participation in the development of its oil and gas sector. They have banned investment and technologies for the development and expansion of gas resources and export infrastructure (see Chapter 3). With few exceptions, almost all major natural gas projects have been either cancelled or abandoned, or substantially delayed, as a result of sanctions, while other projects have faced major difficulties in continuing to operate. Cancellation and suspension of all LNG and some major pipeline exports projects, including the Peace Pipeline and the export pipeline to Europe, made the prospect of Iran becoming a major international gas player highly unlikely.

Any substantial development of the Iranian natural gas industry, to a large extent, depends on the removal or easing of US and international sanctions. If Iran fails to reach a final agreement with the international community, the sanctions will most likely be intensified and will make it almost impossible to see any improvement of the gas industry. Further deterioration seems increasingly likely. In this situation, the gap between the growing domestic market and production capacity will expand further, forcing the country to increase its imports. Frequent interruptions in gas supply would have drastic social and economic consequences as a huge portion of the population – around 75 per cent – consumes gas in household and commercial sectors. Also, a large number of power plants – around 60 per cent of total generation capacity – are gas-fired and without gas they will have to switch to fuel oil, which means depriving the country of a vast source of revenue from fuel oil exports. Continuation (and possible intensification) of sanctions will not only eliminate the chance of expanding Iran's export capacity, but may also force the country to cut off supply to existing export markets, entailing further serious financial damage.

There is, however, an optimistic view that has been strengthened by the coming to power of President Rouhani with his determination to resolve the nuclear crisis with the international community, providing hope that it will be possible to remove sanctions within a relatively short period of time. Although there is scepticism about the timing and scale of sanctions removal, it is reasonable to be optimistic that, in the light of the political improvements achieved since the election of President Rouhani in June 2013, reaching a final agreement, which would include the lifting of sanctions, is a serious possibility by the end of 2014.

Iranian sanctions have hybrid characteristics in terms of their scope and specific national and regional characteristics (see Chapter 3). While it may be more challenging to remove the US and UN sanctions (in the light of the requirement to reach the consensus needed in the UN Security Council or the US Congress), it is possible to see gradual removal of EU sanctions starting from early 2015 if Iran manages to improve its political and diplomatic relations with the EU. US sanctions may also be temporarily suspended if the US President decides to use his authority to grant a waiver, as long as Iran adheres to its commitments under a nuclear deal, and for as long as he remains in office. But permanent removal requires US Congressional approval which, given the complex nature of sanctions, may be difficult and take longer to achieve.

Once sanctions are eased or removed, one should expect a significant flow of investment capital and technologies to the country. In the gas sector, this means development of gas resources which either had never started or which had been suspended, cancelled, or delayed for many years. The development of resources also means an increase in production capacity, which is the source of most of Iran's issues relating to adequate supply of both domestic and export markets. Substantial increases in production can reduce dependency on gas imports and increase export capacity. Although LNG projects may take longer to materialize (see below), Iran can expand its pipeline export capacity in a shorter period of time using existing infrastructure. More importantly, growth in gas production means the availability of more gas for reinjection purposes and hence an improvement in rates of oil recovery, which has significant economic and political importance.

## Politicization of the oil and gas industry

Historical concerns relating to the exploitive and manipulative nature of foreign intervention in the petroleum industry have made it a profoundly politically sensitive sector. The resulting mistrust and suspicion have led to the politicization of the industry with multiple institutions exerting influence on the policy-making process and with politics far outweighing economic considerations. This has created an opaque, hard-to-comprehend system where it is very difficult to identify ultimate decision makers, and this undermines the predictability and stability of the sector's development. This peculiar system is especially problematic in the gas industry, where institutions ranging from the Ministry of Petroleum, National Iranian Oil Company, National Iranian Gas Company, and National Iranian Gas Export Company, to the Parliament, Council of Guardians, Expediency Council, and last but not least the Islamic Revolutionary Guard Corps, all directly or indirectly intervene in its decision-making process (see Chapter 2).

Political interventions have been, and are likely to continue to be, a major impediment in the design and implementation of a comprehensive, medium- to long-term policy for the gas sector. Prolonged debates about the merits of exports versus domestic consumption, which stem from the same syndrome of politicization, are likely to continue, with institutional competition for implementation of different policy agendas. For natural gas exports, which require operation of projects over a long period of time, this means serious uncertainty about secure gas delivery, which might be undermined by a vicious cycle of policy shifts between export and domestic markets. As this increases the political and economic risks, it will significantly diminish investors' confidence in Iran.

It is not hard to imagine that the political debate about natural gas allocation is continuing in the Rouhani administration and is expected to play a major role in decisions relating to the expansion of export projects. The evidence so far shows that the Rouhani government, unlike its predecessor, is pursuing the policy of export market expansion which, in the light of improving international and regional political relations and possible removal of sanctions, may become a near-term option. However, the policy is likely to be challenged by other institutions, particularly the Parliament, through for example, posing challenges on budget ratification, conducting investigations on contract terms and negotiation details, and interfering in bidding processes.

Pessimism regarding confusion surrounding the organizational structure of the gas industry is also likely to persist, as there is no evidence showing that the government is planning to simplify the system or create an integrated structure in which all matters relating to the gas value chain are to be dealt with within one organization.

Also, as experiences of previous gas export negotiations show, one cannot be optimistic about successful conclusion of contract negotiations, due to the problem of political intervention and the prevailing culture of mistrust and fear of foreign dominance (see Chapters 2 and 4). Iranian counterparts are likely to continue to exhibit tough and inflexible negotiating behaviours, and may subsequently seek renegotiations of these same deals, for fear of being deceived and having 'given away' too much to foreigners.

## The foreign investment regime

In the post-Revolutionary era, the foreign investment regime underwent a dramatic transition from an absolute ban on foreign investment, due to the ideologically isolationist path that emphasized self-sufficiency and independence from foreigners, to the attraction and promotion of foreign investment as a result of the country's post-war economic hardship which highlighted the need for attraction of foreign capital and technology. The buyback contracts, introduced to open up the country's petroleum industry to foreign companies, were strictly designed to accommodate the constitutional restrictions on foreign involvement in upstream oil and gas development activities. The result was a contractual regime with rigid, inflexible, and unattractive terms which, despite flourishing investment opportunities in Iran's petroleum sector, did not succeed in attracting substantial investment capital and know-how.

When taking office in summer 2013, the Rouhani government was quick to reform the oil and gas investment regime by, most importantly, revising the upstream contractual regime and abandoning the unpopular buyback contracts which, in the face of increasing international sanctions, damaged hopes for any successful foreign investment. The new contracts are expected to offer flexible and attractive terms and are said to be competitive with contracts offered elsewhere in the region. There is optimism that the new contractual regime, along with the introduction and implementation of investor-friendly laws and regulations such as the Foreign Investment Promotion and Protection Act (FIPPA), can pave the way for the return of foreign investors in oil and gas development projects. These reforms may be particularly attractive for the development of natural gas resources where a long-term, integrated contractual structure is needed to encompass development activities in different segments of the value chain. The government's policy of offering more flexible terms in its future contractual arrangements for the development of joint-fields such as South Pars (from which the Qatari side has been producing gas for many years) can attract capital and technology to speed up development and production from such fields.

This book has shown that there is mounting optimism about the positive role that the new regulatory and contractual reforms can play in attracting foreign investment, and also in encouraging foreign companies to exert pressure on their governments to ease and/or remove sanctions once a final deal is reached on the nuclear issue. However, the shadow of weak governance institutions and systematic corruption in Iran continues to pose serious risks to the participation of foreign investors in oil and gas projects. As reviewed in Chapter 4, the judicial system and bureaucratic administrations responsible for the protection and enforcement of investors' rights are notorious for being influenced by rent-seeking, politically driven incentives, leaving them with limited capacity for the professional performance of their roles. For natural gas developments, particularly those aimed at export markets, the economic viability of projects is dependent on stable and successful operation of long-term (up to 25 year) contractual commitments. Therefore, the absence of an effective, non-corrupt, independent institutional infrastructure which could guarantee the successful implementation of such projects, will influence the investors' decisions on whether to invest in Iran at all, and, if so, may have an impact on any agreement – whose terms may not safeguard both the country's long-term national interests and those of investors.

## Subsidies and domestic market growth

Natural gas consumption after the Revolution experienced skyrocketing growth, making the country the third-largest gas market in the world. Low gas prices, the policy of domestic market expansion, oilfield reinjection, gas for oil substitution, and expansion of energy-intensive industries have been the main drivers of domestic market growth. As the development of natural gas resources slowed, mainly as a result of international sanctions, the country was faced with gas shortages and was forced to increase gas imports from Turkmenistan to meet its deficit.

In order to control the growing rate of gas consumption, the government, as a part of its 2010 energy subsidies reform plan, substantially increased gas prices by as much as 200–300 per cent in some sectors. However, the price rise had little impact on reduction of gas demand in domestic markets. This was mainly a result of the government's policy of domestic market expansion and gas for oil substitution which, since the reform, had added many new users to the network. Also poor implementation of the reform, along with intensification of international sanctions, led to high inflation and devaluation of the national currency, causing a large proportion of subsidies to be restored.

Despite a substantial price increase in the first phase of the reform, expensive cash hand-outs and international sanctions meant that the government fell short of the expected revenues which were initially planned to be allocated for development of natural gas projects. Facing difficulties in making monthly payments, the government also had to distribute a large portion of the funds which should have been allocated to NIOC's and NIGC's budgets, leaving them with virtually no money to invest in development projects.

In the short run, it is hard to be optimistic that subsidies reform and price increases will lead to substantial reduction of consumption, and significant additional government revenues. The subsidies reform should have taken place against a backdrop of stable and strong economic conditions in which inflation and exchange rates could have been controlled. As long as these conditions are not met, one cannot expect major changes in the level of consumption and the availability of gas for other purposes, including exports or reinjection. The situation could worsen if the country does not bring new production capacity on stream. In such circumstances, and in the face of growing domestic demand, it is likely that the country will not be able to continue gas supply to its current export markets, let alone expand volumes to new markets.

The prospect for subsidies reform and its impact on the natural gas market can be positive in the long term if the country succeeds in improving its political relations with the international community and in strengthening its economy. In such a situation, price increases will have real significance and will not devalue in the face of rising inflation or adverse exchange rate movements. Even without a major impact on reducing consumption (as the government's policy of market expansion is likely to continue for many years), price increases can moderate consumption increases and encourage more efficient use of resources. They can also save government revenues, which can be invested in upstream and downstream projects. Better international political relations can also mean access to new technologies and capital to renew and upgrade capital stock, and hence to less wasteful consumption of gas in the industrial sector and power generation.

Participation of foreign investors in the development of Iran's natural gas industry will remain confined to the upstream sector. Deregulation and liberalization of the downstream sector with private investment is highly unlikely for the foreseeable future, due to numerous political, economic, and social considerations. The political imperative of secure supply to the domestic market will reduce the possibility of private investors replacing state-owned companies such as NIGC in downstream activities (processing, transmission, and distribution), despite the fact that new investors might run these sectors more efficiently.

If Iran wants to become a major gas exporter, it must substantially increase its production capacity while controlling the rate of growth of domestic demand. The assumption that export capacity can be increased by raising domestic prices and hence creating gas savings is naïve.

## Natural gas allocation challenges: domestic market versus exports

The issue of optimal allocation of gas resources has gained significant importance in the last few years, in the light of inadequate production capacity which has created serious competition between domestic consumption, reinjection, and exports. The allocation policy in Iran is, to a large extent, driven by political rather than economic considerations. Various political and institutional bodies try to enforce their own set of policies on allocation decisions, making any long-term planning almost impossible. While some political groups, mostly from the Parliament, demand allocation of gas resources to domestic markets on social equity grounds and in response to political objectives, government officials support a gas exports option as a means of strengthening the country's bargaining power in international relations. Closer examination of both groups' justifications shows that little consideration is given to either the country's political and economic conditions or to the realities of global energy market developments which, if taken into account, can have a profound effect on natural gas allocation policies.

If current conditions (limited production capacity, a growing domestic market, and international sanctions) continue, reinjection of gas into oilfields should be given priority after demand from household and commercial sectors has been met, as the latter has top priority, primarily due to social equity objectives. The economic benefits resulting from adequate reinjection of gas are substantially higher than those of other options, while it also strengthens the country's bargaining power – or energy diplomacy – in regional and international spheres. Reinjection can be followed by development of value-added industries including petrochemicals which, given Iran's young and educated labour force, low-priced abundant feedstock, geographical advantages, and favourable export and fiscal policies, can make a significant contribution to the country's economic growth. The export option should only be taken up if there is any gas surplus from the other sectors. In other words, in the light of current gas shortages, it is economically unprofitable for Iran to expand its export capacity (see Chapter 6). Compared with other options, gas exports do not yield significant economic returns. Secondly it is highly unlikely that Iran can use gas exports as a means of bargaining power in a political and diplomatic environment where the country remains under the threat of being further isolated if it fails to reach a final agreement with the international community.

The Rouhani government, in the face of expected improvements in political conditions and removal of international sanctions, has already indicated interest in an expansion of export capacity. Despite comparatively low economic returns, export projects have the strong political attraction of using energy as a means of diplomacy. But, even if political relations improve, energy diplomacy will only be successful if it is not used, or perceived to be intended, as a means of manipulation, antagonism, and blackmail. Energy diplomacy should be accompanied by non-hostile, constructive foreign policy if it is to strengthen trade and commercial ties. Equally important, successful gas exports require long-term policy consistency and adherence to contractual terms, while minimizing domestic political and economic risks and uncertainties which, under Iran's unstable policy-making system and its opaque political/institutional structure, is hard to achieve. The experience of the Ahmadinejad government's radical shift in foreign policy from conciliation to confrontation has created serious doubt about fulfilment and sustainability of such conditions if Iran is to become a major gas exporter.

Even if Iran succeeds in meeting these political and strategic pre-requisites, it may face serious difficulties in building large-scale export capacity in the face of emerging risks and challenges which did not exist when it first embarked on restarting gas exports in the early 2000s. Iran is likely to struggle to create itself a place in the international gas trade given developments such as: substantial cost increases in develop-ing new export infrastructure, changing global gas market dynamics, uncertainties for investors, technological advancements in which it cannot currently share, and uncertainty about the future of natural gas price formation. All of these relatively new phenomena could make it seriously difficult for Iran to compete with already well-established exporters, particularly of LNG, in international markets.

**Iran's gas future to 2020 and beyond: optimism, scepticism, and potential**

Iran's natural gas future to 2020 and beyond involves many uncertain-ties. An important part of the immediate answer to the question of whether Iran can further substantially develop its natural gas resources depends on the country's relations with the international community, particularly the USA. Any major development in the gas sector requires huge capital investment, and technologies which are strictly prohibited under the current sanctions regime. However, the trajectory of nuclear negotiations since the arrival of the Rouhani government has been positive, suggesting serious determination on both sides to resolve their differences. If no major progress is achieved in the negotiations, it is difficult to see any positive changes – and indeed possible further deterioration – for the gas industry. In this scenario, gas production will continue to struggle to keep pace with the increasing growth in domestic demand, most likely leading to increases in gas imports and gas export reductions and interruptions. As the possibility of domestic gas rationing increases, the potential economic loss resulting from insufficient gas supply to oilfield reinjection projects and power generation will be immense. In such circumstances, the prospects for even the maintenance of exports at current levels will be uncertain, and additional expansion of such projects will become almost impossible.

However, improvements in the international political situation can, to a large extent, change the picture of Iran's natural gas future – depending on when a final deal is achieved and on the time frame of sanctions removal. With the required investment and technology, Iran can add up around 50–80 bcm to its production capacity within a five year period, bringing total production capacity up to 210–240 bcm by 2020. This can be achieved if enough investment is available to bring on stream phases 12, 15, 16, 17, and 18 of South Pars which, as of March 2014, had been developed to 80 per cent of their capacity (on average). Beyond 2020, the remaining nine phases of South Pars could be brought on stream which, combined with production from other fields, could increase total gas production to around 350 bcm by 2030.

Up to 2020, domestic demand will continue its upward trend – though at a slower rate – primarily as a result of the government market expansion, and gas for oil substitution policies. If sanctions are removed, new technologies can be utilized to upgrade capital stock and also enhance power generation efficiency. At an average growth rate of 6–8 per cent (as has been the case in the last 10 years), domestic consumption of gas will reach 200 bcm/year in 2020. Such a projection is also supported by the new government's determination to further increase prices, encouraging additional conservation and efficiency in the household and commercial sectors.

The gas export outlook has many uncertainties, but with the above production and consumption projections, by 2020 Iran is likely to have a 10–40 bcm/year gas surplus which can be exported via pipeline. However, as exporting gas needs extensive infrastructure, huge sources of funding, and long-term agreements, the time frame for export of the above-mentioned surplus will most likely be beyond 2020. It is important to bear in mind that even if international sanctions are lifted and favourable fiscal and contractual terms are offered to IOCs for development of the country's gas sector, it would take Iran at least 15 years to develop its export infrastructure to the point where it could become a major gas exporter – of around 100 bcm/year.

By way of comparison, Qatar provides a good example of the time horizon required for achievement of this level of exports, taking into account the requirements of attraction of foreign investment and technologies, the construction of the required infrastructure, and marketing. Qatar adopted the fastest export development programme yet seen in the world,[1] and made remarkable progress, emerging as the world's largest LNG exporter – 105 bcm in 2012 – 20 years from the start of export-oriented gas field development, and 16 years from its first cargo of LNG. The Qatari government adopted policies for fast and effective development of its natural gas resources, including partnerships with international oil companies which were major players in the LNG industry and could provide expertise and experience. It adopted project and legal structures which were attractive to foreign investors and changed the fiscal regime to improve the economic situation and to encourage investment.[2] As reviewed in this book (see Chapters 2–4), these are essential attributes that will take time and, given the past history of petroleum development, may never be seen in Iran. Therefore, taking Qatari gas development as a successful model, it would take Iran 15–20 years to become a major gas exporter, provided that the international sanctions are lifted, and the country is ready to offer attractive legal and fiscal terms to foreign investors. Therefore, adding a lead time of 15 years for the development of export infrastructure, it is difficult to see Iran becoming a major gas exporter prior to 2030.

Even if the required conditions are met, Iran's gas exports projects in a 2030 time frame are most likely to focus on pipeline exports to regional markets, including Iraq, Kuwait, Oman, Pakistan, and possibly increased exports to Turkey and Armenia. It is conceivable that a portion of additional export volumes to Turkey could be delivered to Europe, but any major direct export link to the European market prior to 2030 is difficult to imagine, particularly due to lack of required infrastructure in place, huge investment costs, and the EU's reluctance to rely on unstable suppliers on a long-term basis.

There are also serious doubts about whether the government will resume the development of its abandoned LNG projects prior to 2020, due principally to marketing difficulties and mounting investment costs. However, as the LNG market becomes more mature, and uncertainties arising from shale gas development and modification of terms and pricing of contracts become clearer, Iran might decide to embark on development of LNG capacity. However, given where Iran is starting from, it is almost impossible to see it as a significant LNG exporter prior to 2030, as it is likely to take at least 15 years to successfully design, construct, bring on stream, and market production of a large-scale LNG plant in Iran.

Even beyond 2030, Iran's potential aspiration to substantially develop LNG exports may be curbed by its growing population – more than 76 million in 2013 – and its rapid industrialization policy which encourages excessive expansion of gas-based, energy-intensive industries. Also, as the country's oilfields become more mature, the need for gas reinjection becomes even more pressing, limiting the volume of gas available for export purposes, particularly for new LNG projects. Therefore, in a 2030 time frame, although Iran is likely to have substantially developed its gas production capacity, giving it the potential to boost its exports, it is very important to understand that it is in a completely different situation to countries such as Qatar. Iran has a huge domestic market with massive development capacities and a large young educated workforce, for which the government needs to create employment. Therefore, as the government plans to seriously pursue policies of domestic market expansion and development of value-added industries, it will not be surprising to see a continuation of the competitive tension between allocation to domestic and export markets even beyond 2030, particularly in the light of ongoing increases in domestic gas prices which can significantly increase the economic return of allocating gas to domestic markets, hence reducing export incentives.

Therefore, given reasonable optimism about reaching a final agreement with the international community and the consequent lifting of sanctions, Iran may be able to play a greater role in international gas trade over the next 15–20 years than has been the case since 2000. However, despite huge reserves, the country's internal political constraints and domestic energy requirements mean that Iran should not be expected to become a major exporter of gas to international markets in the period up to 2030.

# NOTES

## Introduction

1   According to the BP Statistics Review 2013, Iran, owning natural reserves of 33.6 tcm, is ranked as the largest natural gas owner in the world followed by Russia and Qatar. For many years, Russian natural gas reserves were ranked first in the world; but BP, following a decision to align the numbers with Western accounting standards, lowered its estimates for proven natural gas reserves in Russia by nearly one third. BP (2013).
2   Wilfried, B. (2000)
3   Thaler, A and et al. (2010, 79)
4   Ibid., 79
5   Ibid., 116
6   Maleki, A. (2002).
7   Thaler, A. et.al. op.cit., 117.
8   Ibid., 116.
9   Ibid., 117.
10  Sadjadpour, K. (2008).
11  Thaler, A et.al., op.cit., 118.
12  Ibid., 113.
13  Ibid., 119.
14  Amuzegar, J. (2004).
15  Ibid.
16  Karshenas. M. and Hakimian, H. (2005, 75).
17  Amuzegar, op.cit.
18  Ramazani (1989).
19  Ehteshami, A. (1995).
20  Pesaran, E. (2011).
21  Bonyads are publicly owned giant charitable organizations.
22  Ehteshami, A. and Zweiri, M. (2011).
23  Ansari, A. (2008).
24  Ansari, A (2013).
25  NBC News (2013).
26  The term 'heroic flexibility' has been used on several occasions by Iran's Supreme Leader Ayatollah Khamenei indicating that in the international political sphere while it is possible to engage in dialogue with enemies, Iranian diplomats and negotiators must be firm in their principled positions and 'take as their model His Holiness Imam Khomeini's steadfastness and manliness'. In a speech delivered to members of the Assembly of Experts in September 2013, he declared, 'artistic and heroic leniency and flexibility in all political arena is desirable and acceptable', but this 'manoeuvring

must not mean crossing redlines, regressing from fundamental strategies, and disregarding the ideals'. Ayatollah Khamenei official website: *http://farsi.khamenei.ir/keyword-content?id=4952*

27   NBC News (2013).
28   Bijan Namdar Zanganeh is the longest serving Minister in Iran with more than 23 years of ministerial experience under the Khamenei, Hashemi Rafsanjani, and Khatami governments as Minister of Agriculture, Energy, and Oil.

## Chapter 1: A background to Iran's natural gas industry

1    E.C.A.F.E Natural Gas Seminar (1964).
2    Soleimanian, R. (2003).
3    Over more than 60 years of flaring, until the country's first attempt to commercialize its natural gas resources in the late 1960s, around 130 bcm (118mtoe) of gas were burned. Vahedi, H. (1977).
4    E.C.A.F.E Natural Gas Seminar op.cit.
5    Shirazi, M. (1974).
6    Soleimanian, op.cit.
7    Behzad, H. (1973).
8    Manoochehri, N. (1970).
9    Ibid.
10   Ibid.
11   Vahedi op.cit.
12   Manoochehri, op.cit.
13   According to Vahedi (1977), Britain's Lord Chalfont had warned the British and US governments about the influence of the USSR on Iran, which he believed could inflict serious financial damage and weaken their political influence over Iran. Vahedi, op.cit.
14   Manoochehri, op.cit.
15   Ibid.
16   Mina, P. (1977).
17   Adibi, S. (2002).
18   Kangan-Iran (1978).
19   Adibi, op.cit.
20   Shirazi, op.cit.
21   Vahedi, op.cit.
22   Pardeli, B. (2008).
23   Ibid.
24   Ibid.
25   Iran Energy Balance (1967–2009). Ministry of Energy.
26   Dehghani, T. (2007).
27   Ibid.
28   Ibid.

29  This Perspective sets the economic development agenda for a 20-year period – from 2005 to 2025 – and is also endorsed by the Supreme Leader.

30  Iran's 20-Year Economic Perspective 2005–2025.

31  Ibid.

32  Iran lost its position as the second-largest gas producer to Iraq as a result of international sanctions on its sale of oil and the increase in Iraqi oil production. In March 2014, Iran ranked as the third largest oil producer in OPEC, but its rank had fallen to fifth in 2013. OPEC (2014).

33  Iran's 20-Year Economic Perspective 2005–2025.

34  Khandan, M. (2012).

35  Mash'al (2005).

36  The issue of 'politicization' of the Iranian petroleum industry; for more detail, see Chapter 3.

37  The eight processing companies are: Ilam, Bid Boland I, Parsian, South Pars, Fajr, Sarkhoon & Qeshm, Shahid Hasheminejad, Bid Boland II. Iran Energy Balance (2012).

38  The provincial gas companies are: Azerbaijan Sharghi, Azerbaijan Gharbi, Ardebil, Isfahan, Ilam, Tehran, Chahar Mahal Bakhtiari, Northern Khorasan, Khorasan Razavi, Southern Khorasan, Khoozestan, Zanjan, Semnan, Fars, Qazvin, Qom, Kordestan, Kerman, Kermanshah, Koh-kilooye Boyerahmad, Golestan, Gilan, Lorestan, Mazandaran, Markazi, Hamedan, Yazd, Bushehr, Hormozgan, and Sistan and Baluchistan. Iran Energy Balance (2012).

39  The administrative companies are: Natural Gas Storage Company, Engineering and Development Company, Commercial Company, and Transmission Company.

40  Tabnak (2012).

41  Shana: *www.shana.ir/fa/newsagency/208688* (2013).

42  Iran Energy Balance (2012).

43  See note 1 of the Introductory chapter. Note that this source changed its methodology in 2012 in a way which significantly downgraded Russian reserves which had hitherto been the largest in the world.

44  Iran Energy Balance (2012).

45  Although many studies reported different figures for the number of South Pars phases, this research follows the data presented at the official website of Pars Oil and Gas Company, the South Pars project managing company; Pars Oil and Gas Company (2014).

46  Ibid.

47  Ibid.

48  Shana. (2011). http://www.shana.ir/fa/newsagency/161038.

49  Shana. (2012b).

50  Ibid.

51  Shana: *www.shana.ir/fa/newsagency/209050* (2013).

52  Shaha: *www.shana.ir/fa/newsagency/209829* (2013).

53  Iran Energy Balance (2011).

54    Pars Oil & Gas Company (2012).
55    BP Statistical Review of World Energy (2012).
56    The gas that accumulates in the upper portions of a reservoir where the pressure, temperature, and fluid characteristics are conducive to free gas. The energy provided by the expansion of the gas cap provides the primary drive mechanism for oil recovery in such circumstances. Schlumberger Oilfield Glossary available at: *www.glossary.oilfield.slb.com/en/Terms/.aspx*.
57    Iran Energy Balance (2012).
58    Iran Energy Balance (2012).
59    Shana: *www.shana.ir/fa/newsagency/210710* (2014)
60    Ibid.
61    Iran Energy Balance (2012)
62    Iran Energy Balance (2011).
63    Ibid.
64    Ibid.
65    Owji, J. (2012b).
66    Iran Energy Balance (2011).
67    Ibid.
68    Owji, J. (2012a).
69    Shana: *www.shana.ir/fa/newsagency/211024* (2013)
70    Iran Energy Balance (2011).
71    Pars Oil & Gas Company (2014).
72    Ibid.
73    Iran Energy Balance (2011).
74    Pars Oil & Gas Company (2014).
75    Iran Energy Balance (2011).
76    Ibid.
77    Ibid.
78    Ibid.
79    Shana: *http://www.shana.ir/fa/newsagency/156664* (2010).
80    Iran Energy Balance (2011).
81    Shana: *www.shana.ir/fa/newsagency/148114* (2009).
82    Iran Energy Balance (2011).
83    Middle East Economic Survey (MEES) (2008).
84    Ibid.
85    Iran Energy Balance (2011).
86    Owji, J. (2012a).
87    Shana (2012a).
88    Iran Energy Balance (2011).
89    Shana (2010).
90    Owji, J. (2012a)
91    Iran Energy Balance (2011).
92    Ibid.
93    In 2012, the actual volume of gas delivered to the network was around 161 bcm. However, as will be mentioned in Chapter 6, a significant portion of the delivered gas to the domestic grid, around 10–12 bcm,

goes missing due to gas leakage and theft.

94 Ibid., BP Statistical Review of World Energy (2013).
95 In 2012, the country's primary energy balance constitutes: oil products 35.75 per cent, natural gas 53.45 per cent, electricity 9.93 per cent, renewables 0.7 per cent, and coal 0.17 per cent. Iran Energy Balance (2012).
96 NIGC (2013).
97 Ibid.
98 Ibid.
99 Shana: *www.shana.ir/fa/newsagency/211003* (2013).
100 Iran Energy Balance (2012).
101 Dehghani, op.cit.
102 Ibid
103 In 2011, the aggregate gas volume reinjected into the Agha Jari oil field was 5bcm. Shana (2011).
104 Iran Energy Balance 2012,
105 Majles Research Centre (2009).
106 NIOC (2010).
107 World Bank (2012).
108 Iran Energy Balance (2012).
109 Ibid.
110 Shana: *www.shana.ir/fa/newsagency/214282* (2013).
111 Iran Energy Balance (2011).
112 Kinnander, E. (2010).
113 Iran Energy Balance (2011).
114 Babali, T. (2012).
115 Platts (2014).
116 Ibid.
117 Shana: *www.shana.ir/en/newsagency/213505* (2014).
118 Platt (2014)
119 Shana: *www.shana.ir/fa/newsagency/213079* (2014).
120 Iran Energy Balance (2012).
121 Shana: *www.shana.ir/fa/newsagency/214208* (2014).
122 Iran Energy Balance (2011).
123 Adibi, S. and Fesharaki, F. (2008); Ebrahimi, I. (2006).
124 The USA is rigorously opposed to further development of the project and has encouraged India to withdraw from the Iran gas import project, suggesting an alternative of constructing nuclear power plants for India. Adibi, S. and Fesharaki, F. op.cit.
125 IHS Global Insight Alert (2012).
126 Energy Information Administration (2012).
127 Pakistan Energy (2011).
128 Shana: *www.shana.ir/fa/newsagency/210737* (2013).
129 Ibid.
130 Nicknamed the 'Japan Crude Cocktail', Japan Customs-cleared Crude (JCC) is the average price of customs-cleared crude oil imports into Japan.

131  Davoodi, M. (2008).
132  Ibid.
133  Nabucco was backed by Austria's OMV, Hungary's Mol, Turkey's Botas, Romania's Transgas, and Bulgaria's Bulgargaz.
134  Adibi, S. and Fesharaki, F. op.cit.
135  TAP (2014).
136  World Gas Intelligence (2008).
137  Davoodi, M. (2008).
138  Shana: *www.shana.ir/fa/newsagency/210239* (2013).
139  Ibid.
140  Shana: *www.shana.ir/fa/newsagency/215366* (2014).
141  Oil and Gas Journal (2013).
142  Adibi, S. and Fesharaki, F. op.cit.
143  Ibid.
144  Shana: *www.shana.ir/fa/newsagency/213887* (2014).
145  Adibi, S. and Fesharaki, F. op. cit.
146  Ibid.
147  Iran Energy Balance (2012).
148  Ibid.
149  Pardeli, B., op.cit.
150  Kassaizadeh, S.R. (2011).
151  Adibi, S. and Fesharaki, F. op.cit.
152  Ibid.
153  Kassaizadeh, S.R. op.cit.
154  Adibi, S. and Fesharaki, F. op.cit.
155  Omidvar, H. (2010).
156  Davoodi, M. op.cit.
157  Adibi, S. and Fesharaki, F. op.cit.
158  Ibid.
159  Ibid.
160  Ibid.
161  Iran Energy Balance (2011).
162  Iran Energy Balance (2012).
163  BP Statistical Review of World Energy (2012).
164  Iran Energy Balance (2012).
165  Owji, J. (2012b)
166  Energy Information Administration (2012).

## Chapter 2: Politicization of the petroleum industry

1    The proximity of Azerbaijan, Gilan, Mazandaran, Khorasan, and Asta-rabad to Russian borders, and the need to recognize Russia's influence and prevent its opposition to the concession, resulted in the exclusion of these regions from the contract. Fakhimi, G. (2008).

2     The provisions stipulated that the concessionaire had 'a special and exclusive privilege to search for, obtain, exploit, develop, render suitable for trade, carry away and sell natural gas, petroleum, asphalt and ozokerite throughout the whole extent of the Persian Empire for a term of sixty years as from the date of the signing.' Draft of D'Arcy Concession

3     Ibid.

4     Hedayati-Kakhki, M.M. (2008, 62).

5     Cited in Hedayati-Kakhki, 63.

6     Ibid.

7     The company was later renamed and called Anglo-Iranian Petroleum Company (AIPC).

8     Zoghi, I. (2001).

9     'The Economy – Role of the Government', United States: US Library of Congress http://countrystudies.us/iran/63.htm.

10    Zoghi, op.cit.

11    L. Elwell-Sutton, *Persian Oil A Study in Power Politics*, London: Lawrence and Wishart, 1955, 67 cited in Elm, M. (1994, 28).

12    Fateh, M. (1979, 286).

13    Katouzian, H. (2010, 222).

14    Alavi, S.A. (1978, 58).

15    Ibid.

16    Hedayati-Kakhki, op.cit. 71.

17    Ibid, 72.

18    Makki, H. (1983).

19    Nadimi, F. (2013, 78).

20    Pollack, K. (2004).

21    Nadimi., op.cit. 78.

22    Ibid., 101.

23    Cavendish, R. (2001).

24    Iranian embassy, cited in Hedayati-Kakhki, op.cit. 105.

25    Zoghi., op.cit.

26    Farmanfarmaian, K. (1955).

27    Elm., op.cit. 271.

28    Ibid.

29    Ibid.

30    Hedayati-Kakhki, op.cit. 107.

31    ICJ Order of 5 July 1951 – Anglo-Iranian Oil Co. (United Kingdom *v.* Iran), 5 July 1951.

32    Elm., op.cit.

33    Ibid.

34    Katouzian (2010, 253).

35    Interview with John Loudon, London, 27 November 1986, interview with Amini, Paris, 22 May, 1983 cited in Elm, op.cit. 324.

36    Elm, op.cit. 325.

37    Ibid, 329.

38    Ibid.

39    Ibid.
40    Ehteshami, A. (2002).
41    In 1973–4, the oil embargo imposed by Arab members of OPEC against the USA and countries supporting Israel in the 1973 Arab-Israeli War, quadrupled the prices of oil per barrel giving rise to the world's first oil price shock.
42    Ramazani, R.K. (1987, 205).
43    Ibid.
44    Iran Energy Balance (2011).
45    Ibid.
46    Pelletiere, S.C. (1992).
47    Ehteshami., op.cit.
48    Amuzegar, J. (1993).
49    Ehteshami., op.cit.
50    Limbert, J. (2009, 16).
51    Katouzian (2010) argues that the tendency towards xenophobia and fear of foreign conspiracies was also, to some extent, a product of arbitrary rule and the habitual alienation of society from the state. Katouzian., op.cit., 10.
52    Abrahamian, E. (1993, 113).
53    Ibid., 116.
54    In the first coup, Tsarist officers bombarded the newly established constitutional parliament in an attempt to support the ailing Qajar monarchy. In the second coup, it was the British officers who helped Colonel Reza Khan to overthrow the government, depose the Qajar Dynasty, and establish the Pahlavi regime.
55    Article 153 of the Constitution, The 1979 Constitution of Islamic Republic of Iran.
56    Limbert, op.cit.
57    Katzman, K. (2011).
58    Ibid.
59    Naficy, H. (2008).
60    Takin, M. (2000).
61    Barkeshli, F. (2012).
62    Ibid.
63    Arjomand, A.S. (2009).
64    The unicameral Iranian Parliament, the Islamic Consultative Assembly or 'Majles-e Shura-ye Eslami', consists of 290 members elected for a four year term. The members are elected by direct and secret ballot. It drafts legislation, ratifies international treaties, and approves the country's budget. All legislation from the assembly must be reviewed by the Council of Guardians. Candidates for a seat in the Majles also require approval by the Council of Guardians.
65    Takin, op.cit.
66    Created by Ayatollah Khomeini in 1988, the Expediency Council has the authority to mediate disputes between the Parliament and the Council of

Guardians. According to the Constitution, the Expediency Council also serves as an advisory body to the Supreme Leader, making it one of the most powerful governing bodies in the country.

67   Twelve jurists comprise the Council of Guardians, six of whom are appointed by the Supreme Leader. The head of the judiciary recommends the remaining six, which are officially appointed by the Parliament. The Council of Guardians is vested with the authority to interpret the Constitution and determines if the laws passed by Parliament are compatible with Shari'a (Islamic law). Hence the council can exercise veto power over Parliament. If a law passed by Parliament is deemed incompatible with the Constitution or Shari'a, it is referred back to Parliament for revision. The council also examines presidential and Parliamentary candidates to determine their eligibility to run for a seat.
68   Naficy, op.cit.
69   Marcel, V. (2006).
70   Ibid.
71   Kassaizadeh, S.R. (2006, 31).
72   Ibid.
73   Ghorban, N. (2005, 6).
74   Ghorban, op.cit.
75   Ebrahimi, I. (2006).
76   Naficy, op.cit.
77   Ibid.
78   Limbert, op.cit., 159.
79   Ibid.

## Chapter 3: The impact of US and international sanctions on oil and gas development

1   Sabatini, R. (2010).
2   The Arms Export Control Act, US Department of State. www.pmddtc. state.gov/regulations_laws/aeca.html.
3   Executive Order 12613-Prohibiting imports from Iran, The National Archives, available at: *www.archives.gov/federal-register/codification/executive-order/12613.html*.
4   Executive Order 12613--Prohibiting imports from Iran, in The National Archives *www.archives.gov/federal-register/codification/executive-order/12613.html*
5   Iran and Libya Sanctions Act of 1996, from the congressional record. *www.fas.org/irp/congress/1996_cr/h960618b.htm*
6   Originally called the Iran–Libya Sanctions Act (ILSA), the Act was also inclusive of Libya, which had been refusing to surrender for trial the intelligence agents suspected in the Pan Am bombing. Libya was removed from the Act in 2006 when the country fulfilled the requirements of all UN resolutions on Pan Am and since then the Act has been called the

Iran Sanctions Act (ISA). Katzman, K. (2005).

7    Katzman, K. (2012).

8    Ibid

9    'Iran–Libya Sanctions Act of 1996', in the Congressional record. *www. fas.org/irp/congress/1996_cr/h960618b.htm*

10   Katzman, K. (2011).

11   Alexander, R.G. (1997).

12   To show its goodwill for the improvement of relations, for example, the US government withdrew its ban on exports of medical and agricultural products to Iran as well as imports of food and luxury products from Iran. Torbat, A.E. (2005).

13   Ibid.

14   Duero, A. (2009).

15   Jentleson, B.W. (2007).

16   The UN Resolutions 1737, 1747, 1803 and 1929.

17   The UN Resolution 1737 U.N. Doc. S/RES/1737.

18   The UN Resolution 1747, U.N. Doc. S/RES/1747

19   The UN Resolution 1929, U.N. Doc. S/RES/1929

20   Article 25 of the UN Charter stipulates that 'the Members of the United Nations agree to accept and carry out the decisions of the Security Council in accordance with the present Charter'. Also Part 1 of Article 43 emphasizes the obligation of the member states to make available to the Security Council on its call any assistance it may need for the purpose of maintaining international peace and security. Charter of the United Nations, 1945.

21   Katzman, K. (2014).

22   Ibid.

23   Secretary of State Clinton in March 2012 in discussing an Iran–Pakistan pipeline: *http://dawn.com/2012/03/01/tough-us-warning-on-iran-gas-pipeline/*.

24   Katzman, K. (2011).

25   This would appear to make sanctionable the activity of global oil services firms in Iran, or the provision to Iran of gear typically used in the oil industry such as drills, pumps, vacuums, oil rigs, and the like. Katzman, K. (2011).

26   'Executive Order 13590 Iran Sanctions,' In.: *www.whitehouse.gov/ the-press-office/2011/11/21/executive-order-13590-iran-sanctions*

27   'Implementation of National Defense Authorization Act Sanctions on Iran,' in (June 2012): US Department of the Treasury *www.treasury.gov/ press-center/press-releases/Pages/tg1409.aspx*

28   'Implementation of National Defense Authorization Act Sanctions on Iran', in (June 2012): US Department of the Treasury *www.treasury.gov/ press-center/press-releases/Pages/tg1409.aspx*

29   Katzman. (2014) op.cit.

30   Ibid.

31   Jentleson, B.W. (2007).

32   Patterson, R. (2013).

33  Ibid.
34  The Iran (European Union Financial Sanctions) Regulations (2010).
35  The policy was in line with the EU's effort to diversify its gas supply options and minimize its dependence on Russian gas imports. Katzman (2011), op.cit.
36  'Iran protestors attack UK embassy in Tehran', *The Guardian*, 29 November 2011, *www.guardian.co.uk/world/blog/2011/nov/29/iran-protesters-attack-uk-embassy-tehran-live*
37  Saudi Arabia's commitment to fill any supply gap in the oil market gave the required reassurance to the European states to proceed with placing an embargo on Iranian crude oil. Chazan, G. (2012).
38  The Iran (European Union Financial Sanctions) Regulations, op.cit.
39  In March 2012, the Belgium-based SWIFT organization also ended its transactions with the Iranian banks blacklisted by the EU, further adding to the pressure of sanctions on Iran. Blenkinsop, P. and Younglai, R. (2012).
40  Cordesman. A.H. (2005).
41  Katzman, K. (2012).
42  Cordesman, A., et.al. (2012).
43  France's Total: Too risky to invest in Iran (2008).
44  Shimbun, Y. (2010).
45  Katzman, K. (2012), op.cit.
46  Garver, J.W. (2010).
47  Garver, J. et.al. (2009).
48  Jentleson, op. cit.
49  Energy Information Administration (2012). The US Department of Energy's country report on Iran: *www.eia.gov/countries/cab.cfm?fips=IR*
50  Press TV (2012).
51  Mehr New Agency (2014).
52  OPEC (2012).
53  Esfahani, H. et.al. (2012).
54  Kinnander, E. (2010).
55  Ibid.
56  Cordesman, A., et.al., op.cit.
57  Comprehensive Iran Sanctions, Accountability, and Divestment Act of 2010: *http://frwebgate.access.gpo.gov/cgibin/getdoc.cgi?dbname=111_cong_reports&docid=f:hr512.111.pdf*
58  'U.N. council brings Iraq closer to end of 1990s sanctions', *Reuters*, 27 June 2013, *www.reuters.com/article/2013/06/27/us-iraq-kuwait-un-idUSBRE95Q0Y320130627*

## Chapter 4: Investment regime in the oil and gas sector

1  Wall, E.H. (1958).

2   Ramazani, R.K. (1962).
3   In the literature on the oil and gas industry, a 'service contract' is referred to as a contract in which the foreign company takes the exploration and feasibility risk in return for a share in the production if the venture is successful. In a 'service contract', the foreign investor agrees to provide services and know-how and to supply materials while having no control of ownership over the project. According to Bindemann (1999), such a contract only works if the mineral sector is well developed and there exists 'a reasonable amount of knowledge about the geological structure of the country'. Early service contracts were signed by Petroleos Mexicanos (PEMEX) and Yacimientos Petroliferos Fiscales in the 1950s. However, the concept became more widely popular in the late 1960s and early 1970s when Iraq and Iran in particular concluded several such agreements. Bindemann, K. (1999).
4   Ebrahimi, S.N. and Shiroui Khouzani, A. (2003).
5   For more detail on Iran's post-revolutionary foreign policy, see introductory chapter.
6   Abrahamian, E. (2006, 33–6).
7   Shiravi, A. and Ebrahimi, S.N. (2006).
8   Ibid
9   Marcel, V. (2006).
10  Bunter, M. (2005).
11  One of the well-known Muslims schools of thought, also known as the 12er Shi'a school of thought, is Jafari. It has derived its name from Jafar Sadeq, the sixth Shi'a Imam and is followed by Twelvers and Ismailis in general. It differs from other Muslim schools of thought and offers different opinions on matters of inheritance, religious taxes, commerce, and governance. Iran has the largest Shi'a Muslim population in the world and its Constitution recognizes Shi'a Islam as the primary religion of the country.
12  Article 4 of the Iranian Constitution reaffirms this principle by stating that all civil, penal, financial, economic, administrative, as well as cultural, military, political, and other laws and regulations must be based on Islamic criteria. The 1979 Constitution of Islamic Republic of Iran.
13  Walied, El-M. (1996). Also there is a hadith (sayings of Imams and Prophet Mohammad) from the Shia's first Imam, Ali Ibn Abu Talib, which describes the ownership scope of the minerals as follow: '*This property is neither yours nor mine, but it is the collective property of Muslims, acquired by their swords. If you had taken part with them in their battle, you would have had a share equal to theirs, otherwise, the earnings of their hands cannot be morsels for others' mouths.*' Nahjol-Balaghah, No. 232, a source of Chapter IV of the Constitution of the Islamic Republic of Iran). Cited in Roberts, P. and Jackson, J. (2001, 159–61).
14  'Mother industries' are large-scale industries with strategic importance to the nation, and generally include: minerals, banking, insurance, power

generations, and dams as well as large-scale irrigation networks, radio and television, post, telegraph and telephone services, aviation, shipping, roads, and railroads; Article 44 of the Islamic Republic of Iran's Constitution.

15 Article 44, The 1979 Constitution of Islamic Republic of Iran.
16 Chapter 5, Foreign Investment Promotion and Protection Act (FIPPA)
17 Ramsay, W.C. (2006).
18 Article 2, The Iranian Petroleum Act of 1987.
19 The Iranian Gazette, 1993 cited in Ebrahimi, S.N. and Shiroui Khouzani, A. op.cit.
20 Iranian official Gazette, 1994 cited in ibid.
21 Shiravi, A. and Ebrahimi, S.N., op.cit.
22 Fesharaki, F. and. Varzi, M. (2000).
23 For more detail of US and international sanctions, see Chapter 3.
24 Bindemann, K. op.cit. 75
25 Zeynoddin, S.M (2014).
26 See Chapter 3.
27 Bindemann, K. op.cit.
28 The MDP is a major component of the buyback contracts and encompasses critical information on each development phase and objectives of the project.
29 Mohammad, N (2009).
30 Shiravi, A. and Ebrahimi, S.N. op,cit., 202
31 Ibid.
32 Ebrahimi, S.N. and Shiroui Khouzani, A. op.cit.
33 Roberts, P. and Jackson, J. op.cit.
34 van Groenendaal, W. J. H. and Mazraati, M. (2006).
35 Hosseini, M. (2014).
36 Dittrick, P. (2009); Me, M. (2009).
37 Dittrick, P. op,cit.
38 Ibid.
39 Ibid.
40 Me, M. op.cit.
41 Ibid.
42 Shana (2014a).
43 Shana (2013).
44 Shana (2014b).
45 Ibid.
46 Ibid.
47 Katzman, K. (2012).
48 Article 3(b), The Iranian Foreign Investment Promotion and Protection Act of 2002 (FIPPA).
49 Shirvani, A. and Ebrahimi, S.N. (2007, 154).
50 Article 3 (b), The Iranian Foreign Investment Promotion and Protection Act of 2002 (FIPPA).
51 Ibid.

52   Shirvani, A. and Ebrahimi S.N. op.cit., 155.
53   Ibid., 163.
54   Gharavi, H. (1999).
55   As of 1 June 2012, Iran has concluded 62 Bilateral Investment Trea-
     ties with: Afghanistan, Albania, Algeria, Armenia, Austria, Azerbaijan,
     Bahrain, Bangladesh, Belarus, Bosnia & Herzegovina, Bulgaria, China,
     Croatia, Cyprus, Ethiopia, Finland, France, Gambia, Georgia, Germany,
     Greece, Indonesia, Italy, Kazakhstan, Kenya, Korea, Democratic People's
     Republic, Korea Republic, Kuwait, Kyrgyzstan, Lebanon, Libyan Arab
     Jamahiriya, Macedonia, TFYR, Malaysia, Moldova Republic, Morocco,
     Oman, Pakistan, Philippines, Poland, Qatar, Romania, Serbia, South
     Africa, Spain, Sri Lanka, Sudan, Sweden, Switzerland, Syrian Arab Re-
     public, Tajikistan, Tunisia, Turkey, Turkmenistan, Ukraine, Uzbekistan,
     Venezuela, Vietnam, Yemen, Zimbabwe; Total Number of Bilateral Invest-
     ment Agreements Concluded. United Nations Conference on Trade and
     Development (UNCTAD), 1 June 2012.
56   Iran's membership to the New York Convention was ratified in October
     2001 and came into force in January 2002: *www.newyorkconvention.org/
     contracting-states/list-of-contracting-states*
57   Shirvani, A. and Ebrahimi S.N. op.cit.
58   2 April 1981, The Council of Guardians' Archives.
59   Legal Newsletter: Atieh Associates, December 2008.
60   Ibid.
61   Hakimian, H. (2009).
62   Davis, K.E. and Trebilcock, M.J. (2008).
63   Perry, A. (2000).
64   Wälde, T. W. (2005).
65   Ibid.
66   Ibid.
67   Dam, K.W. (2006).
68   'Doing Business-Iran, Islamic Republic.', The World Bank, 2014: *www.
     doingbusiness.org/data/exploreeconomies/iran/*
69   Aysan, A., et.al. (2007, 341).
70   Ulen, T.S. (2010).
71   Buscaglia, E. (1999).
72   Higbee, J. and Schmid, F.A. (2004).
73   Mauro, P. (1995).
74   Haggard, S. et.al. (2007, 207).
75   Ibid.
76   Dam., op.cit.
77   Haggard, S. and et.al. op.cit. 211.
78   Transparency International, the international corruption watchdog, ranked
     Iran 133 amongst 176 countries in the index of the most corrupt countries;
     Corruption Perceptions Index 2012. *Transparency International: http://cpi.
     transparency.org/cpi2012/results/.* 2012

## Chapter 5: Energy subsidies and their reform

1   In the last five years before the Revolution, the average natural gas consumption was about 5 bcm/year. After the Revolution and as a result of cancellation of export contracts to the USSR, the gas was redirected to domestic markets, leading to a sharp increase in the domestic consumption rate. Iran Energy Balance (2009).
2   BP (2012).
3   IEA (2010a).
4   Molai, E. (2004).
5   Ibid.
6   Ibid.
7   As explained in Chapter 3, as a part of the 'revolutionary social compact', the nation was even promised to receive oil for free. Harris, K. (2012, 2).
8   Ibid.
9   Nikou, S. (2010).
10  Hassani, S. (2010, 10).
11  Ibid., 11.
12  Around \$0.012/cm based on the early 1960s' average exchange rate of \$1= IRR80.
13  Shiravand, A. (2005).
14  Nasr Esfahani, H. (2008).
15  Khoozestan is given as an example as the city is considered to be the most temperate city in Iran.
16  Nasr Esfahani, H. op.cit.
17  Fattouh and El-Katiri. (2013).
18  Ibid.
19  Victor, D. (2009).
20  Darbouche, H. (2012, 8).
21  Adibi, S. and Fesharaki, F. (2011, 287); According to IEA, the amount of fuel used to generate electricity depends on the efficiency of the generator and the heat content of the fuel. Based on the IEA formula, in standard conditions, 0.28 cubic metres of gas usually generates 1kwh of electricity: *www.eia.gov/tools/faqs/faq.cfm?id=667&t=2*
22  Granado, J. et.al. (2010, 13).
23  Independent Evaluation Group (IEG) (2011).
24  According to the IEA, MENA countries have the most subsidized energy markets in the world. IEA (2008b); also read IEA (2008a).
25  Marcel, V. (2006, 152).
26  Al-Monitor (2014).
27  Baig, T., et.al. (2007).
28  Kobayashi, H., et.al. (2006).
29  The World Bank (1995).
30  Amuzegar, J. (2011).
31  BP (2010).
32  BP (2011).

33   IEA (2009). IEA's estimate for energy subsidies is based on a price-gap approach that compares domestic prices to international prices; meaning that changing prices in international markets will change the amount of subsidies. For example, in 2008, when oil prices reached around $120 bbl, the aggregate cost of fossil-fuel subsidies was estimated at around $550 billion, whereas in 2009, as a result of a sharp drop in oil prices, the world cost of subsidies was reported at around $300 billion. In additional to this methodological complication, the IEA data is also not immune to shortcomings. According to Fattouh and El-Katiri, the most immediate concern over the IEA's estimation of fossil-fuel subsidies is the absence of data for particular types of fuels which, despite their sizeable subsidies, the rate of their subsidization equals zero in the IEA's report. Fattouh and El-Katiri., op.cit., 13.

34   Guillaume, D., et.al. (2011).

35   Global Subsidies Initiative (GSI) (2011).

36   Solomon, J. and Fassihi, F. (2011).

37   Government of Iran (2010).

38   Article 1, Subsidies Reform Act (2010).

39   Due to changing economic and political conditions in the last few years, the Iranian foreign exchange market experienced unprecedented volatility that created different official and free market foreign exchange rates. Hence, to minimize confusion, in this chapter the exchange rate is equivalent to the official rate in the first two years after the reform which was $1=IRR12,260. The official exchange rate has further increased since then, hovering around $1= 25,000 in early 2014.

40   Article 1, Subsidies Reform Act. op,cit.

41   Ibid

42   Ibid

43   The IMF, for example, in its July 2011 report on Iran's subsidies reform plan, presents a very successful picture of the reform. Guillaume, D., et.al. op.cit.

44   International Monetary Fund (IMF) (2014).

45   Clements, B. (2013).

46   Hassanzadeh, E. (2012).

47   IEA (2011).

48   Guillaume, D., et.al. op.cit., 11.

49   Ibid., 12.

50   Ibid.

51   Amuzegar, J. op.cit.

52   Fars News Agency (2012).

53   Gupta, S. et.al. (2000).

54   Iran's Chamber of Commerce, Industry and Mine (2008).

55   ibid

56   The exchange rate at the time of price increases was $1= IRR12,260.

57   See note 39 in this chapter.

58  A year is divided into 5 cold (from November to March) and 7 non-cold months.
59  Donyay-e Eghtesad (2011).
60  The five geographical regions are: cold 1, cold 2, cold 3, temperate and high temperate. Tehran is, for example, classified as a cold 3 region.
61  Guillaume, D., et.al. op.cit. 13.
62  Shana (2014b). The average exchange rate in March 2014 was $1=IRR25,000.
63  Guillaume, D., et.al. op.cit. 8.
64  NIGC (2011).
65  Ibid.
66  Iran Energy Balance (2012)
67  BP (2012).
68  Shana (2012a).
69  Guillaume, D. et.al. op.cit.
70  Mehr News (2012).
71  Shana (2014a).

## Chapter 6: Natural gas allocation policy and prioritization changes

1   Mosleh, K. (2009).
2   Randall, A. (1987).
3   A resource is defined depletable if a) its stock decreases over time whenever the resource is being used, b) the stock never increases over time, c) the rate of stock decrease is a monotonically increasing function of the rate of resource use, and d) no use is possible without a positive stock. Sweeney, J. L. (1992).
4   Allsopp, C. and Stern, J. (2012, 20).
5   Toman, M. and Krautkraemer, J. (2003), 13.
6   For a review of similar problems faced by Middle East and North African countries in respect of their gas industries, see Fattouh, B. and Stern, J. (2011).
7   Barkeshli, F. (2012).
8   For more detail, see Chapter 2.
9   Barkeshli, F., op.cit.
10  Ibid
11  Mash'al (2007).
12  Ibid.
13  Mir Saleh Kohan, L. (2007)
14  Derakhshan, M. (2008).
15  Iran Energy Balance (2012).
16  Shana (2012a).
17  Interview NIGC, October 2013.

18   Interview NIGC, October 2013.
19   Interview NIGC, October 2013.
20   In 2010, 2011, and 2012 the gas equivalent of fuel oil which was burnt in power generation is estimated to have been around 13 bcm, 21 bcm, and 22.3bcm; Shana (2014a). *www.shana.ir/fa/newsagency/209680.*
21   Ibid.
22   Razavi, H. (2009).
23   Ibid.
24   IEA (2005).
25   The cost of gas supply can be assessed at various points of the supply chain. The cost at the city gas includes investment and operating expenses relating to exploration and field development, together with the transmission expenses.
26   IEA (2005).
27   Allsopp and Stern, op,cit., 19.
28   EIA (2014).
29   Bahramian, Y. and Alipour, M. (2011).
30   Ranani, M. et.al. (2008, 123).
31   Jonoobi, P. (2010).
32   Fatwa is a ruling on a point of Islamic law given by a recognized authority.
33   Ranani, M. et.al. (2008).
34   EIA (2013).
35   Iran's average production in the period 2010–11 was about 3.5 million bbl/ day. In September 2012, the country's production rate plunged to a level of only 2.6 million bbl/day, its lowest in the last 25 years. OPEC (2012).
36   EIA (2012).
37   EIA (2013).
38   Stern, R. (2007); Mitchell, J. et.al. (2008).
39   Majles Research Centre (2009).
40   Adibi, S. and Ahmad khani, A. (2005).
41   IEA (2013, 492).
42   Shana (2014b). *www.shana.ir/fa/newsagency/211975*
43   Ranani, M. et.al. op.cit.
44   Jonoobi, P. op.cit.
45   Karimi Zarchi, M. (2010).
46   EIA (2012) op.cit.
47   Mosleh, op,cit.
48   NIOC (2011).
49   Kinnander, E. (2010).
50   Economist (2012).
51   According to the IEA, the construction cost of the Australian Pluto LNG project reached $3,256/tonne of production. The cost for construction of another Australian LNG plant (Ichthys), is estimated to increase even further, reaching $4,048. IEA (2013); Songhurst, B. (2014).
52   Kassaizadeh, S. R. (2011); Songhurst, op.cit.
53   IEA (2012).

54 ibid.
55 Including: unfavourable geology, environmental protests against hydraulic fracturing, water scarcity, and general public opposition to drilling and land disturbance.
56 IEA (2013).
57 Ibid.
58 Rogers, H.V. and Stern, J. (2012).
59 NIGC (2012).
60 Ibid.
61 EIA (2013).
62 Ibid.
63 In 2014, Russia reduced its gas prices to Armenia, making it even more challenging for Iran to compete with Russian gas prices. Nichol, J. (2014).
64 Stern, J. (2005).
65 Herzig, E. (2004).
66 'Russia blackmailing Europe' is an expression widely used by the media during and after the Russia–Ukraine energy crises of 2006 and 2009. See for example: *www.bloomberg.com/apps/news?pid=newsarchive&sid=aqTWszWw XO6o* and *www.theguardian.com/world/2006/may/05/usa.oil*
67 Lough, J. (2011).
68 Ibid.
69 Van den Bossche, P. (2007).
70 Fattouh, B. and El-Katiri, L. (2013).
71 NIPC (2011). NIPC Annual Report.
72 The price of gas for petrochemical feedstock is $0.13 cm. Shana (2014c).
73 NIPC (2010). NIPC Annual Report.
74 Ibid.
75 Ibid.
76 Business Monitor International (2012).
77 Shana (2013).
78 Business Monitor International op.cit.
79 Other plants, which are at the early stages of their construction, are Lordegan and Gachsaran, with estimated capital costs of around $900 million and $850 million, respectively. Shana (2012b).
80 For example, see Ghorban, N. (2010).
81 Glebova, O. (2013, 39).
82 Ibid., 2.
83 Shell (2011); Evans, D. (2008).
84 Glebova, op.cit.
85 Hassantash, G.H. (2006).

## Conclusion

1 Flower, A. (2011).
2 Ibid.

# BIBLIOGRAPHY

## Introduction

Amuzegar, J. (2004). 'Iran's economy: status, problems, and prospects', Woodrow Wilson International Centre for Scholars.

Ansari, A. (2008). 'Iran under Ahmadinejad: Populism and its malcontents', *Review of International Affairs*, no. 84(4).

Ansari, A. (2013). 'Iran: the paradox of sultanism', *International Affairs*, Vol. 89, No.2.

BP (2013). *British Petroleum Statistical Review of World Energy*.

Ehteshami (1995). *After Khomeini: The Iranian Second Republic*, Routledge.

Ehteshami, A. and Zweiri, M. (2011). *Iran's foreign policy: from Khatami to Ahmadinejad*, Ithaca Press.

Karshenas, M. and Hakimian, H. (2005). 'Oil, economic diversification and the democratic process in Iran', *Iranian Studies*, Vol. 38. No.1, Iran Facing the new Century, 75.

Maleki, A. (2002). 'Decision making in Iran's foreign policy: A heuristic approach', *Journal of Social Affairs*, 19, 73: 39–59.

NBC News (2013). 'Iran's president Rouhani: we will never develop nuclear weapons', *www.nbcnews.com/news/other/irans-president-rouhani-we-will-never-develop-nuclear-weapons-f4B11191585*

Pesaran, E. (2011). *Iran's Struggle for Economic Independence: Reform and Counter-Reform in the Post-Revolutionary Era*, Routledge (Political Economy of the Middle East).

Ramazani, R. K. 'Iran's Foreign Policy: Contending Orientations', *Middle East Journal*, 1989, vol. 43, 210.

Sadjadpour, K. (2008). 'Reading Khamenei: The world view of Iran's most powerful leader', Carnegie Endowment for International Peace.

Thaler, A., Nader, A., Chubin, S., Green J., Lynch, C., and Wehrey, F. (2010). 'Mullahs, Guards, and Bonyads: An exploration of Iranian leadership dynamics', Rand: National Defense Research Institute.

The 1979 Constitution of Islamic Republic of Iran.

Wilfried, B. (2000) 'Who rules Iran? The structure of power in the Islamic Republic', The Washington Institute for Near East Policy and the Konrad Adenauer Stiftung.


## Chapter 1: A background to Iran's natural gas industry

Adibi, S. (2002). *Baresi Emkan Tolid Va Saderat LNG Dar Keshvar-e Iran*, Azad Tehran University.

Adibi, S. and Fesharaki, F. (2011). 'The Iranian Gas Industry', in Fattouh, B. and Stern, J. (eds.), *Natural Gas markets in the Middle East and North Africa*, OIES/Oxford University Press .

Babali, T. (2012). 'The Role of Energy in Turkey's Relations with Russia and Iran', *The Turkey, Russia and Iran Nexus: Economic and Energy Dimensions*, Ankara, Turkey, 5.

Bahreini, M. (2010), 'Baresie moghiat-e Iran dar tejarat gaz', *Ekteshaf va Tolid*, No. 77, 16.

Behzad, H. (1973). *Eghtesade San'ate Gaze Iran (the Economics of Iranian Gas Industry)*, University of Tehran, 16.

BP (2012). 'British Petroleum Statistical Review of World Energy'.

BP (2013). 'British Petroleum Statistical Review of World Energy'.

Davoodi, M. (2008). *Baresie Ta'sire Avamele Mohiti Va Estratejihaye Monaseb Dar Saderate Gaze Iran*, Azad Tehran University.

Dehghani, T. (2007). *Model Hadeaxar Sazi Manafe Eghtesadi Hasel az Zakhayer Gazi Iran*, University of Azad.

Ebrahimi, I. (2006). *Saderat-E Gaz-E Iran: Forsat-ha Va Tahdid-ha*, edited by Mostafa Azari: Research Institute of Tadbir-e Eghtesad.

E.C.A.F.E Natural Gas Seminar (1964). 'Recent Status of Natural Gas in Iran', Tehran: The United Nations and the NIOC.

Energy Information Agency (2012). 'Country Analysis Briefs: Iran', the US Department of Energy *www.eia.gov/countries/cab.cfm?fips=IR*

Gulf Oil & Gas. (2011). 'Project focus: Iran–Pakistan–India gas pipeline', www. gulfoilandgas.com/webpro1/projects/3dreport.asp?id=100730

Iran Energy Balance (1967–2009). Ministry of Energy.

Iran Energy Balance (2008). Ministry of Energy.

Iran Energy Balance (2009). Ministry of Energy.

Iran Energy Balance (2010). Ministry of Energy.

Iran Energy Balance (2011). Ministry of Energy.

Iran Energy Balance (2012). Ministry of Energy.

IHS Global Insight Alert (2012). The Iran–Pakistan pipeline – a dangerous proposition.

Kangan-Iran (1978). 'Technical proposal for Kalingas LNG project', vol.10.

Kassaizadeh, S.R. (2011). 'Zanjireyeh Tolid LNG (LNG Production Chain)', *Iranian LNG Conference*, Tehran.

Kinnander, E. (2010). 'The Turkish-Iranian Gas Relationship: Politically Successful, Commercially Problematic', Oxford Institute for Energy Studies Working Paper NG 38, January.

Khandan, M. (2012). 'Ezdiad Bardasht, Challensh-ha, Forsat-ha va Zaroorat-ha', *Ekteshaf va Tolid*, *No.* 91, 5.

Majles Research Centre (2009). 'Baresi Oft Tolide Makhazene Naftie Keshvar Va Manafe Melli'.

Manoochehri, N. (1970). 'Tarhe Shah Looleye Gaz', Tehran: Iranian National Gas Company, 8–9.

Mash'al (2005). *http://mashal.mop.ir/538/pdf/MAIN/MAIN%2005.pdf*

Middle East Economic Survey (MEES) (2008). 'Turkey and Iran sign gas pact', Nicosia, Cyprus: Middle East Petroleum & Economic Publications, 51:47.

Mina, P. (1977). 'Magham San'at Naft Dar Iran Dar Doran Shahanshani Pahlavi' (Status of Oil Industry during Pahlavi Monarchy), Tehran: National Iranian Oil Company.

NIGC. (2010). *www.nigc.ir/utils/getFile.aspx?Idn=12320*

NIGC (2010). 'History of National Iranian Gas Company'. http://en.nigc.ir/Site.aspx?ParTree=11131515.

NIGC (2013). 'Natural gas consumption', *http://cvn.nigc.ir/portal/Home/Default. aspx?CategoryID=dedd41f1-e8ff-460e-9967-591a7dda442e.*

NIOC (2009). Map located in NIOC company archives.

NIOC (2010). National Iranian Oil Company website: *www.nioc. ir/Portal/Home/ShowPage.aspx?Object=News&ID=f8869952-a802-493b-902b-447a28e29446&LayoutID=d2d58b2b-6888-42ca-ba8c-4fdffbf0bd4d&CategoryID=5a83de0d-4c67-4b8a-a794-08e669faf33d.*

Oil and Gas Journal (2013). 'Prospects improve for pipeline natural gas exports by Iran', *Oil and Gas Journal*, 16 December. *www.ogj.com/articles/2013/12/ prospects-improve-for-pipeline-natural-gas-exports-by-iran.html*

Omidvar, H. (2010). 'Iranian LNG, Natural Gas Export Plans Outlined', *Oil & Gas Journal*.

OPEC (2014). Monthly Report, *www.opec.org/opec_web/static_files_project/media/ downloads/publications/MOMR_March_2014.pdf.*

Owji, J. (2012a). 'Rah-Andazie Do Khate Loole Jadid Saderate Gaz', *Mehr News, www.mehrnews.com/detail/News/1682619.*

Owji, J. (2012b). 'Tavafogh Jadid Iran Va Torkamanestan', *Shana. www.shana. ir/fa/newsagency/198142.*

Pardeli, B. (2008). *Tahlil Hazine Fayedeye Eghtesadi Asarat Tabdile Gas Tabi'i Be LNG* (Cost-Benefit Analysis of Converting Gas to LNG), Azad Islamic University.

Pars Oil & Gas Company (2012). 'Gaz-e pars jonoobi tabestan-e 92 be Baghdad miresad', *http://pogc.ir/Default.aspx?tabid=94&ctl=Detail&mid=448&Id=10393*

Pars Oil & Gas Company (2014). 'About South Pars gas field', see *www.pogc. ir/Default.aspx?tabid=136*

Platts (2014). 'Turkey–Iran arbitration split into two cases', *Platts European Gas Daily*.

Ramazani, R.K. (1989). 'Iran's Foreign Policy: Contending Orientations', *Middle East Journal*, vol. 43, 210.

Shana (2009). 'bakhshe nahai khate hashtom sarasari gaz', www.shana.ir/fa/ newsagency/148114.

Shana (2010). *www.shana.ir/fa/newsagency/160656*

Shana (2010). 'Aghaze amaliat tazrighe gaz', *www.shana.ir/fa/newsagency/160656.*

Shana. (2011). 'Recorde bi nazire hamzaman tose'eye 18 faze pars jonoobi', www.shana.ir/fa/newsagency/161038.

Shana (2011). 'Ersale 7.5 miliard metre moka'ab gaz baraye tazrigh', *www. shana.ir/184322-fa.html.*

Shana (2012a). 'Ehdase khat looleye gaz dahome sarasari', *www.shana.ir/fa/ newsagency/191812.*

Shana (2012b). 'Pishraft Matloobe Hafarie Chah-Haye Tose'eye Meidan Gaze Kish', *http://shana.ir/193428-fa.html*.

Shirazi, M. (1974). 'Gas Industry in Iran', edited by NIGC, Tehran: Iranian Petroleum Institute for Public Relation Affairs.

Soleimanian, R. (2003). *Takhmine Taghazaye San'ate Gaze Tabi'i Dar Iran*, Azad Tehran University, 26.

Tabnak (2012). 'Laghv-e Mosavabey-e Shekate Saderate Gaz', *www.tabnak.ir/fa/news/270070*.

TAP (2014). 'Shah Deniz Consortium selects TAP as European export pipeline', *https://www.trans-adriatic-pipeline.com/news/news/detail-view/article/414/*.

Vahedi, H. (1977). 'Naft va Gaz Dar Rabete Ba Tahavolat Iran Dar 50–70', NIGC Archives.

World Bank (2012). 'World Bank Sees Warning Sign in Gas Flaring Increase', 3 July, *www.worldbank.org/en/news/press-release/2012/07/03/world-bank-sees-warning-sign-gas-flaring-increase*

World Gas Intelligence (2008). 'Uncertainties Behind EGL's Iran Gas Buy', *World Gas Intelligence*, 19 March.

## Chapter 2: Politicization of the petroleum industry

Abrahamian, E. (1993). *Khomeinism: essays on the Islamic Republic*, I.B Tauris & Co Ltd, 113.

Alavi, S.A. (1978). *History of the Oil Industry in Iran*, California Institute of Asian Studies, 58.

Amuzegar, J. (1993). *Iran's Economy under the Islamic Republic*, London: I.B. Tauris.

Arjomand, A.S. (2009). *After Khomeini: Iran under His Successors*, Oxford: Oxford University Press, 152.

Barkeshli, F. (2012). 'Iran's energy diplomacy: Challenges and opportunities', *Middle East Economic Survey*, 3.

Cavendish, R. (2001), 'The Iranian Oil Fields Are Nationalised', *History Today*, 51, no. 5.

Ebrahimi, I. (2006). *Saderat-E Gaz-E Iran: Forsat-Ha Va Tahdid-Ha*, edited by Mostafa Azari: Research Institute of Tadbir-e Eshtesad.

Ehteshami, A. (2002). 'The Foreign Policy of Iran', in Hinnebusch, R. and Ehteshami, A. (eds.), *The Foreign Policies of Middle East States*, Lynne Rienner: Boulder & Co, 286.

Elm, M. (1994). *Oil, power, and principle: Iran's oil nationalization and its aftermath*, Syracuse University Press, 28.

Fakhimi, G. (2008). *30 Sal Nafte Iran-Az Melli Shodan Ta Enghelabe Eslami*, Tehran: Mehr Andish.

Farmanfarmaian, K. (1955). 'An Analysis of the Role of the Oil Industry in the Economy of Iran', University of Colorado.

Fateh, M. (1979). 50 sal nafte iran, Tehran, Pyam publications, 286.

Ghorban, N. (2005). 'The Need to Restructure Iran's Petroleum Industry (Revisited after Eight Years)', *Middle East Economic Survey* XVVlll, 6.

Hedayati-Kakhki, M.M. (2008). 'A Critical Analysis of Iranian Buy-Back Transactions in the Context of International Petroleum Contractual Systems', University of Durham, 62.

Iran Energy Balance (2011). Ministry of Energy.

Kassaizadeh, S.R. (2006). 'Sherkat-E Melli Gaz Parcham Dar-E Energy Dar Keshvar', *Chashmandaz*, 31.

Katouzian, H. (2010). *The Persians: ancient, mediaeval, and modern Iran*, Yale University Press, 222.

Katzman, K. (2011). 'Iran Sanctions', Congressional Research Service.

Limbert, J. (2009). *Negotiating with Iran: wrestling ghosts of history*, United States Institute of Peace, 16.

Makki, H. (1983). *Tarikh-E Bist Saleye Iran*, Tehran: Amir Kabir.

Marcel, V. (2006). *Oil Titans: National Oil Companies in the Middle East*, Brookings Institution Press.

Nadimi, F. (2013). 'The Role of Oil in the Outcome of the Iran–Iraq War', in Ashton, N. and Gibson B. (eds.), *The Iran-Iraq War: New International Perspectives*, Rootledge, 78.

Naficy, H. (2008). 'Resource Depletion, Dependence and Development – Country Commentary Iran', Chatham House.

Pollack, K. (2004). *The Persian puzzle: Deciphering the twenty-five year conflict between United States and Iran*, Random House.

Pelletiere, S.C. (1992). *The Iran–Iraq War: Chaos in a Vacuum*, Greenwood Publishing Group.

Ramazani, R.K. (1987). *Revolutionary Iran: challenges and response in the Middle East*, Johns Hopkins University Press.

Takin, M. (1996). 'Future Oil and Gas: Can Iran Deliver?', *World Oil*, v. 217(11); November, 96–106.

Takin, M. (2000). 'Oil and gas – Can Iran Produce?', Centre for Global Energy Studies, *http://igs.nigc.ir/STANDS/ARTIC/NG-00.PDF*.

Zoghi, I. (2001). *Masaele Siasi Eghtesadi Nafte Iran*, Tehran: Pazhang.

## Chapter 3: The impact of US and international sanctions on oil and gas development

Alexander, R.G. (1997). 'Iran and Libya Sanctions Act of 1996: Congress Exceeds Its Jurisdiction to Prescribe Law', *Washington and Lee Law Review*, 54.

Blenkinsop, P. and Younglai, R. (2012). 'Banking's SWIFT says ready to block Iran transactions', *Reuters, www.reuters.com/article/2012/02/17/us-iran-sanctions-swift-idUSTRE81G26820120217*.

Chazan, G. (2012). 'Sanctions choke off Iran oil output', *Financial Times www.ft.com/cms/s/0/50079b60-6df7-11e1-b98d-00144feab49a.html#axzz24xCOM0fY*.

'Comprehensive Iran Sanctions, Accountability, and Divestment Act of

2010', *http://frwebgate.access.gpo.gov/cgibin/getdoc.cgi?dbname=111_cong_reports&docid=f:hr512.111.pdf*

Cordesman. A.H. (2005). 'The changing balance of US and global dependence on Middle Eastern energy exports', Center for Strategic and International Studies.

Cordesman, A., Bosserman, B., and Khazai, B. (2012). 'US and Iranian Strategic Competition: The Sanctions Game: Energy, Arms Control, and Regime Change', a report of the CSIS Burke Chair in Strategy, Center for Strategic and International Studies, April.

Duero, A. (2009). *The Iranian Rentier State: Rentierism, Political and Economic Development in Iran*, VDM Verlag.

Energy Information Agency (2012). The US Department of Energy's country report on Iran, *www.eia.gov/countries/cab.cfm?fips=IR*

Esfahani, H. et.al. (2012). 'Oil Exports and the Iranian Economy', Faculty of Economics, University of Cambridge.

France's Total: Too risky to invest in Iran (2008). *Washington Post www.washingtonpost.com/wp-dyn/content/article/2008/07/10/AR2008071000026.html*

Garver, J. et.al. (2009). 'Moving (Slightly) Closer to Iran China's Shifting Calculus for Managing Its "Persian Gulf Dilemma" ', *Asia–Pacific Policy Papers* Washington D.C.: The Edwin O. Reischauer Center for East Asian Studies.

Garver, J.W. (2010). 'China's Investment in Iran Oil and Gas', Sam Nunn School of International Affairs, Georgia Institute.

'Implementation of National Defense Authorization Act Sanctions on Iran', in (June 2012): US Department of the Treasury *www.treasury.gov/press-center/press-releases/Pages/tg1409.aspx*

Iran Sanctions (2012). 'Congressional Research Service'.

Jentleson, B.W. (2007). 'Sanctions against Iran: key issues', The Century Foundation.

Katzman, K. (2005). 'The Iran–Libya Sanctions Act', in *CRC Report for Congress*, *www.dtic.mil/cgi-bin/GetTRDoc?AD=ADA475663.*

Katzman, K. (2010). 'Iran Sanctions', Congressional Research Service.

Katzman, K. (2011). 'Iran Sanctions', Congressional Research Service, June.

Katzman, K. (2012). 'Iran Sanctions', Congressional Research Service.

Katzman, K. (2014). 'Iran Sanctions', Congressional Research Service.

Kinnander, E. (2010). 'The Turkish-Iranian Gas Relationship: Politically Successful, Commercially Problematic', Oxford Institute for Energy Studies Working Paper NG 38, January.

Mehr New Agency (2014). *www.mehrnews.com/detail/News/2225885.*

OPEC (2012). 'Growing Impact of Emerging Economies on the Oil Market', *OPEC Monthly Oil Market Report*, August.

Patterson, R. (2013). 'EU Sanctions on Iran: The European Political Context', *Middle East Policy*, Vol. XX, No.1.

Press TV (2012). 'China to invest $20bn to develop Iranian oil fields', *Press TV: www.presstv.ir/detail/2012/07/08/249976/china-to-invest-usd-20-bn-in-iran-oil-fields/*

Sabatini, R. (2010). 'Economic Sanctions: Pressuring Iran's Nuclear Program', Monterey Institute for International Studies, Nuclear Threat Initiative.

Shimbun, Y. (2010). 'Japanese Firm to Withdraw from Iran Oil Field Project', *Daily Yomiuri Online, www.yomiuri.co.jp/dy/business/T100930005106.htm.*

The Iran (European Union Financial Sanctions) Regulations (2010). The National Archives *www.legislation.gov.uk.*

The UN Resolution 1737 U.N. Doc. S/RES/1737.

The UN Resolution 1747, U.N. Doc. S/RES/1747.

The UN Resolution 1929, U.N. Doc. S/RES/1929.

Torbat, A.E. (2005). 'Impacts of the US Trade and Financial Sanctions on Iran', *The World Economy*, vol. 28, issue 3, March, 407–34.

## Chapter 4: Investment regime in the oil and gas sector

Abrahamian, E. (2006). *Khomeinism: Essays on the Islamic Republic*, University of California Press, 1993, 33–36.

Aysan, A., et.al. (2007). 'Governance Institutions and Private Investment: An Application of the Middle East and North Africa', *The Developing Economies*, XLV, no. 3 (September), 341.

Bindemann, K. (1999). 'Production-Sharing Agreements: An Economic Analysis', Oxford Institute for Energy Studies Working Paper WPM 25, October.

Bunter, M. (2005). 'An Introduction to the Islamic (Shari'a) Law and to Its Effect on the Upstream Petroleum Sector', *CEPMLP Publication*.

Buscaglia, E. (1999). 'Law and Economics of Development', Hoover Institute, Stanford University, 563.

Dam, K.W. (2006). *The Law Growth Nexus: The Rule of Law and Economic Development*, Washington D.C.: Brookings Institution Press, 93.

Davis, K.E. and Trebilcock, M.J. (2008). 'The relationship between law and development: Optimists versus Skeptics', New York University Law and Economics Working Papers, New York University School of Law, July.

Dittrick, P. (2009). 'Yadavaran Buyback Contract Signals Better Iranian Terms', *Oil, Gas & Energy Law Intelligence* 7, no. 1.

Ebrahimi, S.N. and Shiroui Khouzani, A. (2003). 'The Contractual Form of Iran's Buy-Back Contracts in Comparison with Production Sharing and Service Contract', edited by Society of Petroleum Engineers: Middle East Oil Show.

Fesharaki, F. and. Varzi, M. (2000). 'Investment Opportunities Starting to Open up in Iran's Petroleum Sector', *Oil & Gas Journal*, 14 February.

Gharavi, H. (1999). 'The 1997 Iranian International Commercial Arbitration Law: The UNCITRAL Model Law', *International Arbitration* 15, no. 1.

Haggard, S., MacIntyre, A., and Tiede, L. (2007). 'The Rule of Law and Economic Development', Annual Review of Political Science, 16:7.

Hakimian, H. (2009). 'Iran's Free Trade and Special Economic Zones: Challenges and Opportunities', *Conference on Iranian Economy at a Crossroads: Domestic and Global Challenges*, University of Southern California.

Higbee, J. and Schmid, F.A. (2004). 'Rule of Law and Economic Development', *International Economic Trends*.

Hosseini, M. (2014). NIOC website article: *www.nioc.ir/portal/Home/ShowPage.aspx?Object=NEWS&ID=d1be8e8e-5bc9-4967-afab-734b3dabbda7&LayoutID=d088303e-229d-4bfc-a0be-2cc0e11ea34c&CategoryID=40295507-1e70-49ec-af82-e5eeba6870bc*

Katzman, K. (2012). 'Iran Sanctions', Congressional Research Service.

Marcel, V. (2006). *Oil Titans: National Oil Companies in the Middle East*, Brookings Institution Press.

Mauro, P. (1995). 'Corruption and Growth', *Quarterly Journal of Economics* 110, no. 3, 681–712.

Me, M. (2009). 'The Iranian Buyback Model and Its Efficiency in the International Petroleum Market – a Legal View', OGEL.

Mohammad, N. (2009). 'The New Face of Iranian Buyback Contract: Any Hope for Foreign Investment?', *Oil, Gas & Energy Law Intelligence*, 11.

Perry, A. (2000). 'Effective Legal Systems and Foreign Direct Investment: In Search of the Evidence', *International and Comparative Law Quarterly* 49, no. 784.

Ramazani, R.K. (1962). 'Choice-of-Law Problems and International Contracts: A Case Study', *The International and Comparative Law Quarterly* 11, no. 2,517.

Ramsay, W.C. (2006). 'Security of Gas Supplies in Europe', in *Nabucco: Conference of the Ministers of Energy (Austria, Bulgaria, Hungary, Romania and Turkey*, International Energy Agency.

Roberts, P. and Jackson, J. (2001). 'The Iranian Buyback Concession: The Principle and the Prospects', *International Energy Law and Taxation Review* 7, 159–61.

Shana (2013). *www.shana.ir/fa/newsagency/208574*

Shana (2014a). *www.shana.ir/fa/newsagency/211694*

Shana (2014b). *www.shana.ir/fa/newsagency/pdf/212407*

Shiravi, A. and Ebrahimi, S.N. (2006). 'Exploration and Development of Iran's Oilfields through Buyback', *Natural Resources Forum* 30, 201.

Shirvani, A. and Ebrahimi S.N. (2007). 'Legal and Regulatory environment of LNG projects in Iran', *Journal of Energy and natural resources law*, vol.25, no.2, 154.

The 1979 Constitution of Islamic Republic of Iran.

Ulen, T.S. (2010). 'The Role of Law in Economic Growth and Development', the Bonn Law & Economics Workshop, University of Bonn.

Wälde, T.W. (2005). 'Law, Contract & Reputation in International Business: What World?', *CEPMLP Internal Journal 3*.

van Groenendaal, W.J.H. and Mazraati, M. (2006). 'A Critical Review of Iran's Buyback Contracts', *Energy Policy* 34, 3713.

Wall, E.H. (1958). 'The Iranian-Italian Oil Agreement of 1957', *International and Comparative Law Quarterly* 7, no. 4.

Walied, El-M. (1996). 'State Ownership of Minerals under Islamic Law', *Journal of Energy & Natural Resources Law* 14, 313.

Zeynoddin, S.M. (2014). 'New models of oil contracts are consistent with macroeconomic policy', NIOC website, *www.nioc.ir/portal/Home/ShowPage.aspx?Object=NEWS&ID=ba12dd70-3486-44f3-a9db-b78081f54fdc&LayoutID=d088303e-229d-4bfc-a0be-2cc0e11ea34c&CategoryID=40295507-1e70-49ec-af82-e5eeba6870bc*

## Chapter 5: Energy subsidies and their reform

Adibi, S. and Fesharaki, F. (2011). 'The Iranian Gas Industry' in Fattouh, B. and Stern, J. (eds.), *Natural Gas markets in the Middle East and North Africa*, OIES/Oxford University Press.

Al-Monitor (2014). 'Iran needs Reform of Gas Sector', Iran Pulse, *www.al-monitor.com/pulse/originals/2014/01/iran-needs-gas-sector-reform.html*

Amuzegar, J. (2011). 'Iran's Subsidy Reform: A Progress Report', *Middle East Economic Survey*.

Baig, T., Mati, A., Coady, D., and Ntamatungiro, J. (2007). 'Domestic Petroleum Product Prices and Subsidies: Recent Developments and Reform Strategies', Washington D.C.: The World Bank, Fiscal Affairs Department.

BP (2010). 'British Petroleum Statistical Review of World Energy'.

BP (2011). 'British Petroleum Statistical Review of World Energy'.

BP (2012). 'British Petroleum Statistical Review of World Energy'.

Clements, B. (2013). 'Energy subsidy reform: lessons and implications', International Monetary Fund, *www.imf.org/external/np/pp/eng/2013/012813.pdf*.

Darbouche, H. (2012). 'The Pricing of Internationally-Traded Gas in Mena and Sub-Saharan Africa', in Stern, J. (ed.), *The Pricing of Internationally Traded Gas*, 8.

De Moor, A. and Calamai, P. (1997). 'Subsidizing Unsustainable Development: Undermining the Earth with Public Funds', edited by Institute for Research on Public Expenditure: Earth Council, 53.

Donyay-e Eghtesad (2011). 'Baztab ghabz jadid gaz', www.donya-e-eqtesad.com/news/648070/.

Fars News Agency (2012). *Government's violations of Subsides Reform Act*, retrieved from: *www.farsnews.com/newstext.php?nn=1391020200146920*.

Fattouh, B., and El-Katiri, L. (2013). 'Energy and Arab Economic Development', *Arab Human Development Report*, United Nations Development Programme, 11.

Global Subsidies Initiative (GSI) (2011). 'Iran Makes Drastic Cuts to Subsidies for Energy and Other Goods'.

Government of Iran (2010). 'The press should prepare the society for grand economic surgery', retrieved from: *www.dolat.ir/NSite/FullStory/News/?Serv=0&Id=183990*.

Granado, J., Coady, D., and Gillingham, R. (2010). 'The Unequal Benefits of Fuel Subsidies: A Review of Evidence for Developing Countries', in *IMF Working Paper*, Washington: International Monetary Fund, 13.

Guillaume, D., Zytek, R., and Farzin, M.R. (2011). 'Iran: The Chronicles of the Subsidy Reform', IMF Working Paper, Middle East and Central Asia Department, July.

Gupta, S., Verhoeven, M., Gillingham, R., Schiller, C., Mansoor, A., and Cordoba, J. P. (2000). *Equity and Efficiency in the Reform of Price Subsidies – a Guide for Policymakers*, IMF, available at: *www.imf.org/external/pubs/ft/equity/index.htm*.

Harris, K. (2012). 'The End of Iran's Revolutionary Social Compact?', in *The XXVI International Sociology Association World Congress of Sociology*, Gothenburg, Sweden: Department of Sociology, John Hopkins University, 2.

Hassani, S. (2010). 'Vezarat-e Bazargani Va Hadafmandi Yaraneha', Tehran: Ministry of Commerce, Paeez, 10.

Hassanzadeh, E. (2012). 'Recent Developments in Iran's Subsidies Reform: Lessons and Recommendations', Global Subsidies Initiative, International Institute for Sustainable Development.

IEA (2008a). 'Betwixt petro-dollars and subsidies', in *Surging energy consumption in the Middle East and North Africa States*, IEA Information Paper, OECD/IEA, October.

IEA (2008b). 'World Energy Outlook: Middle East and North Africa Insights'.

IEA (2009). 'World Energy Outlook'.

IEA (2010a). 'Economic Cost of Fossil-Fuel Subsidies'.

IEA (2010b). 'IEA Analysis of Fossil-Fuel Subsidies', in *World Energy Outlook*, 509.

IEA (2011). 'IEA Analysis of Fossil-Fuel Subsidies', in *World Energy Outlook*.

International Monetary Fund (IMF) (2014). 'Statement at the Conclusion of the 2014 Article IV Consultation Mission to the Islamic Republic of Iran', Press Release No. 14/50, IMF, 12 February, *www.imf.org/external/np/sec/pr/2014/pr1450.htm*.

Independent Evaluation Group (IEG) (2011). 'Social Safety Nets: An Evaluation of World Bank Support 2000-2010', edited by. Washington D.C: The World Bank.

Iran's Chamber of Commerce, Industry and Mine (2008). 'Eghtesad-E Bimar-E Iran Va Yaranehai Ke Hadafman Mishavad', *http://iccim.ir/fa/index.php?option=com_content&view=article&id=2737:-----s----&catid=38:---&Itemid=63*.

Iran Energy Balance (2009). Ministry of Energy.

Iran Energy Balance (2012). Ministry of Energy.

Kobayashi, H., Arif, S., and Fernando, L. (2006). 'Mainstreaming Environment in the Energy Sector – the Case of the Energy–Environment Review for Iran', Washington D.C: The World Bank.

Marcel, V. (2006). *Oil Titans: National Oil Companies in the Middle East*, Brookings Institution Press.

Molai, E. (2004). 'Tarikhcheye Pardakhte Yaraneh Dar Eghtesad Iran', *Resalat Eghtesadi*.

Mehr News (2012). *http://mehrnews.com/detail/news/2175814*

Nasr Esfahani, H. (2008). 'Ghimat Gozari Gaz Tabi Dar Iran', *Eghtesad Energy*, no. 113–14.

NIGC (2011). *Energy consumption annual report.* *www.nigc.ir/Site.aspx?ParTree=111 013&LnkIdn=68601.*

NIGC. (2014). 'Ta'rafeye gaz baha dar sale 1393'. *www.nigc-mpgc.ir/newsdetail-1359-fa.html.*

Nikou, S. (2010). 'The Subsidies Conundrum', Centre for Conflict Analysis and Prevention, US Institute of Peace.

Oxford English Dictionary (2010). Oxford University Press.

Shana (2012a). 'Tavafogh Jadid Iran Va Torkamanestan', www.shana.ir/fa/newsagency/198142.

Shana (2014a). *www.shana.ir/en/newsagency/208786*

Shana (2014b). *www.shana.ir/fa/newsagency/214368;*

Shiravand, A. (2005). 'Baresi Mechanism Ghimat Gozari Baraye Gaz Tabi'i Motale'eye Moredi Iran', Azad University.

Solomon, J. and Fassihi, F. (2011). 'Iran Redistributes Wealth in Bid to Fight Sanctions', in *Iran va Jahan*, *www.iranvajahan.net/cgi-bin/news.pl?l=en&y=2011&m=07&d=28&a=1.*

Subsidies Reform Act (2010). Islamic Republic of Iran.

The World Bank (1995). 'Islamic Republic of Iran Environment Strategy Study', edited by Natural Resources & Environment Division, Maghreb and Iran Department and Middle East and North Africa Region, 58–9.

Victor, D. (2009). 'The Politics of Fossil-Fuel Subsidies', in *Untold Billions: Fossil-fuel subsidies, their impacts and the path to reform*, Geneva: The Global Subsidies Initiative (GSI) of International Institute for Sustainable Development (IISD).

## Chapter 6: Natural gas allocation policy and prioritization changes

Adibi, S., and Ahmad khani, A. (2005). 'arzyabi eghtesadi porojehaye tazrigh-e gaz be makhazene naftie keshvar', Motaleate Eghtesadi Energy, no. 4.

Allsopp, C. and Stern, J. (2012) 'The future of gas: What are the analytical issues relating to pricing?', in Stern, J. (ed.), *The Pricing of Internationally Traded Gas*, Oxford: Oxford University Press.

Bahramian, Y. and Alipour, M. (2011). 'Barasi Zarib Oft Tolid Dar Mayadin Naft Va Gas', E*kteshaf va Tolid*, no. 84, 23.

Barkeshli, F. (2012). 'Iran's energy diplomacy: Challenges and opportunities', *Middle East Economic Survey*, 3.

Business Monitor International (2012). 'Iran Petrochemicals Report Q3 2014', 14 May, *www.marketresearch.com/Business-Monitor-International-v304/Iran-Petro-chemicals-Q1-7896306/*

Derakhshan, M. (2008). 'ba saderate gas rah be jai nemibarim', also available at: *http://naftnews.net/view/7223/*

Economist (2012). 'A Liquid Market', *www.economist.com/node/21558456.*

EIA (2012). 'Country Analysis Briefs: Iran', Energy Information Administration, the US Department of Energy

EIA (2013). 'Country Analysis Briefs: Iran', Energy Information Administration, the US Department of Energy

EIA. (2014). Glossary. *www.eia.gov/tools/glossary/index.cfm?id=R*.

Evans, D. (2008). 'Pearl GTL Set for Big Payback', *Upstream*.

Fattouh, B. and Stern, J. (2011) 'Introduction', in Fattouh, B. and Stern, J. (eds.), *Natural Gas markets in the Middle East and North Africa*, OIES/Oxford University Press.

Fattouh, B., and El-Katiri, L. (2013). 'Energy and Arab Economic Development', *Arab Human Development Report*, United Nations Development Programme, 11.

Ghorban, N. (2010). 'Chera LNG?', *Iran Economics*.

Glebova, O. (2013). 'Gas to Liquid: Historical development and future prospects', Oxford Institute for Energy Studies Working Paper NG 80, 39.

Hassantash, G.H. (2006). 'Iran's Gas Export: From Illusion to Plan', in *Mosalas*, edited by Kaveh Karegar, 50.

Hajarizadeh, H.A. (2004). 'Ezdiad bardasht naft', National Iranian Oil Company, www.nioc.ir/portal/File/ShowFile.aspx?ID=36292448-d621-4dde-847b-a0a8bd429fb1.

Herzig, E. (2004). 'Regionalism, Iran and Central Asia', *International Affairs* 80, no. 3.

IEA (2005). 'World Energy Outlook', Middle East and North Africa Insights.

IEA (2012). World Energy Outlook.

IEA (2013). World Energy Outlook, 492.

IEA (2013). 'Developing a natural gas trading hub in Asia: Obstacles and opportunities', IEA Partner Country Series.

Iran Energy Balance (2012). Ministry of Energy.

Jonoobi, P. (2010) 'Lozoome Tavajoh Bishtar Be Sarmaye-Gozari Dar Bakhshe Gaz-e Keshvar', National Iranian Gas Company, *www.nigc.ir/utils/getFile. aspx?Idn=5075 2010*.

Karimi Zarchi, M. (2010). 'Analysis of Optimal Allocation of Iran's Gas Resources with a Particular Focus on Reinjection and Export', *Ekteshaf va Tolid* no. 77.

Kassaizadeh, S. R. (2011). 'Zanjireyeh Tolid LNG (LNG Production Chain)', Iranian LNG Conference, Tehran.

Kinnander, E. (2010). 'The Turkish-Iranian Gas Relationship: Politically Successful, Commercially Problematic', Oxford Institute for Energy Studies Working Paper NG 38, January.

Lough, J. (2011). 'Russia's Energy Diplomacy', Russia and Eurasia Programme, Chatham House, May: www.chathamhouse.org/sites/default/files/19352_0511bp_lough.pdf.

Majles Research Centre (2009). 'Baresi Oft Tolide Makhazene Naftie Keshvar Va Manafe Melli'.

Mash'al (2007). 'Gas Export Gives Iran Stronger Position', *Mash'Al* (The Weekly Publication of the Iranian Petroleum Industry), No. 364, New Edition 30 September.

Mir Saleh Kohan, L. (2007). *Arzyabi Eghtesadi Arzeye Gaze Iran Be Bazare Orupa*,

Azad Tehran University.

Mitchell, J., Stevens, P., and Cassinadri, E. (2008). 'Resource Depletion, Dependence and Development: Iran', London: Chatham House.

Mosleh, K. (2009). *Estefadeye Behine Az Manabe Gazi Iran*, Majles Research Centre.

Nichol, J. (2014). 'Armenia, Azerbaijan, and Georgia: political developments and implications for US interests', US Congressional Research Service.

NIOC (2011). 'Bahre Bardai Az Bozorgtarin Projeye Tazrigh Gaz Khavarmianeh', *http://ekteshaf.nioc.ir/55/pdf/55-04.pdf*.

NIGC (2012). 'Saderate Gaz'.

NIPC (2010). NIPC Annual Report.

NIPC (2011). NIPC Annual Report.

NIPC (2012). NIPC Annual Report.

OPEC (2012). 'Growing Impact of Emerging Economies on the Oil Market', *OPEC Monthly Oil Market Report*, August.

Rahimi, G. (2006). 'Olaviat bazarhaye saderat baraye gaze Iran', *Iran Energy*, 41.

Ranani, M., Sharifi, A., Khosh-Akhlagh, R., and Din-Mohammadi, M. (2008). 'Cost–Benefit of Various Natural Gas Consumption Options with Emphasis on Oil-Field Reinjection', *Tahghighat-e Eghtesadi Journal*, No. 84..

Randall, A. (1987). *Resource economics*, New York: John Wiley.

Razavi, H. (2009). 'Natural Gas Pricing in Countries of the Middle East and North Africa', *The Energy Journal* 30, no. 3, 15.

Rogers, H.V. and Stern, J. (2012). 'The Transition to Hub-Based Gas Pricing in Continental Europe', in Stern, J. (ed.), *The Pricing of Internationally Traded Gas*, Oxford: Oxford University Press.

Shana (2012a). 'Tahaghoghe Ahdafe San'ate Gaz'.

Shana (2012b). 'Construction of 8 New Petrochemical Plants', National Iranian Oil Company.

Shana (2013). *www.shana.ir/fa/newsagency/210276*

Shana (2014a). *www.shana.ir/fa/newsagency/209680.*

Shana (2014b). *www.shana.ir/fa/newsagency/211975*

Shana (2014c). *www.shana.ir/fa/newsagency/214368*

Shell (2011). 'Shell overview', *www.shell.com/global/aboutshell/our-strategy/major-projects-2/pearl/overview.html*.

Songhurt, B. (2014). 'LNG plant cost escalation', Oxford Institute for Energy Studies Working Paper NG 83, February.

Stern, J. (2005). *The Future of Russian Gas and Gazprom*, Oxford Institute for Energy Studies/OUP.

Stern, R. (2007). 'The Iranian Petroleum Crisis and United States National Security', *International Journal of Economic Sciences* 104, no. 1, 377–82.

Sweeney, J. L. (1992). 'Economic theory of depletable resources: An introduction', in Kneese, A.V. and Sweeney, J.L. (eds.), *Handbook of natural resource and energy economics*, North Holland.

Toman, M. and Krautkraemer, J. (2003). 'Fundamental Economics of Depletable Energy Supply', RFF Discussion Paper 03-01, November.

Van den Bossche, P. (2007). *Law and policy: World Trade Organization, Text cases and Materials*, Cambridge University Press.

## Conclusion

Flower, A. (2011). 'LNG in Qatar' in Fattouh, B. and Stern, J. (eds.), *Natural Gas markets in the Middle East and North Africa*, OIES/Oxford University Press.

# INDEX